Psychoanalytic Reflections: Training and Practice

Psychoanalytic Reflections:
Training and Practice

Sandra Buechler

IPBOOKS.net
International Psychoanalytic Books

International Psychoanalytic Books (IPBooks),
30-27 33rd Street, #3R
Astoria, NY 11102
Online at: www.IPBooks.net

Interior book design by Maureen Cutajar, gopublished.com

ISBN: 978-0-9980833-9-1

For Daphne, Isaac, Eva, Phoebe, their parents, and George

Introduction to Psychoanalytic Reflections

My friend Peter Shabad quotes Soren Kierkegard, who said that life can only be understood backwards, but it must be lived forwards. In thinking about the papers that make up this volume, I see themes that took a good deal of time to coalesce in my own mind. For example, I wrote papers on the analyst's hope, courage, and integrity long before they emerged in my mind as "clinical values," and formed the nucleus of my first book.

How do we each create a personally resonant way of thinking about treatment? I believe that most people who have had only graduate school training have not yet developed what I would call their signature style. They may have many styles, or techniques they have learned. But, often, they do not have a clinical identity, a core of strongly held beliefs about what is important to them in the work they do. Post graduate training is a place to develop those beliefs. To me, most of the work in any identity building task is accomplished through contrasts. By seeing what goes on in his friend's home, the ten year old child understands that his parents' way of functioning is not the only possibility. Similarly, in training, by hearing how differently various teachers and supervisors think about treatment, we can examine, validate, and modify our core beliefs about the work, and eventually forge that signature style. This style does not tell us what to say in any session. Nothing can, fortunately, I would say. Treatment always has to remain a live response to real moments with another person. It can never be reduced to formulas, recipes, manuals, pre-programmed sound bites.

But training can tell us about the experiences of other clinicians who have faced and thought through a variety of clinical dilemmas. I came to analytic training to become a better clinical instrument. As you can tell from many of the papers in the first section of this book, training has always meant a great deal to me. I deeply wanted to "join" the psychoanalytic culture, (1988) to have the strength to bear its stresses (1992) and, later on, to develop ideas about how training can be more growth enhancing (2009, 2011, 2013) and less shaming (2008). More recently I have been concerned with how I can sustain passion for the work (2014) and communicate it to others (2015).

Development as an analyst is so deeply personal. An analogy comes to mind. Unfortunately I don't remember the artist's name, but I once read an interview, in which she said she found her sculptures in the materials she used. She didn't think of her process as creating something, but as finding it. To me, that is as good a description of treatment, and training, as any I have read. Hopefully, in treatment, analysts help find the patient and, in training, supervisors, and others, help find the developing analyst. In both processes, we are not creating something new but, rather, following the contours of what already exists.

In the second part of this volume the papers describe what I have found, in myself, to use in my work with patients. At least some of the time the ingredients include hope, (1995) the strength to face loneliness, (1998) passion, (1999) joy, (2002) and the capacity to atone (2009) and bear sorrow (2000). Life has given me more than just a theoretical acquaintance with pain (2010) and many reminders of being more simply human than otherwise (2002). I hope my clinical and personal experiences taught me enough of the right stuff (1997) to help people. Of late I have gone back to re-read H.S. Sullivan, (2014) whose work made such as impression on me early in my career. It still does. Despite some regrets that have haunted me from mid career on, (2015) I feel immensely grateful to my teachers at the W.A. White Institute, who furthered my understanding of Sullivan's thinking and Erich Fromm's contributions, among many others. Some I worked with were able to model these ideas, in the way they lived the teaching relationship. Most of all, they showed me who I would like to become. Guidance about who we would like to be, and like not to be, comes from what I call the clinician's "internal chorus". Especially in training, but throughout our careers, we are auditioning people for parts in this chorus. That is, our analysts, supervisors, teachers, and others become internalized mentors who are always available to guide, support, and inspire. They accompany us in our loneliest hours, and help define us to ourselves. We can turn to them when we are confused, or bored, or deeply sad. They can help us avoid burnout, and, in a Winnicottian sense, give us something to play with, no matter what is going on interpersonally. If they are primarily benign, they help us bear vicarious traumas, conflict laden, and painful exchanges. They are the mentors who became especially meaningful, partially because they resonated enough with who we already were.

Some members of my own chorus, like Sullivan and Fromm, are people that I never met personally, but encountered through their writing and through their students, who were my teachers. To be internalized, I think an analytic model needs to have enough integrity, or wholeness, to be easily digested. That is, the way he or she works clinically has to be consonant with the way the mentor treats supervisees.

We each search, our whole careers, for what really helps anyone have a richer life. For me, the poet, Rilke best captured what makes our work so hard, and so worthwhile. In his *Letters to a Young Poet* (pp. 23–24) Rilke says, "...at bottom, and just in the deepest and most important things, we are unutterably alone, and for one person to be able to advise or even help another, a lot must happen, a lot must go well, a whole constellation of things must come right in order once to succeed."

Rilke, R.M. (1934). *Letters to a Young Poet*. New York: W.W. Norton.

Table of Contents

I. Training

INTRODUCTION

The papers in this section span twenty seven years of my career. During that time, many professional and personal experiences have affected my view of the training process. In 1988 I had only five years of experience as a graduate analyst. I was still struggling to find my place in an analytic community, to find my voice as a writer, and to solidify what I have come to call my "signature style" of doing treatment.

I hope I can continue to evolve, but it seems like a good time to look back and consider how my thinking about training has changed, and what has remained the same. Training was an important part of my professional identity even before I became an analyst. Working in a New York State hospital, I became a supervisor as a very young psychologist. Looking back, now, I see myself as rather ill prepared to supervise and, perhaps partially as a result, working extremely hard, as an attempt to compensate for my shortcomings.

Not surprisingly, this work ethic (supported by aspects of my character) had an impact on what I expected of those I trained. I imagine that most veterans of state hospital systems can predict that I was in for many disappointments. While I met some highly dedicated and talented professionals, I also encountered many who hoped for nothing more than to serve their time, and collect a pension.

It means a great deal to me to include experiences from early in my career, in my reflections about training. I want to bring everything I have learned, from every walk of life, to my work as an analyst and as a supervisor. In every session I am still a woman, a reader, and everything else I have ever been. I am the same human being who faced the challenges of working in a state hospital system, where the despair of the patients was sometimes matched by the despair of the staff.

One of my most significant lessons from those early professional experiences is about "serving time." State hospital workers and their patients are not the only ones hoping to get through the hours, the days, the weeks. Those years taught me that the price of this schizoid survival mode can be an enervating alienation from oneself.

I think this is part of why, as an analyst and supervisor, I am attracted to Erich Fromm's passionate approach. Fromm imbues my work with vitality. His spirit tells me to make every session count, whether it is a session with a patient or someone in training. "Biophilic," life enhancing analysis is a "practice" in that, like the rest of life, we must work at it.

I see Fromm as informing all of the papers in this section. In the first, "Joining the psychoanalytic culture," Fromm is in the background, urging me toward my own self actualization. His phrase, ". . . because I have eyes, I have the need to see; because I have ears, I have the need to hear; because I have a mind, I have the need to think; and because I have a heart, I have the need to feel" (Fromm, 1968, p.72) inspires me to fight for the full use of my own resources, and for candidates' full use of theirs. In this early paper I was searching for a voice that uses my personal strengths and also honors my forbears.

Each of the subsequent papers on training asks what helps and what hinders candidates' development as analytic instruments. What stresses, what attitudes, what professional rivalries, what insecurities in those who train limit our cultivation of candidates' analytic growth? How do our own cultural biases and flagging energy, inspiration, passion, curtail our ability to pass the torch? Most importantly, how can we do better?

CHAPTER ONE

Joining the Psychoanalytic Culture[*]

INTRODUCTION

This paper was published five years after I graduated from the William Alanson White Institute. In it I treat the profession as a culture and training as a process of acculturation, wherein we learn a language, a set of clinical values, and taboos. We start to forge a role for ourselves in this culture, and begin to understand the rewards it offers, as well as its hardships. I explore biographies of several analysts who have written about their struggles to develop an individual voice, while still honoring the legacies of their analytic mentors.

Looking back, I would say that becoming an analyst required an act of self appointment, in addition to the more formal process. How did this come about? While the development of an analytic identity took some time, it came to feel like I was finally recognizing an aspect of myself. Gradually I understood that I could "re-purpose" the poet inside me, to nurture interpretations.

I think of the analyst's professional appointment as a kind of non-religious annunciation. That is, we find our life's purpose by being inspired. In the religious annunciation, the Angel Gabriel announces that the Holy Spirit has entered Mary, and she becomes aware of her

* *Contemporary Psychoanalysis*, 1988, 24:3, pp. 462–470.

calling. For me, while nothing that dramatic happened, I certainly felt that my first analyst filled me with inspiration.

In this paper I highlight one aspect of the achievement of an analytic identity: the delicate balancing of loyalty to an analytic tradition with the need to develop one's own, unique, personally resonant voice. Many of us continue to struggle to find this equilibrium. Joining an analytic culture is just the first step toward creating a satisfying professional identity.

JOINING THE PSYCHOANALYTIC CULTURE

In this paper I would like to treat the profession of psychoanalysis as though it were a culture. We are not born into this community, but choose to enter it. During our initial period of acculturation, we must learn its language, its moral codes, its behavioral ethics. We adapt to its hardships and find ways of enjoying the rewards it offers. Depending on our natural endowments, personalities, and experiential backgrounds we fashion different roles for ourselves in this culture. Some of us become leaders, perhaps even heroes or heroines, by venturing into the field's intellectual frontiers, or by pursuing political activities. Most are content to work the field, so to speak, largely applying the formulations of others. Our culture has its outlaws, renegades who violate the spoken and unspoken rules. Our language has many dialects, some so self-contained that even members of neighboring groups may find them hard to follow. We have our fads, and fashions, and those who try to capitalize on their glamour. We have our traditionalists, keepers of the faith, who remind us of the riches to be found in the writings of our forefathers. Customs also vary from group to group, though we may all be more alike than different if seen from a vantage point outside the entire culture.

This paper is the product of my contemplation on the initial period of adjustment into the psychoanalytic culture. It begins with a brief glimpse at the autobiographical and biographical statements of several psychoanalysts, who have written of their early career experiences. From these writings a composite picture is drawn, a picture that may fit no one precisely but, perhaps, many of us approximately.

I'd like to begin with Helene Deutsch, relying primarily on her autobiographical work, *Confrontations With Myself* (1973), and on Paul Roazen's study of her life and contribution to psychoanalysis, *Helene Deutsch: A Psychoanalyst's Life* (1985). Although in her autobiography Deutsch was not extremely forthcoming about the inner process of becoming a psychoanalyst, she left behind many letters, principally to her husband Felix, that are quoted at length by Paul Roazen, and give a rather unique glimpse into one person's struggle with the difficulties of becoming and remaining a psychoanalyst. Though her early career development took place in a very different context, I was struck with the number of conflicts she raised that had a familiar, contemporaneous ring.

For example, when at the age of 29, Deutsch was trying to decide whether to leave Vienna in the hope of richer professional experiences, she wrote to Felix about her need for a theory to lend coherence to her clinical experience and to function as a guide in doing treatment. In her words:

> I became convinced—and this was confirmed by experienced people—that in no field so much as in this one, which I want to choose, *one concept* must serve as a guideline, without which everything must remain dilettantism, cheap stuff on the marketplace of science. That key word is: *school*(Roazen, p. 106).

The search for a school may take on the messianic quality of the craving for religion, or a political cause. The fledgling analyst may look to teachers and supervisors for a concrete manual on how-to-do-psychoanalysis. For Helene Deutsch this search for a professional belief system combined, I think, with her emotional hunger for a more experienced male mentor, and resulted in a public adherence to Freudian ideology, regardless of her private misgivings. Deutsch writes of the urge for what she called the "Sunday happiness" of a platonic relationship with a working superior. It is fascinating to me that this woman who has so frequently been criticized for a seemingly unquestioning acceptance of Freudian thinking privately wrote the following:

> I don't want to practice my profession, as until now, with complete engagement of my personality, and above all, not with this

rigid adherence to the phantom of "Freudian Method, " which, as I now realize, I must regard as an *area of research* and not as a therapeutic method. The 'swindle' is based on the fact that certain people (Professor himself!) in full awareness, for the purpose of scientific and material exploitation, do not openly disavow the therapeutic—whereas others, on the one hand out of identification, and on the other hand out of the narcissistic need to have some special ability, unconsciously elevate psychoanalysis to be their battle cry, to be the one and only path to blessedness (Roazen, p. 261).

This, written in 1926, still fairly early in her career, expresses, with arresting bluntness, what may be our common plight—the need to believe in a system, perhaps to elevate it to the level of absolute truth, which may inevitably result in disillusionment, and, in some, despair. Added to this is the fact that adherence to an ideology is also a public, political act in our field, entails the joining of a particular society or group, so that the early identifications one makes under the sway of the great yearning for a belief system can become ties that bind when subsequent experience yields some misgivings.

To further complicate matters, at the same time as there is a pull toward belief in a system, and a relationship with a more experienced mentor, there is also an injunction to develop one's own style. Just when Deutsch was groping for a belief system with which to wholly identify, she also wanted complete freedom from any supervision or restraint, to be allowed to find her own way. For example (Roazen, p. 119), at 29 she wrote to Felix, saying how glad she was to have the full responsibility for her patients. Though aware she is lacking in knowledge, she says having authority is extremely important to her. I wonder whether the entrance into our field isn't especially conducive to conflicts with an adolescent ring, expressed sometimes in exaggerated needs to repudiate professional "parental" figures in order to feel able to individuate. I will elaborate on this possibility later.

Helene Deutsch often used her own experiences, thinly veiled as "case" illustrations, and in these she poignantly describes the clash between her professional and personal needs. All her life these aims seem to have been to some extent in conflict. Sometimes she describes this opposition as a peculiarly female problem in that the balancing of career and motherhood is especially difficult. Our work is so inevitably personal, requiring intellectual pursuit, emotional investment, and self-scrutiny. The long period of preparation takes up our early adulthood, when many of our friends, contemporaries, spouses are beginning to establish themselves professionally and economically. We are forced to be out of tune professionally with our developmentally appropriate personal needs, and this, I feel, must create some disharmony. Helene Deutsch humorously describes her own plight:

> I saw in myself a conflict of interest between my intellectual preoccupations and my emotional self. I felt like the personification of a children's song my grandsons loved: A peculiar creature turns up in a chicken yard. She feels out of place and unwanted and moves on to the goose yard. But here too she is greeted by protesting cackles. In despair she asks herself, 'Who am I? I am not a chicken, I am not a goose. I am a chirkendoose!' My grandsons enjoyed this song without knowing how much their grandmother identified herself with this strange animal (Deutsch, p. 193).

We must develop, within ourselves, a patient attitude of intellectual curiosity, a willingness to submit to a life-long process of self-scrutiny, an ability to forgo immediate gratifications. We must have the intellectual's patience, curiosity, respect for reflection, leisurely attitude toward time. Yet we can't be obsessively distanced from immediate emotional experience, we must be quickened by it and aware of our responsiveness.

It seems to me that inherent in our work is the potential for several conflicts:

1. Discord, especially early in our careers, between our own age-appropriate personal needs and our professional requirements.

2. Difficulty serving well both the intellectual and emotional demands of the profession.

3. Conflict between differing aspects of the therapeutic role. Because of its unfamiliarity, this problem may be exacerbated early in our careers. In a recent article on therapeutic burnout, Arnold Cooper (1986) delineates some of the seemingly contradictory expectations of the analyst, and the pitfalls that may be inherent at each stage of our careers. Early in our professional development, we must learn to maintain subtle balances:

> The suggestion that optimal therapeutic efficacy depends on maintaining a stance which includes both zeal and distance, both devotion to the patient and exclusion of the patient from one's personal life, leads to the self-evident conclusion that this optimal stance will be difficult to maintain. It is this difficulty of maintaining the balance of therapeutic determination and remoteness, of deep empathy and emotional detachment, of shared responsibility between patient and analyst, of therapeutic persistence and willingness to let go—it is these difficult balances that give rise to appropriate therapeutic modesty. It is wise to be aware of how easily we can become de-skilled and of how difficult it is for us to maintain an optimal balance as analysts (Cooper, p. 578).

In short, early in our careers we, as analysts, must learn the delicate balancing of private and professional needs, intellectual and emotional professional requirements, responsiveness and detachment from our patients. Our particular characters and defensive styles no doubt shape our personal answers to these challenges.

At this point I'd like to turn to a very different personality, Melanie Klein, for further insights into some of the issues we face as beginning psychoanalysts. I am drawing principally from Grosskurth's recent biographical work, *Melanie Klein, Her World and Her Work* (1986).

Klein, born in 1882 in Vienna, spent a good deal of her career in opposition to many of the people most closely aligned with Freud and Deutsch, but nevertheless fought inner battles that sound strikingly similar to those faced by Deutsch. Some early commonalities are especially clear. Klein also voiced the pressing need for a mentor who would validate for her that she had some promise as an analyst. I feel that the nature of our field may leave us especially dependent on such validation, since we have to make such an extensive commitment to the profession before we have had much opportunity to practice it and develop confidence based on experience. To further complicate things, since our instrument is ourselves and our products are intensely personal moments, making an "objective" judgment of one's own worth may seem impossible.

Klein wrote of another problem, the analyst's position of perpetually dealing with issues that are painful and evoke our own resistances. Writing to Winnicott in 1940, she said of psychoanalysis:

> It is true—this work may go under and might be rediscovered again;—that has happened before but its very nature, the fact that even each of us, of those who have got most hold of it have to keep great vigil not to let it slip ... because it makes such very great demands and there is a constant temptation to cover it up or to turn away from the points where it strikes terror or causes pain (Grosskurth, p. 260).

Klein wrote of other obstacles to be overcome in achieving an analytic identity. For example, she had to contend with her own high expectations of her success as an analyst, since she'd done well in academic work. The great difference between the process of learning how to be a psychoanalyst vs. other, more academic kinds of learning in which we may have excelled, can create painful gaps between our expectations and our performance.

Klein also wrote of the long period of training necessary to our profession and of how it complicates other aspects of our life-course. While mid-life may, for most people, be a time of beginning to come to terms with one's limitations, with what is evidently not within our professional and creative grasps, we, as psychoanalysts, are just beginning to come into our own. As was suggested by some of Helene Deutsch's comments, in many respects we are out of sync with the developmental life cycle.

Klein also wrote of the conflicts surrounding joining one school of thought, since some demand an almost religious fervor and loyalty before one has had enough experience to make a personally valid choice. She wrote, in her letters, of the problems of establishing a relationship to an institute, of institutional transferences, of the potential for generational conflicts with the older, more established generation wishing to see its work carried on and the newer, younger members needing to find their own voices.

It is probably also true that we are more vulnerable to our psychoanalytic version of medical students' disease early in our careers, to add to our self-doubts. Our little bit of knowledge can probably easily become a dangerous thing when misapplied to our spouses, parents, children, and ourselves. Much controversy surrounded Klein in this regard, since she treated her own children as analysands and as material for her writing.

Another difficulty Klein made clear is the pressure to prove oneself in more than one capacity in our field. It may not feel like it is enough to excel as a clinician and teacher. One must also prove adept at formulating theory.

It may be so that, especially as our field has expanded, it has become necessary for each of us early in our careers to discard some possible identities. In some sense, of course, this has always been a necessary part of establishing a professional persona. At the age of 30, in 1909, Ernest Jones wrote to Freud:

> The originality-complex is not strong in me; my ambition is rather to know, to be 'behind the scenes,' and 'in the know,' rather than *to find out*. I realize that I have very little talent for originality; any talent I may have lies rather in the direction of being able to see perhaps quickly what others point out: no doubt that also has its use in the world (Brome, p. 70).

Jones, it seems, was quite consciously defining his future place in psychoanalytic circles, partly on the basis of what he felt he was *not* cut out to be.

A few references to the life of Harry Stack Sullivan will illustrate some similarities in the issues he faced as a beginning professional. Helen Swick Perry, in her biography, makes it clear that crucial to Sullivan's career was his reliance on several mentors, who played the role of encouraging him, and facilitating the development of his sense of professional competence. William Alanson White and Ross McClure Chapman surely were two such figures for Sullivan. Perry writes that, "like White, Chapman had the rare gift of not having to compete with his own staff, so that Sullivan's experimental approach delighted him" (p. 190). Perry suggests that Sullivan felt White "had rescued his career and set him on his way" (p. 184) but that Sullivan always "yearned for a fuller appreciation of himself by White than he ever received" (p. 186). Both White and Chapman seem to have provided, for Sullivan, figures he could respect intellectually and an atmosphere with enough latitude and trust to enable Sullivan to develop and actualize his conceptual framework. Thus Sullivan, like Deutsch and Klein, was dependent on a mentor who offered both instruction and validation. Sullivan, like Deutsch, benefited from a situation, provided relatively early in his career, to be allowed to experiment and fashion his own way.

At this point I would like to draw a composite picture, to summarize some of the issues mentioned thus far. The beginning analyst faces disquieting uncertainty about his or her present competence and potential ability. To deal with this self-doubt and the ambiguity about how analysis should be done, the beginning analyst may search for certainty in the form of a school of thought or an idealized mentor. Either or both may provide, initially, a sense that one knows where one is going and has the ability to get there. Some eventual disappointment may be inherent in this process, since the early identification with a school or mentor may elevate to the position of absolute truth what is, in reality, only a point of view. The hunger for the structure and guidance of a school exists side by side, in the beginning analyst, with the urge for complete independence. We wish for a place that will give us enough latitude to encourage our development of an individual style. This particular combination of anxiety, the yearning to be molded by an authority, and the pressing need for freedom and individual experimentation may lend a peculiarly adolescent coloring to the early stages in the career of an analyst. Adding to that adolescent quality may be the need to weed out and discard potential analytic identities that don't fit one's particular personal equipment. Furthermore, the beginning analyst, like the adolescent, has to engage in a long period of patient training and preparing, despite burgeoning personal needs. For both it is a time of rapid self discovery, an exhilarating time that nevertheless presents new difficulties in the integration of a stable identity.

It is my belief that the adolescent position of the beginning analyst may rekindle issues from his or her chronological adolescence. In particular, I think, struggles over dependence and independence, the fierce need to belong, coupled with an equally passionate need to emerge as an individual, may be evoked.

I would like to quote from Ruth Moulton's comments on Clara Thompson's career, which can be found in the book *Women and Analysis* (Strouse, 1974). Moulton ends her chapter with a description of Thompson by Erich Fromm. When I read it, it seemed to me to suggest that Clara Thompson had found a way to resolve many of the issues sprung from adolescence that I have been trying to describe as renewed challenges for those just entering the society of psychoanalysts. Fromm said of Thompson that she was a

> thoroughly independent person, averse to rules and principles with which she did not agree; at the same time she did not endow her own theoretical principles with a halo that would make her fight all others. But while she was never a fanatic or one to intimidate others, it was one of her remarkable characteristics that she could not be intimidated. ... This integrity within and loyalty to friends made it possible for others to trust her and rely on her. She was a person with fine appreciation of theory and, at the same time, with excellent common sense (Moulton, p. 328).

It seems that Thompson has surmounted the hurdles of joining the psychoanalytic culture. She developed outlets for her needs for independence and belonging. She found ways to use the various facets of her creativity. She traversed the generational issues and became able to impart her vision. She evolved an identity, a place in her profession that fit who she became as a person. This is the extremely arduous challenge that the beginning analyst has to face.

My own personal version of these adolescent issues affected my entrance into the psychoanalytic culture by giving it the quality of a headlong dash. Barely restrained impatience precluded taking the time needed to develop conviction about my place in this new culture. I was too anxious about making sure I would have a place to take the time to find it. I am, for that reason, moved by Rilke's words written to the young poet for whom he served as a spiritual and intellectual mentor. Although Rilke was addressing the question of how one enters the community of poets, I would want to be able to apply his words to my entrance into the psychoanalytic culture. In the *Letters to a Young Poet*, Rilke advises:

> Leave to your opinions their own quiet undisturbed development, which, like all progress, must come from deep within and cannot be pressed or hurried by anything. *Everything* is gestation and then bringing forth (Rilke, p. 29).

REFERENCES

Brome, V. 1983 *Ernest Jones: Freud's Alter Ego.* New York: W. W. Norton.

Cooper, A. 1986 Some limitations on therapeutic effectiveness: the 'burnout syndrome' in psychoanalysis. *Psychoanalytic Quarterly* 55:576–598.

Deutsch, H. 1973 *Confrontations with Myself.* New York: W.W. Norton.

Grosskurth, P. 1986 *Melanie Klein: Her World and Her Work.* New York: Alfred A. Knopf.

Moulton, R. 1974 The role of Clara Thompson in the psychoanalytic study of women. In: *Women and Analysis* ed. J. Strouse. New York: Dell, pp. 319–333.

Perry, H. 1982 *Psychiatrist of America: The Life of Harry Stack Sullivan.* Cambridge: Belknap Press.

Rilke, R. M. 1934 *Letters to a Young Poet.* New York: W.W. Norton.

Roazen, P. 1985 *Helene Deutsch: A Psychoanalyst's Life.* New York: New American Library.

CHAPTER TWO

Stress in the Personal and Professional Development of a Psychoanalyst*

INTRODUCTION

This paper discusses some sources of stress for analytic candidates and practitioners. It highlights challenges inherent in our role with patients, and pressures that can come from collegial relationships. It takes as its basic premise that human dilemmas inform both our personal and professional lives. This can have both positive and negative consequences. On the positive side, what we learn in one arena can enrich us in the other. But it is also true that we can suffer from a kind of psychological carpal tunnel syndrome, an over-use of certain capacities. It is a common complaint of clinicians that we want a break from interpersonal interaction when we reach home at the end of the day, but our partners and children may have other plans for us.

Looking back, I see this paper as foreshadowing my book, "Still Practicing: The Heartaches and Joys of a Clinical Career" (2012). The intervening twenty years brought me ample evidence of the painful burdens of clinical work, as well as its uplifting highs. In "Still Practicing" I

---

* *Journal of the American Academy of Psychoanalysis* 1992, 20: 183–191. Presented at the 33rd Annual Meeting of the American Academy of Psychoanalysis, May 1989.

better understood shame and sorrow as two concomitants of clinical (and personal) life, at least for me. Shame, or a sense of insufficiency, often lurks in a session. And the inevitability of the loss of every treatment partner makes sorrow equally unavoidable. As a clinician (and as a human being) I am "still practicing" bearing shame and sorrow with all the grace I can muster.

But this paper, published less than ten years after my graduation, approaches life as an analyst from the standpoint of a relative novice. Implicitly it asks whether I will be able to use my personal experience to deepen my clinical work, and my clinical work to good effect in my personal life. Will each help me stretch in moments of insufficiency and live sorrow with courage?

STRESS IN THE PERSONAL AND PROFESSIONAL DEVELOPMENT OF A PSYCHOANALYST

> But yield who will to their separation
> My object in living is to unite
> My avocation and my vocation
> As my two eyes make one in sight.
> Only where love and need are one,
> And the work is play for mortal stakes
> Is the deed ever really done
> For heaven and the future's sakes.
>
> —Robert Frost (1942), "Two Tramps in Mud-Time"

For us, as analysts, making our love and need one contributes to the fulfillment but also to the stress of our work. Our lives are enriched and suffer from a peculiar degree of integration of the professional and the personal. Presumably, had we not had both love and need for a professional life centered on human issues we would not have chosen to become analysts. An analyst who only *loves* this work, in the expectation that it will provide every emotional fulfillment, will complicate the treatment with his or her personal investment. On the other hand, one who only *needs* this work, and does not love it, for whom it is a deadly serious business, who tries to obtain all pleasure from outside avocation, not only splits himself or herself, but also robs the work of its essential playfulness.

The following pages present a series of dilemmas that result from being an analyst. The common thread is that in each the strain of the work and personal stresses exacerbate one another. At such times, rather than providing a safe haven from personal concerns, our work focuses our awareness on them more sharply. In situations such as the following we suffer because both vocationally and avocationally we are continuously involved in self-observed interpersonal interactions.

To begin, a word about what is meant by "stress." The dictionary provides several meanings. Stress is "importance, significance, or emphasis placed upon something." In music, of course, it is an accent. In other terms, it may be used to mean a force that tends to deform a body. It may also suggest a mentally or emotionally disruptive influence, a stress that can distress. It is interesting that the same word can connote greater emphasis, distortion, and disruption. Perhaps, like an overworked muscle, any part of our human equipment that we call on for both vocational and avocational purposes may be strained just by virtue of the overemphasis.

So, on to the stresses of the analyst, whose accent is so prevailingly on human interactions. Some analysts have been chroniclers of their own as well as their patients' experience and have, through their writings, provided glimpses into the stresses they feel. Melanie Klein, for example, wrote of her work as an analyst that it" makes such very great demands and there is a constant temptation to cover it up or to turn away from the points where it strikes terror or causes pain" (Grosskurth,1986, p. 260).

In addition to serving other resistances, the temptation to "cover up" may be a wish to avoid shame from self-exposure. The stress of self-exposure is perhaps never more burdensome than during our years of analytic training. In a thoughtful article on "The Emotional Stresses of Psychotherapeutic Practice," O. Spurgeon English (1976) reflects on his feelings of exposure during training:

At first, I responded to my analyst's expectations of me to think about myself and others, and reveal to him what I was thinking with no pleasure in the procedure. People used to remark how interesting it must be to have the opportunity to study oneself with the help of a guide and mentor. I don't recall disagreeing very actively, probably out of some apprehension that if I did so, they would think I must have had a terrible past. I resisted the process of self-revelation, often quite painfully. (p. 192)

The candidate, whose character and work is observed in any number of contexts, is subject to scrutiny by supervisors, the training committee, teachers, classmates, and patients, not to mention the candidate's analyst who may also have a role in the training process. It is demanded that, as candidates, we see ourselves and that we are seen by others. In some instances, in addition to being seen, we are also being judged, as fit or unfit to move on in our preparation to be an analyst.

Of the shame of public exposure an emotion theorist (Izard, 1977) writes:

Shame occurs typically, if not always, in the context of an emotional relationship. The sharp increase in self-attention (and sometimes the increased sensitivity of the face produced by blushing) causes the person to feel as though he were naked and exposed to the world. Shame motivates the desire to hide, to disappear. Shame can also produce a feeling of ineptness, incapacity, and a feeling of not belonging. (p. 92)

Others (e.g., Schecter, 1980) wrote of "shame anxiety," emphasizing how much of our sense of security depends on how we feel we are being seen by significant others.

While the potential for shame from self-exposure is present for everyone, the analytic candidate is in an unusual position with regard to this emotion. The candidate has maximal opportunity to feel shame but minimal opportunity to hide. Although presumably equipped with the human capacity for shame, although highly exposed, the candidate may feel pressure to be comfortably self-revealing rather than self-protective. The candidate may come to feel ashamed of his or her shame, or anxious that the shame itself might be exposed.

Stress, in the sense of distress, may thus result from stress, in the sense of emphasis, on the candidate's self-exposure. Lines of demarcation between professional and personal, public and private, vocation and avocation become unclear in the years of analytic preparation. No wonder candidates struggle over how much to reveal of themselves to their patients, with some attempting an artificially sterile neutrality and others tempted to abandon the constraints of the therapeutic role. Persistent uncertainty about how much to reveal of ourselves in our analytic work may be a legacy we carry over from the stress of potential exposure and shame in our candidacy.

Stress, of course, does not end with the conferring of an analytic certificate. The newly minted analyst faces another set of potential insecurities, so exceedingly different from the first that the transition itself can be disconcerting. After having been acutely observed, taught, and confronted for the years of training, the new analyst suffers the opposite extreme, a total absence of structure. Of course, many continue in analysis, in supervision, and in theoretical course work, but there is a distinct difference. Training provided a clear, recognizable goal and guidelines for shaping a course of self-development. After training, the new analyst is expected to know what he or she needs to learn and how to obtain whatever input is necessary. In addition, there may follow a nebulous period in terms of professional standing in the analytic community, in which goals are unclear, progress is hard to chart, status difficult to measure.

The source of the stress, I would suggest, is not the ambiguity itself but the sense that one *should* know what one may not know. Roy Schafer (1979) wrote about the need, especially early in one's career, to have a place in an analytic community, and to believe in its school of thought. This gives a feeling of belonging and a sense of clarity and conviction about the work itself. Schafer discusses the difficulty of developing outside an analytic community and the equally hard task of fully embracing any one analytic tradition:

In working and developing within a tradition, one is not left with the impossible job of making oneself up totally. There is a sense of authenticity that comes from working within a form, a form that is a set of constraints as well as opportunities. You would be engaged in living out a rather simple-minded, romantically individualistic fantasy to think that you could simply make yourself up from moment to moment: you would be disregarding the necessarily interpersonal matrix of adaptation. Nevertheless, with all of the advantages of working within one's school wholeheartedly, there are also advantages to questioning the traditions within which you work. As time goes on, you inevitably become aware that there are gaps and contradictions....

The time is likely to come when you ask yourself, "To whom would I refer someone I love?" or "To whom would I go for a second analysis?" All too often, these are not easy questions to answer. You may well wonder then what your uncertainty implies about the extent of your confidence in the official point to view and the methods of your school. How much is actually shared in practice by the members of one group? (pp. 350–351)

The need to "know" one's theoretical stance can be felt as a prerequisite for membership in one or another analytic establishment. It may also be felt as a deep inner necessity, a strong desire for faith in a proven method of treatment.

In his reflective essay, "Sorrows and Joys of the Psychotherapist" Kepinski (1981) writes:

When I look back on my professional activity I can hardly refrain from an ironic and indulgent smile. At the beginning one literally pounces upon the first patient and, filled with ambition and the wisdom of book-learning, expects to penetrate their innermost affects, to fathom the furthest reaches of their souls, to even cure and redirect their distorted life-lines. Soon deep disappointment enters. Somehow everything is other than according to the texts. There everything was simple and clear; here on the other hand everything is changing, in flux, and foggy. The key that appeared during the lecture like a *passé partout* will not fit. One tries other keys, looks for other personality theories and concepts of psychopathology. The new keys are just as worthless. One loses faith both in any proffered key to the human psyche and in one's own therapeutic ability. Listlessness overtakes us. The only comfort and stimulus to further investigation is the circumstance that at times the patient's condition improves—and we are not even clear as to why. Thus for example it happens that, proud of a singular therapeutic success, we meet by chance the patient on the street in obvious tender harmony with a female being. In thinking about this encounter with the patient's real life, doubts soon appear about our "successful" treatment. In no time at all we begin to think that the success may be perhaps best ascribed to "her." (p. 393)

The injunction to have a way of knowing the right method of treatment is amplified by other sources. Often one is trying on other professional hats, perhaps for the first time. Experience as a new supervisor can be replete with moments of identification with an uncertain supervisee's wish for firm direction. Patients also contribute their anxious need for clear directives and guidance, for a sure sense of where they are going and whether they will get there.

This cursory tour of the stresses in the analyst's early development has briefly reviewed the candidate's overexamined life, and the new analyst's pressure to know the unknowable about his or her own professional development, and the efficacy of various theoretical stances and treatment modalities. Next is brief mention of a situation that may be intrinsic to analytic work for the whole of one's career: the stress of conflicting injunctions. As has been suggested by Roy Schafer (1979), our work is a series of responses to conflicting demands:

On the one hand, you don't want to be exactly the same for all analysands; that is the way of rigidity. On the other hand, you don't want to try to be altogether different for each analysand, for then in addition to lacking authenticity, you will not develop any baseline for comparing analysands with one another or comparing one analysand with himself or herself from one time to another. As in other respects, the tension consists in finding and continuously redefining a balance between remaining the same and yet changing appropriately. The problem is to calibrate yourself as an analyst. (p.355)

In a similar vein, Arnold Cooper (1986) wrote of the analyst as subjected to sharply conflicting internal and external pressures:

The suggestion that optimal therapeutic efficacy depends on maintaining a stance which includes both zeal and distance, both devotion to the patient and exclusion of the patient from one's personal life, leads to the self-evident conclusion that this optimal stance will be difficult to maintain. It is this difficulty of maintaining the balance of therapeutic determination and remoteness, of deep empathy and emotional detachment, of shared responsibility between patient and analyst, of therapeutic persistence and willingness to let go —it is these difficult balances that give rise to appropriate therapeutic modesty. It is wise to be aware of how easily we can become de-skilled and of how difficult it is for us to maintain an optimal balance as analysts. (p.578)

Every moment with a patient can be felt as a challenge to maintain that optimal balance between empathic involvement and therapeutic distance. Stress, in the sense of distress, can result from the stress in the sense of frequent emphasis on the reassertion of this balance. Just as the emotionally exposed candidate is also subject to examinations in his or her private life, and the new analyst is pressured toward (impossible) certainty privately as well as professionally, so the strain of conflicting injunctions will be a recurring professional and personal dilemma.

Many (Cooper, 1986; Knutsen, 1977; Marmor, 1953, 1982; Searles, 1979) have written of the personal strains associated with the analytic role. One aspect of this stress is the pressure the analyst may feel to be above human frailties. This expectation may come from several sources, aside from the particular character issues of the analyst. First, the psychoanalyst is the target of the unrealistic (transferential) expectations of his or her patients, who may need to see the analyst as an all-knowing, ever-sensitive model of perfection.

Second, as has been explored by Marmor (1953), the particular anxieties inherent in the psychotherapeutic role may foster dependence on a defensive grandiosity:

> All of these factors, then—the lack of fixed standards, the necessity of adapting to constantly changing and shifting problems, the complexity of the material, the realistic difficulties involved in achieving success, the constant need to make corrections for subjective blind spots, the disparity between the therapist's human limitations and the expectations of his patients and the public— are a constant potential source of anxiety to the psychotherapist and may create in him defensive tendencies to bolster his threatened ego by maximizing his successes, by minimizing his shortcomings and in extreme cases by taking refuge in the character traits of the God complex. (p. 283)

Third, it seems implicit in the psychoanalytic culture that the analyst should be able to put aside all thoughts of his or her own human physical and emotional needs while at the analytic task. Knutsen (1977), in a discussion of the emotional well-being of psychiatrists, notes how difficult this selflessness may be to achieve, especially since the therapist is engaged in helping patients legitimize concern about the quality of *their* lives. The therapist's failure to put self-concern aside may result in a sense of fraudulence or, perhaps, envy of the latitude accorded his or her patients.

A fourth, subtle source of pressure to be superhuman may come from the relative lack of open discussion among colleagues of actual case material. Partially because of the requirements of confidentiality but also, most likely, for defensive reasons, we seldom create the opportunity to show each other the human frailty evident in our actual interchanges.

The gap between the analyst's realistic capacities and these excessive expectations creates "role strain" (Marmor, 1982). The analyst is supposed to excel in the human qualities of intelligence, idealism, interpersonal sensitivity, and integrity, among other virtues. This standard is applied to professional work as well as family relationships and friendships.

When Sullivan (1953) said that "everyone is much more simply human than otherwise ..." (p. 32) he did not exclude the psychoanalyst. And yet we, as analysts, suffer the strain of introjecting inordinate role expectations. We feel we should "handle" the anxiety of our tremendous responsibilities without observable stress, without our own needs becoming evident, whether dealing with the violent, the suicidal, the patient whose issues are uncomfortably similar to our own, or any other of a wide array of challenges. We are expected, and, therefore, expect of ourselves, consistently to rise above the simply human.

Our professional stresses come from the fabric of the human interchange with patients, a fabric cut from the same cloth as our personal lives. All of our professional concerns are more human than otherwise. Hence, we meet the same issues in our private lives that we have to face professionally, and often at the same period of time. Generally, we are young adults as candidates and new analysts. We have chosen self-examination in the context of work in a helping profession as a way of life. We are likely to be people who create personal relationships in which self-examination and knowing how to help are prominent features. In our young adult years, antidotes to shame and the sense of inadequacy from not knowing enough may not yet be available to us. A young perspective may contribute too much of a sense of urgency, too pointed a focus on the present, too narrow an egocentric concern, to meet these issues with equanimity. Professional and personal exposure can deeply threaten a young unsure, unproven, self-absorbed, eager person urgently focused on his or her viability. The professional and personal pressure to "know" is probably exacerbated by a youthful faith in the possibility of controlling life's outcomes. And whose personal life does not abound in conflicting pressures? But, unlike the statistician, for whom these pressures are personally highly relevant but professionally mainly incidental, for us as analysts they are *everywhere*. As Erving Goffman (1961) said about the patient in a mental hospital, there is no time out, away, in a separate compartment with a different set of issues. We are 24-hour-a-day participants in human interactions, in our personal as well as our professional lives. We suffer the stress of overworked interpersonal skills. Certain basic dilemmas in various permutations come at us from all sides. Of course, we also benefit from the redundancy. Our attempts at coping with a human issue professionally enrich our personal adaptations, and our private struggles inform our work. Our avocation and vocational interests mingle, cross-pollinate. Since our work is human interchange, no experience, public or private, is irrelevant. As observers we are always on the job, always perfecting our instruments. This is the stress, that is, the emphasis that can be distressing, but this is also the unlimited opportunity for integration and the joy of being an analyst.

REFERENCES

Cooper, A. (1986), Some limitations on therapeutic effectiveness: "The burnout syndrome" in psychoanalysts. *Psychoanalytic Quarterly* 55:576–598.

English, O. S. (1976). The emotional stress of psychotherapeutic practice. *Journal of the American Academy of Psychoanalysis and Dynamic Psychiatry* 4:119–210

Frost, R. (1942). *The Complete Poems of Robert Frost.* New York: Holt, Rhinehart and Winston.

Goffman, E. (1961). *Asylums.* New York: Anchor Books,

Grosskurth, P. (1986). *Melanie Klein, Her World and Her Work.* New York: Alfred A. Knopf.

Izard, C. E. (1977). *Human Emotions.* New York: Plenum Press.

Kepinski, A. (1981). Sorrows and joys of the psychotherapist. *Journal of the American Academy of Psychoanalysis and Dynamic Psychiatry* 9:391–398. http://www.pep-web.org/document.php?id'jaa.009.0391a

Knutsen, E. (1977). On the emotional well-being of psychiatrist: Overview and rationale, *American. Journal of Psychoanalysis* 37:123–129. http://www.pep-web.org/document.php?id'ajp.037.0123a

Marmor, J. (1953). The feeling of superiority: An occupational hazard in the practice of psychotherapy, in *Psychiatry in Transition.* New York: Brunner/Mazel, 1974, pp. 279–290.

——— (1982). Some factors involved in occupation-related depression among psychiatrists, *Psychiatry Annals* 12:913–920. http://www.pep-web.org/document.php?id'joap.027.0001a

Schafer, R. (1979). On becoming a psychoanalyst of one persuasion or another, *Contemporary Psychoanalysis* 15:345–360. http://www.pep-web.org/document.php?id'cps.015.0345a

Schecter, D. (1980). Early developmental roots of anxiety. *Journal of the American Academy of Psychoanalysis and Dynamic Psychiatry* 8:539–554. http://www.pep-web.org/document.php?id'jaa.008.0539a

Searles, H. (1979). The countertransference with the borderline patient, in *Essential Papers on Borderline Disorders*, New York: New York University Press, 1986, 498–526.

Sullivan, H. S. (1953). *The Interpersonal Theory of Psychiatry*, New York: W.W. Norton,

CHAPTER THREE

The Legacies of Shaming Psychoanalytic Candidates*

INTRODUCTION

Are some painful shame experiences inherent in analytic training, and, therefore, unavoidable? Does shame make any positive contribution to our professional growth? After exploring some sources of candidates' shame I discuss its immediate and long term effects. Briefly, I believe that our shame experiences in training can have a profound impact on our careers, and a lasting effect on our subsequent ability to deal with shame as it arises in either participant in the treatments we conduct.

From my point of view, no one has depicted shame more clearly than Thomas Mann. In his great short story, "Little Lizzy" (1997) an obese lawyer, Jacoby, literally dies of shame. He is taunted by his beautiful but cruel wife, Amra, into a public humiliation that is too much for him to bear, and he collapses in the middle of his "performance."

Shame in analytic training is usually (but not always) more private. The mentor who prioritizes making a point over all other considerations can do damage to the confidence of the vulnerable supervisee. The

---

* *Contemporary Psychoanalysis* 2008, 44:1, 56–64. An earlier version of this paper was presented at Symposium 2006 Journals Conference on Shame, March 5, New York City

teacher who insists that candidates pay tribute to one way of thinking theoretically may spawn competition for who will become the most favored disciple. This exacerbates our already competitive professional climate. Furthermore, bearing these experiences without protest can have its own damaging, and long lasting, impact on candidates.

While, unlike Jacoby, we may not literally die of shame, I think it is frequently a major factor in the death of a promising career. Some candidates eventually graduate, but hide what they really think for the rest of their careers. I have seen quite a few who end their practices early, having found themselves unable to recover from wounds inflicted in training. As is often true of shame, it creates absences. A silent majority of our colleagues feel unequal to contributing to our literature, our conferences, our faculties, and our efforts to convince the public of the value of psychoanalysis. Can we afford to continue these practices?

ABSTRACT

Given that analytic training involves profound self-examination, self exposure, and personal and professional assessment, it should come as no surprise that candidates often suffer from anxious shame. To what extent should we consider shame inevitable, and perhaps even a necessary aspect of the training process? What constructive uses might it have? What are the sources of shame in analytic training, and how might unnecessary, deleterious shame be avoided? The long-term consequences of inducing shame in candidates are considered. Shame in training can have a tremendous impact on the analyst's professional identity, ambition, and personal sense of worth.

I think it's a good idea not to overwhelm a supervisee with all the clever ideas that you as a supervisor think you have. This is one of the ways in which I tend to err in supervision. I get very stimulated, and sometimes I talk too much, and it can have a deleterious effect on the work of the supervisee. Occasionally, supervisees who are working through the problems of speaking up against authority in their own analyses begin to indicate to me that I sort of make them feel stupid-things like that.

With those refreshingly candid remarks Roy Schafer (1984, p. 225) named some of the potential sources of candidates' shame. Who among us has not felt inadequate when we compared ourselves with a renowned supervisor? Are some painful shame experiences inherent in analytic training and, therefore, unavoidable? Does shame make any positive contribution to our professional growth? I believe that our shame experiences in training can have a lasting effect on our subsequent ability to deal with shame in the treatment relationship.

Sources of Shame in Analytic Training

Shame occurs typically, if not always, in the context of an emotional relationship. The sharp increase in self-attention (and sometimes the increased sensitivity of the face produced by blushing) causes the person to feel as though he were naked and exposed to the world. Shame motivates the desire to hide, to disappear. Shame can also produce a feeling of ineptness, incapacity, and a feeling of not belonging [Izard, 1977, p. 92].

It is difficult to imagine an educative process more acutely conducive of shame than analytic training. Every aspect of Izard's definition fits the analytic training process. When we are candidates our relationships with our analyst, supervisors, teachers, patients, colleagues, and even the institute itself are all emotional relationships. These people matter to us, and we care what they think and feel about us. Self-attention is intense in training, since heightened self-awareness plays such a crucial role in every part of the learning process. A candidate must be extremely self-observant. Without self-observation, every aspect of analytic training, from personal analysis to supervision and even theoretical coursework would be a disembodied, sterile exercise.

So, in training all the ingredients needed to induce shame are present. Candidates are looking intensely at themselves as they are being evaluated by people whose opinion of them matters deeply. But yet another pressure is often added. Candidates are frequently aware of an expectation that not only should they be able to reveal themselves while being evaluated, but they should be able to do so relatively *comfortably*. To put it briefly, candidates are expected to open themselves to an unusual degree of personal scrutiny and still maintain enough equanimity to function in their new professional roles. Since they often incorporate these expectations, they also expect themselves to be comfortably self-revealing. At the same time, they are involved in a personal treatment process that facilitates less reliance on accustomed defenses, and therefore they are confronting anxiety their defenses previously kept at bay. They are learning a new, highly ambiguous task, absorbing complicated theoretical material, making new friendships, and attempting to integrate this new life with their previous responsibilities and relationships. And, often, any discomfort with this process is seen as problematic by the candidate himself, as well as others. Here is one graduate's self-reflections, 50 years after his training was completed:

> At first, I responded to my analyst's expectations of me to think about myself and others, and reveal to him what I was thinking with no pleasure in the procedure. People used to remark how interesting it must be to have an opportunity to study oneself with the help of a guide and mentor. I don't recall disagreeing very actively, probably out of some apprehension that if I did so, they would think I must have had a terrible past. I resisted the process of self-revelation, often quite painfully [English, 1976, p. 192].

Thus English suffered from shame about his shame. His discomfort at revealing himself felt as if it was, itself, something to hide and be ashamed of. It is the shame about feeling shame that, I think, is unequivocally harmful, unnecessary, and potentially avoidable in training.

We train people to do something that is intensely personal. If we were teaching people how to be carpenters, we would pass judgment on what they produce, but our judgment would not reflect so exquisitely on who they are as human beings. An analyst's hopes for her patient reflect her deepest, intensely personal values about life. The outcome of the treatments she conducts can have a powerful impact on her own sense of self.

So, for many reasons, a candidate's self-worth is likely to be deeply affected by how his control cases seem to be going. A competitive climate can also foster candidates' shame. We subtly promote competition among candidates by, for example, comparing one class with another, or candidates with each other or with candidates in golden analytic eras in the past. It is not difficult, in classes, to privilege certain kinds of contributions to the discussion, thus valuing one type of intellect over others.

Candidates often become adept at avoiding mention of certain extracurricular activities. I have regularly encountered women candidates who seem to feel their personal experience as mothers is a source of shame. It almost seems as though they feel disqualified from the higher echelons of analytic intellect, by being sullied by life experience. A version of this is the comment, "I am just clinical," as though those who contribute theory breathe more rarified air than can a mere clinician. I believe the tendency to value the theoretician over the clinician has a subtle, but long-lasting effect on our feelings about doing clinical work. Can we feel proud toward the end of our careers if we have been "just clinical"? Can we maintain belief in the value of our work, over the long haul, even though it is frequently challenged by our patients, if we start our careers ashamed of being "just clinical"? I think our analytic jargon, while sometimes a useful shorthand, often obfuscates, thereby further promoting elitism. How frequently we value a sharp intellect over plainer voices of human wisdom and experience!

So a candidate, with her professional life at stake, comes to supervision, where her countertransference is often a central focus. It is less likely that the supervisor's countertransferences (to the candidate, as well as the candidate's patient) will be similarly scrutinized. We do not have as firmly established a tradition of looking at supervisory countertransference as we have for examining an analyst's countertransference in treatment. Given the power differentials, this omission can hardly be accidental. I believe there are also many ways to engage in outright, but unacknowledged competition with a candidate, and these, too, can foster the candidate's feelings of inadequacy and shame. The context hardly creates a level playing field. As Edgar Levenson (1982) suggests, supervision derives its clarity from its level of abstraction. The supervisor can address himself to the *class of* patients to which a particular patient belongs. In addition, the supervisor has the advantage of being removed from the patient's pressures. Also, he is already "stamped" with the institute's seal of approval. Competition between supervisor and candidate is, thus, unfair and potentially shaming.

Especially conducive to evoking a candidate's shame is the situation we create when we provide the candidate with a patient who is fundamentally unanalyzable and then judge the candidate on his ability to conduct an analysis. An example would be assigning the candidate a patient who spends 40 out of every 45 minutes campaigning to break the frame and considers the analytic interpretive process a poor substitute for unlimited contact. In this situation the candidate is extremely likely to feel like a failure with the patient and with the supervisor. In the treatment he feels he is not helping the patient feel better. The patient's troubles are urgent and require relief. What the treatment provides is too slow, abstract, removed from the patient's crises. With the supervisor the candidate feels equally inadequate, but for a contradictory set of reasons. He feels he has been too concerned with the patient's life and not sufficiently focused on the patient's analysis. He is too easily drawn into the patient's mood of urgency. He has let himself be bullied, perhaps even blackmailed by the patient's implicit threat to leave treatment if he isn't more forthcoming with personally revealing, openly caring, concretely advising behavior. In short, with the patient the supervisee feels inadequate about his ability to help, while with the supervisor he feels ashamed because he is not doing enough to analyze.

A more subtle source of shame is the candidate's temptation to imitate the supervisor, rather than developing his own, unique style. We foster this self-disrespect if we collaborate in the attitude that the way the patient will get an optimal treatment is for the supervisee to absorb as much as possible in the supervisory hour and hold on to it with all his might until he next sees the patient, when he must dispense these precious drops into the patient's ear. What the candidate "learns" from this dehumanizing experience is that the best he can be is a fairly accurate imitation of someone else.

But even supervisors who are uncomfortable with authoritarian self certainty can subtly foster lasting shame in the candidate. Depending partly on his tone of voice, a supervisor who suggests how he would have responded to the patient may invite comparison, shame, and envy, even while he may also be making valid and valuable points. Although we may intellectually understand shame as generally the product of an interpersonal process, often we do not see how the supervisor contributed to it, because we are relatively unaccustomed to examining automatically the countertransferences of supervisors. Not looking at the supervisor's emotional contribution, we treat the candidate's shame as though it had a virgin birth, conceived entirely by the supervisee.

For example, a candidate in analytic training presents his work with an obsessive patient whose language is at a 45 degree angle away from direct communication. He says he is upset rather than angry to avoid the part of the message that might make him anxious. As the supervisor, I hear in the material a kind of contagion. The patient's indirectness seems to elicit something similar in the language of the candidate. When I point this out, I am very likely to elicit the supervisee's shame. While seeing any countertransferential defensiveness may evoke some shame, becoming aware of obsessive language is particularly shame inducing, at least in my supervisees. I wonder if this reaction is partially a product of my own attitude. Perhaps not unlike Schafer (1984), I can feel tremendous zeal at these moments. I am excited to impart something I think of as potentially highly mutative. My excitement may lend intensity to my voice. My supervisee may then feel his obsessive defenses have been all too eagerly exposed.

Another kind of supervisory situation is likely to elicit shame in my supervisees. When I see the content of the session, that is, *what* is being communicated, being *enacted* in the session, and I point this out, I think it can evoke in the candidate the kind of shame that we feel when we did not know our slip was showing or that or there is a hole in our shoe and someone comments on it. In this situation, as with contagious obsessive language, I believe some shame in the supervisee may be inevitable, but my own emotions will affect the manner and timing of my comments, which may affect the intensity of the supervisee's shame. Do I interpret with glee, with unnecessary emphasis, or with compassion for the courage it takes to train as an analyst?

LEGACIES OF CANDIDATES' SHAME

We cannot be too surprised that candidates often develop a lingering sense of incapacity that is not dispelled upon receipt of their certificates. Many harbor vague feelings that other graduates are doing "real" analysis, while their own inadequacies confine them to some analytic equivalent of the peanut gallery. Even before training begins, self-selection and admission policies probably favor candidates who are likely to develop shame. A serious student who has always studied hard for good grades may well be troubled with anxious shame when evaluated on his conduct of a process that is as unpredictable as analysis. Unlike in graduate school, in psychoanalysis there is no way to cram for sessions with patients. In fact, trying too hard to do well can deaden the process, rendering the candidate obsessively controlling and the treatment stultified.

Again in analytic training, unlike in any other learning process, a person being evaluated is expected to comfortably shine a spotlight on his personal difficulties. Any discomfort while doing so itself can create anxious shame, since the analytic culture prizes nondefensive openness. I believe this priority can inculcate shame about shame, which, I suggest, is potentially much more detrimental than the shame itself. One of its legacies is a persistent uncertainty about how much of our inner experience to reveal to our colleagues and patients. Lately, we have been challenging ourselves, and each other, to be more and more self-revealing in a kind of escalating game of truth or dare, making reality TV out of many of our conferences. In what seems to me a macho display, our case presentations become competitions for who can confess to the worst analytic sins and still seem relatively at ease. And no wonder we have so many schools of thought on the uses of self-disclosure. Expected to be gracefully self-revealing during training, after graduation some of us idealize self-revelation, overburdening our patients, while others maintain a self-protective, emotionally hidden withholding stance.

Inculcating anxious shame about shame, then, delivers the coup de grâce. Elsewhere (Buechler, 2004) I have written about the emotion related values that I feel are essential to the analytic endeavor, such values as avid curiosity, hope for change, interpersonal courage, a powerful sense of therapeutic purpose, replenishing emotional reserves, personal integrity, and a well-developed capacity to bear loss. When we elicit in a candidate shame, especially anxious shame about shame, I believe we undermine his development of these crucial strengths. The candidate who is thus ashamed is not likely to feel much wholeness or integrity, since she feels she cannot herself practice the openness she advocates for others. She may feel too worried and self-protective to be curious, hopeful, or courageous, and her sense of purpose will be blunted by the more pressing need for safety. Shame about shame tempts the candidate to hide in the shadows to wait out her training and perhaps enter her analytic career without some of the strengths that can sustain alive involvement. This experience makes it easy to burn out early, blaming managed care, difficult patients, and our bottom line-driven culture. While these factors can be genuinely demoralizing, I think anxious shame about shame leaves us much more vulnerable to their impact.

I can envision reasons some shame may be inevitable, and even adaptive, in analytic training. The functions shame serves in training may be similar to shame's role in early life. Shame motivates a child's development of objective self-awareness. The children we all were needed this perspective to become socially attuned. The analysts that candidates are becoming need a high degree of attunement, self-awareness, and sensitivity to their interpersonal effect. Candidates are preparing for a professional life uniquely dependent on painstaking self awareness, honest self-scrutiny, and a willing acceptance of responsibility for negative interpersonal impact. It is human nature to feel shame when a spotlight is thrown on our significant limitations. As Sullivan (1953) suggested, we learn to be social creatures partly through experiencing varying degrees of failure, with its attendant discomfort. So perhaps shame in analytic training is inevitable and even has its adaptive functions. In other words, a candidate revealing how her limitations as a human being affect her clinical work inevitably feels some shame, as would any other human being acculturated in our society. Nevertheless I think shame about shame is avoidable, destructive, and can leave a lasting, demoralizing legacy. I would like to close with a series of thoughts about how we might delimit anxious shame, and shame about shame, in analytic training.

1. As I suggested earlier, I think shame comes in different flavors, depending on the intrapsychic and interpersonal context. My own intense curiosity about my shame will modulate it. And feeling partnered in analyzing my shame can decrease its loneliness and, perhaps, sadness. Most debilitating, I think, is anxious shame, that deer in the headlights, struck dumb, dysfunctional state we enter in some of our worst moments.

    Anxious shame is what I think Sullivan (1953) was describing when he likened anxiety to a blow on the head. Cognitive powers are limited, the mind is blank, we feel alone and exposed. We may then connect with our own private history of shame, but the yearning to flee often diminishes useful self-observation and learning from the experience. Hence curiosity and other strengths are unavailable to us when anxious shame renders us desperate. We cannot hope to understand when we can only long to escape.

2. Understanding that analytic training involves exposure and human beings react to exposure with shame, we can *expect* some shame in training and communicate that it is a natural response, so that we do not *exacerbate* shame about shame. Candidates are not spineless because they wish they could hide their weak points when they are being evaluated.

3.   Supervision itself deserves to be taught and studied much more. It should not be assumed that one has the necessary skill, on the basis of other attainments, such as years post graduation, publications, or popularity among colleagues. Analytic supervision is an extremely difficult and subtle art, for which some people are better suited than others. Since supervisors play key roles in training, including whether that training inculcates shame, supervisory positions should not be treated as rewards for scholarly, social, or political services rendered.

4.   Emotions themselves are the most powerful modulators of other emotions. Thus, deeply felt pride and curiosity can be relied on to modify painful shame in training. When we are proud of the courage that self examination takes, that healthy pride can modulate shame about the content of what the process is uncovering. This is true, I believe, in any treatment, including the training analysis. In addition to healthy pride, curiosity can lend us a kind of analytic attitude toward ourselves that modulates shame.

5.   Finally, we must give up the worship of isolated intellect in favor of wisdom. In seeking analytic rigor we run the risk of developing rigor mortis. It is not helpful to create elitist hierarchies. Feelings and cognition, Sigmund Freud and Emily Dickinson, Mary Cassatt and John Bowlby all have something valuable to teach us about human life. Candidates who find education and inspiration in their experience as parents are no less worthy than those who resonate with Marcel Proust or Helene Deutsch. Privileging an esoteric jargon shames candidates who find it impenetrable, limits our communication with scholars from other fields, and contributes to our isolation, even from our own colleagues. Perhaps most vitally, it promotes disembodied intellect over wisdom. Personally, I connect wisdom with a kind of savoring. Like the gourmet

whose educated palate discerns the whiff of rosemary in the sauce, the psychoanalyst savors life by noticing its separate psychic ingredients. This educated, heightened awareness of psychological nuance in oneself and others is possible only when our senses are not hobbled by anxious shame. The wisdom to apply the gourmet's focus to life itself, and notice its nuances, and thereby savor it, is born of curiosity that is relatively unhampered by shame. By creating an atmosphere that is free of excessive shame and, most especially, excessive shame about shame, we encourage candidates to acquire the wisdom to appreciate shades of difference in their own, and their patient's words, tones, muscle movements, and other ingredients of human self-expression. Noticing nuance, the psychoanalytic gourmet feels too stimulated to burn out. Hers is the wisdom to take in everything an hour has to offer and live it to its fullest.

REFERENCES

Buechler, S. (2004). *Clinical Values: Emotions That Guide Psychoanalytic Treatment*. Hillsdale, NJ: The Analytic Press.

English, O. S. (1976). The emotional stress of psychotherapeutic practice. *Journal of the American Academy of Psychoanalysis and Dynamic Psychiatry* 4:119–210.

Izard, C. E. (1977). *Human Emotions*. New York: Plenum Press.

Levenson, E. (1982). Follow the fox: An inquiry into the vicissitudes of psychoanalytic supervision. *Contemporary Psychoanalysis* 18:1–15.

Schafer, R. (1984). Supervisory session with discussion. In: *Clinical Perspectives on the Supervision of Psychoanalysis and Psychotherapy*, ed. L. Caligor, P. M. Bromberg & J. D. Meltzer. New York: Plenum Press, pp. 207–230.

Sullivan, H. S. (1953). *The Interpersonal Theory of Psychiatry*. New York: W.W. Norton.

CHAPTER FOUR

A Letter to My First Supervisor[*]

INTRODUCTION

In 2009 I edited a special issue of *Contemporary Psychoanalysis*, dedicated to the study of psychoanalytic education. Along with 16 other analysts I tried to describe what goes right, when training genuinely enhances candidates' natural abilities.

As part of my contribution, I wrote a "letter" to my first analytic supervisor, in an effort to find words for what he imparted to me. Although not a letter in the usual sense, since he had died long before it was written, nevertheless it expressed my gratitude as well as some ideas about effective supervision.

Editing this issue was a valuable experience for me. Aside from teaching me a profound respect for the painstaking work of a journal editor, it acquainted me with the breadth of opinion about what "works" when supervision goes well. Senior analysts ranged from endorsing common practices to advocating scrapping institute training altogether.

My letter was a very personal statement about my supervisor's impact on my life and work. More than anything else, his integrity profoundly affected me. As an analyst and supervisor, his actions were consonant with his words. He was a man who truly practiced what he

[*] *Contemporary Psychoanalysis,* 2009, 45:3, pp. 422–427.

preached. How he treated me, in supervision, conformed with the values that informed his work as a clinician. This wholeness, this seamlessness, greatly contributed to the impression he made.

ABSTRACT

Twenty-five years later, the author examines the impact of her first analytic supervisor on her growth as an analyst and as a human being.

Dear Ralph [M. Crowley, M.D.],

I am writing to thank you for being my first analytic supervisor. I know you helped me enormously, but I wish I could figure out just how you did it. I have been trying to understand this for 25 years now. I am hoping that writing this letter will help me formulate what made you such an inspiring model for me.

I spoke at your memorial service, since I was the last candidate you worked with in supervision. I thought I could tell people what you taught me and how you gave me confidence. I thought it would be easy, for I knew that you made a huge difference in my training. But when I sat down to write, I drew a blank.

Well, not exactly a blank. I could see your whimsical half-smile. I could hear your refrain, "Now, Sandy, let's look at what you *do* know about the patient." I could remember how often you had new articles waiting for me. You introduced me to the minimalism of Louis B. Hill's writing. You taught me that the simplest, most direct expression of analytic ideas can be profound. You heightened my respect for contributions that address specific clinical dilemmas, rather than sweeping theoretical statements. Those papers, waiting on my chair for our 9 A.M. supervision, meant to me that my education as an analyst mattered enough for you to bother to find them. At the time, I think that was their greatest impact.

But is that all you did? Was I so needful of someone to believe in me that you were simply the right person at the right time? Just a nice guy who communicated a positive attitude about my potential? Is that what beginning candidates most need?

I don't think it is that simple. At the memorial I spoke of your integrity. You had a consistency of word and deed. Your way of being with me was consonant with the values you were teaching. I learned something about how to be with my patient from how you were with me. Somehow you balanced curiosity with patience. For me, then, curiosity was a drive that obliterated patience. It sometimes still works that way. Patience is not one of my virtues. But you taught me about it in the way you contrasted with me. With you, for the first time, I was conscious of how powerfully contrast teaches.

My patient seemed at the brink of disaster. She came to me poised between functioning and giving up. She demanded that I keep her afloat, and, in retrospect, I can see that I asked the same of you. I needed to believe that you could (magically) give me the words that would keep the analysis going long enough for it to take hold. I wanted it, the patient, and me to have a chance. Just give us a chance. I'll work hard. I promise. Just give me a chance in the beginning.

I felt that you saw beyond the beginning, when I was still embroiled in it. You reminded me of an earlier teacher, who taught me how to drive a car and told me to look not just in front of the car, but "far, high, and wide." Even back in those early days I recognized that that advice applied to more than just driving cars.

You were not flashy. Others dazzled with their keen intelligence and sharp wit. And, I admit, sometimes I was dazzled. Like so many of the young, I confused intelligence with wisdom. I was overly impressed by a razor-sharp wit. I took its failure to help me clinically as *my* failure. Like so many others, I was tempted to undervalue you, because you didn't bellow. You weren't trying to be impressive. You were trying to be Ralph.

Time passed, the treatment did take hold and, with many misgivings, I stayed in training. It was a tough choice. I felt drawn to go back to academia. But my wish to forge an adequate clinical instrument prevailed. In a way, you prevailed. I can now see that what didn't happen with you was as important as what did happen.

You didn't make me choose between you and what I believed was right clinically. It wasn't that we never differed. But you just let the difference hang in the air. You seemed to believe that was enough. It was.

You didn't seem horrified by my passion. In fact, you didn't seem to believe it would disqualify me. I thought that to become an analyst I would have to tame and cloak it beneath a veneer of "neutrality." You helped me feel that it was an aspect of who I am, something to use rather than something to suppress.

I wondered why you seemed amused by me. I don't mean that you were laughing at me. Just slightly amused or, perhaps, bemused. Was it my earnestness? How did you come to understand me so well? I didn't know how fully you grasped me until our last long talk, which took place at the annual society retreat just after I graduated. You and I searched for, but never found, a trail you thought you remembered. You spoke of your family and then asked me how things had been going for me since graduation. I began to talk about my uncertainties about the direction of my career at that point. I was unsure where I was going in that and other areas of my life. You looked at me with your humorous but wholly friendly smile and said, "You don't *consciously* know where you are going." I wouldn't have felt so profoundly understood and accepted without the smile.

It was through you I became convinced about Sullivan. I had studied him in graduate school, and I understood some of the theory, but I had not yet made it my own. I hadn't found how it could help sharpen my focus in a session. I heard you do that out loud in the supervision. You told me what Sullivan would say about the material I presented. You made the theory useful, not just interesting. You showed me how theory can inspire an intervention. I began to think about what guides our focus, as we listen to patients. How the theories we have read and, most especially, the apt phrases we have incorporated shape what we hear, forget, respond to, privilege.

Others amplified the lessons I learned from you, but you gave me a foundation. Intuitively, I sensed that I had grown. But I couldn't formulate what I had learned, and how you taught it. What I most regret is that I don't think I told you how grateful I am.

So, I am telling you now. But, like many other things, perhaps you knew. I would like to think so. I would like to think that was part of your smile and what gave your eyes their brightness. I hope you knew how much I would come to respect profound insight expressed in simple, accessible language.

You taught me that our all being "simply human" could be taken to mean that we all have some acquaintance with basic human experiences, such as anxiety and frantic efforts to avoid its escalation. While each hour and each human being offers surprises, there are also consistencies. What can be predicted are the fundamental struggles that are part of being a person. As Rilke, my favorite poet, wrote in his *Letters to a Young Poet*, "Do not be bewildered by the surfaces; in the depths all becomes law."

Did you know that we would still be talking to each other? After you died you took up a permanent place in what I like to call my "internal chorus." I see it as essential that candidates audition their supervisors and others for inclusion in this chorus. In training (I hope) we internalize some of our relationships to our analyst, supervisors, teachers, and others. These voices can make even the loneliest clinical moments less painful. For me, the quality of the experience of intense aloneness depends on who I am with when I am alone. Ideally, analytic training can provide graduates with an array of internalized mentors who guide, support, and inspire them in their loneliest hours, enabling them to bear vicariously traumatic, conflict-laden, and other painful exchanges without significant burnout.

So, if, with a particular patient, my internal chorus of analysts gives me acceptable feedback, I don't feel too lonely. I can turn to these familiar mentors, with their characteristic ways of expressing themselves. Then my aloneness feels less absolute. Even if the patient completely withdraws from me, I can probably bear it because I still have my good opinion of myself. I can think about why the patient is withdrawing, find meaning in the transference and countertransference, and explore it in my mind theoretically. I have plenty to play with, in a Winnicottian sense. But if, with a patient, the chorus cuts me off, and especially if that feels permanent, I am cast out in space, lost forever. This, to me, is true loneliness. It does not end after the 45 minutes are up.

Another way to express this is that an analyst needs a relative absence of persecutory inner objects. This allows her to bear what the patient evokes, most of the time. We each probably have a different Achilles heel, that is, the coping style in patients that evokes undue harshness from our internal chorus. A withdrawn, schizoid patient may leave us feeling as though we are sending messages in bottles into an expanse of sea or trying to play tennis when the ball isn't coming back. Like brides left at the altar, we may feel as though we are the only ones who care enough to make a commitment. Depending on our own character issues, this feeling can be more profoundly or less profoundly disorienting, but it always leaves us without the human responsiveness we all use in order to know, literally and figuratively, where we are with each other. But, for some of us, our responses to the schizoid, withdrawn patient incur great wrath from our internal chorus, evoking a profoundly guilty loneliness, while other analysts can maintain a curious, creative aloneness with withdrawn patients, but feel tremendously self-critical about their responses to narcissistically entitled patients. For each of us, there are probably certain patients who most easily drive us into a harshly self-critical state in which we are cut off from the comfort of positive, internalized professional objects.

For me, personally, the worst form of loneliness, the one in which I most profoundly lose myself, is signaled by my effort to coast through a session. I am convinced that the temptation to coast is a dangerous form of burnout. It can be born of many parents, including a marriage of loneliness and fatigue. Unsure whether I will have the stamina for the overly demanding schedule I have created, I feel tempted to look for an hour I can slide through, half-attending. Snapping back after one of these un-scheduled mini vacations, I feel guilty enough to force myself to focus on what is being said to me, hoping to glean what I have missed from what follows. At such moments, just getting through relatively unscathed feels like a triumph. To survive undetected can seem ambitious enough. We are scrutinized hour after hour, and we scrutinize ourselves. We hear common and uncommon human misery, as well, of course, as other subjects. It can be tempting to steer clear of pain. And yet coasting has a predictable aftermath, at least for me. It leaves an empty, demoralized, un-connected feeling. Like so many other time killers, such as television and internet addiction, just getting through promises a relief it does not deliver. It does not bring peace or comfort. It does not ease the burden of the work. It is a false hope, a mirage, seeming to offer smooth sailing, but actually depriving me of the meeting that might bring genuine solace.

I would say that some of our most painful loneliness results from losing touch with ourselves. Ideally, training is the time to equip ourselves to withstand the rigors of a lifetime of practice. A nurturing internal chorus, a supply of theoretical ideas to play with, and a well-developed sense of clinical purpose can certainly help. But also crucial, I think, is how we each feel about the effort doing treatment entails. It will not surprise you that Rilke best expressed my feelings about the effort the work requires of us:

> People have (with the help of conventions) oriented all their solu-tions toward the easiest side of the easy; but it is clear that we must hold to what is difficult; everything alive holds to it, everything in Nature grows and defends itself in its own way and is characteris-tically and spontaneously itself, seeks at all costs to be so and against all opposition. We know little, but that we must hold to what is difficult is a certainty that will not forsake us. (pp. 67-68).

You made a difference for me, Ralph, by becoming a depend-able part of me. With your wit, belief in human potential, and absolute integrity, you will always have a significant role in my internal chorus. As it has in the past, your voice will continue to guide and strengthen me. How many times have I remembered the moment when I told you that I worried that my patient wanted to use the treatment to become perfect enough to go to heaven and, with your usual dry wit, you leavened my seriousness by saying, "I think you should let her know that you're not an expert in that." You helped me put the treatment, the patient, and myself in broader perspective. Aside from your wit and patience, I so deeply appreciated your eagerness to teach. You seemed to actually enjoy it, and not just tolerate it. Your attitude was contagious. Now, I love it, too.

Most of all, I hope you understood that you helped me by believing in me before I could. You extrapolated from who I was, to who I could become. I hope you knew you would be a touchstone for the rest of my career; for the rest of my life.

With love,
Sandra

References

Rilke , R.M. (1934/1984). *Letters to a Young Poet.* New York: Random House.

CHAPTER FIVE

Early Career Development[*]

INTRODUCTION

This paper makes some suggestions as to how we can nurture analytic talent. More specifically, it names some challenges facing analytic training institutes, and how they might be met. Among the questions it raises are the following:

1. Can good supervision be defined? Is it the same, regardless of the institute's theoretical leanings? What are its goals?
2. How can we facilitate the development of a clinician's capacity to meet the inevitable challenges of an analytic career, including its many unavoidable uncertainties?
3. What values/goals inherent in conducting analyses can be modeled, and thereby nurtured, in the training process?
4. What do we want to avoid promoting in analytic training? How might we go about this?
5. Going beyond just the supervision, can we describe the "ideal" or "optimal" preparation for becoming an analyst? What are some of the most essential ingredients?

---

[*] This paper was presented at Division 39 of the American Psychological Association, April 16, 2001.

In this paper I crystallize the idea that in analytic training the medium is the message. That is, how the candidate is treated registers indelibly, forever affecting their treatment approach and many other aspects of their professional and personal conduct.

EARLY CAREER DEVELOPMENT

How can we nurture analytic talent? More specifically:

1. What is good analytic supervision? What are its goals?
2. How can we facilitate the development of a clinician's capacity to bear uncertainty?
3. What values/goals inherent in analytic treatment also pertain to analytic training?
4. What do we want to avoid promoting in analytic training? How might we go about this?
5. Can we describe the "ideal" or "optimal" analytic training? If so, what are its defining characteristics and goals?

BASIC CONCEPTS ABOUT TRAINING

1. THE INTERNAL CHORUS

I think it can be a constructive part of analytic identity formation to take in the voice of an analyst, supervisor, or teacher. Personally, I am sure I incorporated some of my training analyst's ideals, as well as some of the ideals of my supervisors and teachers, and I feel I benefited from it. Any process of identity formation, much like adolescence, includes taking in values. Over time the candidate develops her own unique amalgam of personal, clinical, and cultural values. But without the inter-generational transmission of clinical values much that is precious would be lost to us all. Elsewhere (2004) I have considered these voices as a kind of "internal chorus" that, hopefully, accompanies, guides, and sometimes comforts the analyst for the rest of her career. Without this compass many forty-five minute hours would be lonelier, more confusing, and sadder than they have to be.

50

2. THE MEDIUM IS THE MESSAGE

If the process of becoming an analyst gratuitously shames, it won't enhance the candidate's capacity to treat self-esteem issues. If analytic education stifles the candidate's unique voice, it won't hone his ability to help his patients individuate. How we teach shapes *what* is learned. The medium is the message.

It is implicit in my work that the process and content of analytic education must be isomorphic. That is, for example, we can't facilitate the expression of curiosity without demonstrating it in the supervisory process. The supervisor has to talk about the clinical uses of curiosity in an openly curious way. Perhaps it takes a whole, passionately curious village to nurture this quality in the developing analyst.

The values enacted in the supervision, and whether they are consonant with the supervisor's stated approach, are core to the supervision's impact. Thus, a supervisor who preaches kindness to patients but, in the supervision, behaves contemptuously will confuse, at best. On the other hand, hopefully, we have all experienced the powerful effect of supervisory integrity, that is wholeness, or consistency between word and act. A supervisor makes a mistake, forgets something, needs help, etc. Does she live the moment palpably valuing self-discovery and clinical effectiveness over her own pride? Is there evident courage, tactful truth, in how she teaches? Does intense clinical purpose impassion the supervision? Does the supervisor embody realistic hope? Can she gracefully bear losses, including the end of the supervision process itself? In other words supervision should manifest the meaningfulness of clinical values.

3. WHOLENESS

This is about encouraging people to use who they are as human beings in their clinical work. I can't tell you how many times people entering training have seemed to me to be apologetic about former careers, being parents, or having interests other than psychoanalysis. Perhaps the cumbersome jargon analysts often use tells them they don't belong in analytic training unless they are willing to act as though they were just born and had no clinically useful experience at all! A striking contrast to this was the philosophy of Ralph Crowley, M.D. who was a superb supervisor, and always tried to capitalize on the supervisee's personal resources. When we come to work as analysts we are still parents, readers, art lovers, etc. We bring our whole selves to the office in the morning, and we had better learn to call on all our resources for our difficult task.

4. ENHANCING THE SENSE OF CLINICAL PURPOSE.
The sense of purpose is, to me, far more important than any particular goal in treatment. It is an attitude of purposefulness that looks for meaning, assumes the quality of a life is important, and believes that treatment can contribute to life's richness. Nietzsche once remarked, "If we have a 'why' we can live with any 'how'." As analysts and as patients we can bear the pain of treatment if we have a strong sense of its ultimate purpose. In the moving play, "Angels in America," a character advises us all to reach for "more life." To me, reaching for more life is the central goal in treatment. It is also the main reason training is worthwhile. As clinicians we are our own instruments. To become the best possible clinical instruments, to do our utmost to promote more life, we have to learn to use every potential personal resource we have, to its utmost.

5. DEVELOPING THE USE OF COUNTERTRANSFERENCE AS VITAL INFORMATION, ABOUT BOTH TREATMENT PARTICIPANTS.
Very often when people enter supervision they feel as though some of their countertransference is a secret shame, a response that would disqualify them from the profession if it were found out. The change that is often helpful is to become better able to use countertransference as information, not as self-castigation. Like fire, countertransference is, in itself, generally neither good nor bad, but it can be constructive or destructive, depending on how it is used.

6. FACILITATING ENTRANCE INTO THE CULTURE OF PSYCHOANALYSIS.
I have elaborated elsewhere (2004) that I believe psychoanalysis is a culture, with a language, tradition, a history, mores, and even a kind of system of values, which include courage, integrity, hope, honoring truth,

treasuring individuality, and fostering personal freedom. As is true for any profession, we undergo changes in our identities when we enter the field. Of course, we remain ourselves, but we also become members of a new group. This transition can be difficult, as can any adolescence. It can bring up issues left unresolved in our own, personal teen years. Were we rebels, conformists, leaders, reluctant followers, or always perched on the fence? Training can often facilitate transition into the field by bringing out the distinctiveness of each analytic voice, encouraging difference, as it also passes on a rich heritage. It should nurture what I call the process of self-appointment. We each have to appoint ourselves as therapists and analysts. No one else can truly do this for us. We have to *feel* we are clinicians in order to bear the responsibility of working with our first patients. As we, hopefully, gain confidence, self-appointment becomes a more natural, automatic, smooth process.

7. DEVELOPING OUR CAPACITY FOR PRIMARILY NON-NARCISSISTIC INVESTMENTS IN LIFE AND GROWTH.

Describing how her work has changed over the span of her long analytic career Alberta Szalita once said, "It boils down to one thing: to what degree you are concerned with yourself and to what degree you are, as a therapist, concerned with the other person"(Issacharoff, 1997, p. 627). Supervision is, to me, the art of nurturing a predominantly non-narcissistic capacity to foster life.

8. AVOIDING GRATUITOUS SHAMING IN TRAINING.

We can not nurture candidates' capacity for non-narcissistic commitment to the field if we gratuitously shame them during their training. Shaming candidates debilitates the centeredness they need in order to face a lifetime of clinical challenges. Only a confident, centered analyst with a strong, independent voice, and a passionate love for the truth, can make an abiding commitment to life and growth.

Shame is likely to result if the candidate feels she has to hide what she does with patients that would be deemed "not analytic" if it were exposed. I will not attempt to address the vast question of whether psychoanalysis and psychotherapy differ quantitatively and/or qualitatively. Regardless of our position on this matter, the assumption that what is analytic is more intellectual and superior is a prejudice that breeds what prejudices usually breed-scapegoating. If we create such an atmosphere we tempt candidates to lie about what they really do with their patients. This will surely foster shame but, perhaps just as importantly, it will fail to nurture what I have elsewhere (2004) called "clinical values." Faith in the value of truth, authenticity, curiosity, hope, courage, a sense of purpose, and integrity, are necessary to the analytic process, as I see it. These values play a role in enhancing our conviction that our work has inherent meaning and purpose. They give us strength in the painful, confusing, challenging moments we all face clinically. They also protect us from early burnout. Without sufficient hope, courage, and clarity of purpose we can too easily succumb to the forces of cynicism about whether our field has a future.

It seems to me to be very important to distinguish gratuitous shame induction from other sources of shame. Elsewhere (2008) I have tried to distinguish anxious shame from angry shame and regretful or guilty shame. I think when shaming feels gratuitous it often evokes an angry shame. The intensity of the feeling comes from the combination of the emotions. When the training process feels unnecessarily shaming the candidate may feel something like, "You didn't have to make me feel this. It was not necessary. You chose to shame me, when you could have chosen otherwise. Maybe you like to see me squirm, or you enjoy feeling superior to me, or you revel in your power."

Part of the legacy of these shaming experiences can be the painful feeling that in her silence the candidate collaborated. The feeling that one has collaborated in being shamed oneself, or in allowing another to be shamed, can be especially damaging. The candidate who sits in silence as her work is trashed in class, or in supervision, goes home with the shame of feeling exposed but, perhaps even more painfully, the feeling of having betrayed herself by not standing up for herself. I believe that this can be one of the most damaging shame experiences in training (or elsewhere). "Going along to get along" when we are being shamed gratuitously leaves a destructive legacy that, I suggest, is especially difficult to bear and especially hard to alter.

Seeking advanced clinical training seems to me to be a tremendous act of faith. Candidates trust that their investment of time, money, and effort will pay off in the long run. Personally, I believe training *is* worthwhile, since it *can* cultivate the candidate's talents. I have often said that the violinist, painter, and surgeon take care of their instruments, and we do, too, but in analysis our instrument is our own psyche. Analytic training should optimize each candidate's potential as a clinical instrument.

9. RESILIENCE

A further requirement is the analyst's emotional resilience. I have tried to understand this quality in many different ways. What allows us to bounce back, after a difficult moment, or session, or a longer stretch of time? What helps us regain our emotional balance, after we have been knocked off kilter? Where do we find the strength to learn from our mistakes and move on?

Emotional resilience is at the heart of empathy, from my point of view. I differentiate empathy from sympathy. The sympathetic listener feels something similar to what she is hearing. But the empathic listener goes further. She feels in tune with the other person, recovers her balance, and learns something potentially useful from this process. To illustrate, it is generally not empathic to join a child having a tantrum by having one of your own. Empathy requires us to feel the edge of the tantrum, so we emotionally reverberate with it, but then right ourselves, and, finally, understand something potentially useful about what happened, so we can help ourselves and the child grow from the experience. Resilience comes from our own need to recover balance. Perhaps we have felt intense, contagious rage or anxiety or sorrow in a session. Being available for this mutual experience is the first stage of a healing empathy but, by itself, it is not enough, in my judgment. Curative empathy requires us to dig deeper into ourselves than that. We need to call upon all our emotional resources, to come back to a curious holding. Once we have done that, we can wonder about the whole journey, and, hopefully, learn something about ourselves and the patient. Sometimes in living through an unbearable sadness, we may better understand the patient's losses and our own. If the process stopped there it might be comfortingly sympathetic and, therefore, alleviate loneliness in both people. While certainly not a bad outcome that is often not enough, in my judgment. I agree with conceptions of analysis as a process of structural change, and not just amelioration of painful feelings. That is, analysis aims at changing how people function; how they process their experiences, and not just what those experiences are. In analysis it is not enough to help someone feel better today. We aim to help them know life differently, to take it in differently. Structural change means to me hearing with new ears and seeing with new eyes. We don't just help people hear or see something more positive today. We help them hear and see more life today and forever after. They no longer waste one ear and one eye in trying *not* to hear and see, that is, in defensiveness. They spend less of their resources defending **against** their experiences and more of their resources having their experiences. Through bearing something along with the patient we feel how they take life in. And then we use whatever we have inside to regain the capacity to wonder and to connect. And then both of us stop, look back, learn, and, maybe change. Engaging empathically takes tremendous emotional resources. Every positive feeling, from joy to hope, to curiosity and love must be recruited, and it is necessary to have a capacity for bearing every negative feeling, from loneliness, to anger, to fear, to sorrow. This work requires us to be human beings *who can think feelingfully and feel thoughtfully.* Training must bring out our natural potential for empathic relatedness.

10. THE CAPACITY TO BECOME A TRANSITIONAL OBJECT

I will add just one more ability to this list of requirements for the budding analyst: the capacity to become a transitional object. As material to be molded I, like the teddy bear or blanket, have limitations. I have a reality of my own, that is not a product of the patient's fantasy. A teddy bear can probably be seen as a sweet baby bear or a jungle tyrant, but it is hard to make it into a convincing waterfall. Similarly there are limits in how I can be experienced. A blanket comes with its own contours, and so do I. But, within these boundaries, I believe I should be malleable enough for the patient to transform me into the analyst he or she most needs. Training brings out our capacity to become a transitional object to the extent that it helps us recognize what I call the textural aspects of the work.

More specifically I mean that patients affect the frequency of my interventions, the tone of my voice, the direction of my gaze, the posture of my body, the length of my sentences, the pace of the interchange, (from rapid fire staccato to slow and measured) and the use I make of silence. I am calling these elements "textural" to emphasize their relationship to the feel of the experience of being with me.

Thus, I need to be able to be both theme and variations. As theme I am always myself, with my particular signature style. But, within these contours, it is my job as an analyst to be capable of being transformed and, therefore, transformative. I believe that training should aim to bring out the candidate's transformative capacities.

REFERENCES

Buechler, S. (2004). *Clinical Values: Emotions that Guide Psychoanalytic Treatment*. Hillsdale, NJ: The Analytic Press.

——— (2008). *Making a Difference in Patient's Lives: Emotional Experience in the Therapeutic Setting*. New York: Routledge.

Issacharoff, A. (1997). "A Conversation with Dr. Alberta Szalita". *Contemporary Psychoanalysis* 33:615-632.

A Raid on the Inarticulate: Questioning Assumptions in Analytic Training[*]

INTRODUCTION

In this paper I elaborate on the disparity between our belief in the subjectivity of all of our perceptions, as analysts, versus our greater certainty about our perceptions as analytic supervisors and teachers. As clinicians most of us have fully accepted that there is no objectively perceived reality in treatment. But when we put on our other hats, as supervisors and teachers, a mantle of authority seems necessary in order to complete the outfit. What are the consequences of these disparities between our fundamental assumptions as analysts and our most basic assumptions as educators? More specifically, how do we train a candidate to respect differing perspectives but also develop sufficient confidence in her own "signature" style?

---

[*] Paper presented at the Unbehagen, New York City, 2013.

A RAID ON THE INARTICULATE: QUESTIONING ASSUMPTIONS IN ANALYTIC TRAINING

.....Trying to learn to use words, and every attempt
Is a wholly new start, and a different kind of failure
Because one has only learnt to get the better of words
For the thing one no longer has to say, or the way in which
One is no longer disposed to say it. And so each venture
Is a new beginning, a raid on the inarticulate
With shabby equipment always deteriorating
In the general mess of imprecision of feeling,
Undisciplined squads of emotion.

—T. S. Eliot, "East Coker," pp. 30–31

My task, today, is to raid some of the unarticulated assumptions embedded in analytic training. This personal foray is likely to leave out many suppositions that come to your minds and, perhaps to include some you will think unnecessary to name. I hope to entice you to perform a raid of your own. I elaborate on the disparity between our fundamental belief in subjectivity, as analysts, vs. what we seem to believe as analytic supervisors and teachers. As analysts most of us have fully accepted that there is no objectively perceived reality, in treatment as elsewhere. But when we put on our other hats, as supervisors and teachers, a mantle of authority seems necessary in order to complete the outfit. The result is insufficient integrity, or wholeness. That is, we are failing to preach what we practice, and practice what we preach. We are treating candidates like children who must be indoctrinated in religion until they are old enough to give up the faith, as we, ourselves, have done. Some of our field's most serious problems stem, in part, from these often unarticulated, contradictory assumptions.

1. I think that psychoanalytic treatment can lose its meaning without sufficient clarity about how the analyst's training prepares him or her to contribute to the process differently from the ways the patient contributes. In bidding farewell to

60

the original Freudian patriarchs and Sullivan's psychiatric expert, we have lost our belief in our own expertise.

2.   In an effort to rid our training programs of the excessive authoritarianism and logical positivism of previous eras we have purged them of some of what used to be considered essential to the education of an analyst. To avoid seeming old fashioned we expunge courses on specific diagnostic categories, and play down anything that smacks of character issues that existed before the analytic dyad was co-created. I suggest that this has truncated the candidate's passionate sense of purpose. How can we cultivate a passionate desire to treat what can't be named?

3.   At the same time, as previously mentioned, we are inconsistent in our application to training of the relativism we espouse clinically. As clinicians we believe all knowledge is subjective, but, as educators we operate as though it is not.

4.   Toting diagnostic manuals only to satisfy the requirements of insurance companies, we have dispensed with most notions of pathology, making it hard to define progress in treatment. Lacking clear goals we are bleached of passion about our work and cannot convey its profound meaning to anyone else, because we no longer inhabit it ourselves.

5.   And yet, although this is contradictory, everyone at a case conference breathes a sigh of relief when a candidate's patient is once again able to engage in social and professional activities. That sigh gives away our ambivalence about relativism. When a patient's depression is incapacitating, when paranoia is rampant, when schizoid withdrawal is completely isolating, when obsessive ritual takes over a human life we seem, once again, to believe we can define a pathology that is not, primarily, in the eye of the beholder, but is, painfully,

constricting the life of the patient, and can provide both treatment participants with a burning need to take up the work of an analysis.

The assumption of the subjectivity of all perspectives on clinical data has dominated the consulting room for decades, but it has not yet fully infiltrated the training process. What would training programs that take subjectivity seriously look like? If we really believed there is little the analyst objectively knows about the patient, what is still worth teaching the candidate? Should analytic training, much like some forms of religious indoctrination, emphasize the development of profound humility? Should our courses be geared toward helping the budding analyst become aware of how little she knows, while still remaining capable of conducting treatment and charging a fee? Can this brand of chutzpah be taught? What would the curriculum look like? What would be the criteria for deeming a candidate ready to graduate? Should the certificate mention that the successful newly minted analyst has attained the capacity to admit how scanty is his basis for clinical judgment calls?

Hoffman (1991) sums up the analyst's position by stating (p. 77) that "what the analyst seems to understand about his or her own experience and behavior as well as the patient's is always suspect, always susceptible to the vicissitudes of the analyst's own resistance, and always prone to being superseded by another point of view that may emerge." While a bit later I will question aspects of this position, I think there is no doubt, today, that the all-knowing analyst has been de-throned. Yet, when the candidate presents a case in supervision or in class we generally expect him to formulate its dynamics, and we assess his capacity to do so. If we asked the candidate what she knows about the patient and, somewhat like Cordelia, King Lear's youngest daughter, the candidate answered "nothing," we might be as dissatisfied with that answer as was the displeased king, who chastised his daughter that "nothing comes from nothing."

Taking this argument a bit further, how should we select our programs' teachers and training analysts? What qualities indicate that someone will be able to facilitate the candidate's development of comfort with how little he can claim to know?

I find myself in a dilemma that is, for me, quite familiar. As a supervisor I am unhappy with the limitations in the foundation of knowledge in training today, and yet I am in sympathy with the idea that all perceptions in treatment are inherently subjective. But, just as patients tend to want to believe their analysts know something more definite than they do, so candidates want to believe they are accruing knowledge they can rely on in the confusion of clinical exchanges. It is hard to sell people therapeutic or educational processes that eschew claims of knowing what is being treated. I am aware that one can argue that we train candidates to be able to engage their patients in a process of exploration. Once again, this is fine, but for anxious candidates yearning to have a sense of what to prioritize in their first analytic sessions with patients, it often doesn't feel like enough. When I was in charge of a clinic staffed by very inexperienced doctoral student clinicians, a sincere young man preparing to conduct his first therapy session knocked on my door to say, "I have just one question. When the patient arrives, what do I do?" Like that young man, candidates want to feel they increasingly know something about what they are treating, and how to tailor the treatment to the patient's dilemmas. I think supervisors often imply that the candidate's desire to feel prepared is a sign she is hopelessly controlling, or obsessively perfectionistic, or wedded to logical positivism, or grandiose. But we wouldn't say to the novice in any other field that there is something wrong with their desire to feel they know what they are doing and why they are doing it. On the contrary, we probably would find this praiseworthy in a medical student. Are we claiming that psychoanalysis is of a different ilk from all other subject matter, so the initiate's job is to embrace uncertainty rather than try to dispel it? How is the candidate to attain a sense of competence if we tell him that everything that can be said about his patient is only a subjective perspective? Will candidates be content to spend at least four years of their lives devoted to a training process that makes such modest claims?

Personally, I agree with Maroda, when she says (1999, p. 162) that "It seems to be too much of a pendulum swing in the opposite direction of the analyst being all-knowing." I am not taking this position merely because I think we will fail to interest patients and candidates in a process that makes so few claims. I believe that in our efforts toward egalitarian treatment and training processes that adequately reflect human subjectivity we have left ourselves without an adequate compass, without a strong sense of purpose, and without sufficient courage, belief, and confidence in what we do. We have left ourselves too vulnerable to early burnout, which can easily take the form of cynicism about the worth of psychoanalysis today. Instead of questioning our assumptions we question the worth of psychoanalysis, and/or our own worth as individual clinicians. We don't look at what has brought us to this precipice, but only at the precipice itself. In our enthusiasm about embracing the idea that there is no "truth" or reified "reality" we have cleansed ourselves of much of what distinguishes us from other listeners. No wonder we find it hard to justify our worth to insurance companies and skeptical patients. And no wonder that by the last phases of a long career many of us succumb to burnout. Under these circumstances can our eventual capitulation to self-doubt come as a surprise?

INEVITABLE VS. AVOIDABLE PAIN IN TRAINING AND BEYOND

Life hurts. Eventually, clinical work acquaints us with much of the pain inherent in the human condition. In training, we begin adjusting to being in the vicinity of pain, every hour of our professional lives. We become secret, and not so secret sharers. From my point of view sorrow, loneliness, regret, shame, and guilt are inevitable during training and beyond. Along with our patients, we sorrow over losses, like the trauma victim's loss of an unharmed self. Hour after hour we face the loneliness of seeing situations from a vantage point that we may not yet be able to share. We may feel regret, shame, and/or guilt when we coast through a session or, more generally, for missed opportunities.

In a way, all of my books are discussions of the avoidable and unavoidable shame and sorrow inherent in a clinical career. One way or another, we lose every treatment partner we ever have. There is no way around this. In offering us an introduction to the clinical task, training has to acquaint us with the feelings of insufficiency and loss that will punctuate our professional lives. But, I will argue, training could also offer us some measure of inoculation.

We train people to do something that is intensely personal. If we were teaching people how to be carpenters we would pass judgment on what they produce, but it wouldn't reflect so exquisitely on who they are as human beings. An analyst's hopes for her patient reflect her deepest, intensely personal values about life. The outcome of the treatments she conducts can have a powerful impact on her own sense of self.

So, for many reasons the candidate's self-worth is likely to be deeply affected by how his control cases seem to be going. A competitive climate can also foster candidates' shame. We subtly promote competition among candidates by, for example, comparing one class with another, or candidates with each other, or with candidates in golden analytic eras in the past. It is not hard, in classes, to privilege certain kinds of contributions to the discussion, thus valuing one type of intellect over others.

At the same time candidates frequently feel uneasy revealing their previous accomplishments and theoretical allegiances, as well as certain extracurricular activities. I think they often feel they are supposed to act as though they have come to analytic training straight from kindergarten, with no prior professional expertise, like blank chalk boards, immaculate and ready for the imprint of their supervisors, teachers, and analyst. Any claim to professional expertise (even though it may have been required for entrance into the training program!) and any already acquired clinical style will be seen as a form of resistance to training, or grandiosity. It is as though clinically experienced professionals are expected to have no deeply held values, beliefs, and theoretical commitments! What impact does it have on candidates if they acquiesce to this expectation? What is the potential for instilling lasting shame, if we subtly require the candidate to deny a vital aspect of her professional self?

Another dimension of the candidate's life is frequently felt to be a hindrance to training. I have regularly encountered women candidates who seem to feel their personal experience as mothers is a source of shame. It almost seems as though they feel disqualified from the higher echelons of analytic intellect, by being sullied by this form of life experience.

So the candidate, with her professional life at stake, comes to supervision, where her countertransference is often a central focus. Work on countertransference seems to me to be especially conducive to evoking shame in the candidate. The analysis of countertransference in supervision has much in common with the analysis of defense in treatment, with one major difference. In treatment, we explore the patient's defensive style in the genetic context, as well as in its current manifestations. We look at why the analysand needed to develop her defenses. But in supervision, while the candidate's defenses are also an important focus, the genetic situations that necessitated their development are generally not mentioned. Thus my analysand and I understand, together, why he had to become the person he is. But my supervisee and I only examine the defensive outcome of his life experience, but not the life experience itself. We don't have the shared understanding of the historical context that explains the need for just these defensive patterns. In supervision, as opposed to treatment, the candidate does not have the opportunity to identify with my empathic attempt to contextualize his defenses, to help make sense of them. In treatment we can understand the struggling person whose only way to survive may have been to develop these defensive maneuvers. In supervision, we focus on their professional impact, but, generally, not on their genetic sources. The candidate often feels ashamed that he needs these defenses, afraid they make him unfit to be an analyst, unforgiving toward himself for these "inadequacies." This may elicit his self-contempt, scorn, and shame, unmodulated by the compassion he might feel more easily in a treatment context.

I do not mean to suggest that we should explore the candidate's genetic history in supervision. Generally I do not inquire into the candidate's personal life, although if a candidate chooses to disclose I do not discourage it. But I leave the decision entirely up to the candidate. Since most candidates limit how much of their early life they share in supervision, I think they find it easier to feel compassion for themselves in their treatment than in their supervision. I believe that in treatment compassionate love for oneself, as a struggling human being doing the best she can, more often modulates shame than in supervision.

I think it adds to the potential for shame in the candidate that it is so infrequent that the supervisor's countertransferences (to the candidate, as well as the candidate's patient) get scrutinized. We do not have as firmly established a tradition of looking at supervisory countertransference as we have for examining an analyst's countertransference.

A more subtle source of shame is the candidate's temptation to imitate the supervisor, rather than developing his own, unique style. Perhaps, to some degree, this is unavoidable, but we foster this self disrespect if we collaborate in the attitude that the way the patient will get an optimal treatment is for the supervisee to absorb as much as possible in the supervisory hour, hold onto it with all his might until he next sees the patient, when he must dispense these precious drops into the patient's ear. What the candidate "learns" from this dehumanizing experience is that the best he can be is a fairly accurate imitation of someone else.

MISSED OPPORTUNITIES IN TRAINING

I am suggesting some ways that our training procedures may fail to emotionally prepare candidates to do their job without burning out.

In training candidates we often fail to clearly describe our own experience of what doing analysis has required of us, as human beings. This misses a crucial opportunity to adequately prepare candidates to do their jobs. Partially as a consequence of this, they often begin doing analytic treatment feeling at a loss. This, naturally, contributes to their lack of professional confidence. I suggest that this early career experience can have lasting deleterious consequences, paving the way for early burnout.

Why don't we teach more effectively, and help candidates feel better equipped for their profession? While it is genuinely hard to define the analytic task, and we have real differences of opinion about what it entails, I believe that this is not enough to explain how unprepared graduates frequently feel.

I would suggest that our own unmet narcissistic needs, as analytic educators, play a significant role. I think we are afraid to speak clearly and simply about analysis. For one thing, we fear being accused of oversimplification. Having been accused of this many times, I can certainly attest to the sting of this criticism. It can be hard to be clear without reducing the process to an over-simplified formula. Yet, I would rather over-simplify than obfuscate, if these were the only choices. At least then, listeners would understand what I am saying, and could disagree. But when we mystify the treatment process we may leave candidates dumb-founded, in several senses. They are struck dumb, in that they feel afraid to speak up and show how little they understand. But they also feel dumb, or unintelligent, ignorant, and inadequate. Perhaps most important, unless we are clear about theory we prevent candidates from comparing it with their own clinical and personal experience, and determining for themselves whether or not they find it relevant to their work. Out of our own narcissism, do we need to seem as though we have mastered esoteric theory? While many have promoted demystification for patients, I think we have not done enough to demystify the treatment process for candidates and graduate analysts as well. Are we afraid that, along with our mysteries, we would lose our status in the hierarchy of treatment forms? In the name of clarity, are we willing to drop unnecessary jargon and are we willing to expose our own clinical work?

As I have already discussed, in my judgment we are in love with the inscrutable. Of course, an appreciation of it is vital. Without sufficient attention to the limits of our knowledge we are in danger of the hubris of our analytic ancestors. In brief, analysts don't have any special knowledge about whether or not someone should live in Westchester, have three children, or get a dog. We are not experts, in that sense. But if we were not expert in something, why would people pay us? We do have a knowledge base. We know more than non-professionals about patterns of defense, character issues, and some of the ways people tend to cope with their emotions. Like dentists, lawyers, and other professionals, we are schooled in a kind of pattern recognition. The pediatrician has seen countless cases of chicken pox, and so can usually diagnose it easily. Being able to recognize an example of a familiar pattern is a skill that contributes to her sense of professional competence. Having this skill helps her feel she earns her fee, and helps her transmit to patients a sense that they are getting something valuable. In the long run, her knowledge of how chicken pox looks will contribute to her feeling useful. I believe that the analytic practitioner needs a similar base. But, almost by definition, those who train analytically are a generation older than those who are being trained. Since the current vogue is for dwelling on our uncertainties, I think as teachers we may emphasize what interests us most, at the expense of transmitting what candidates most need, in order to graduate with a fundamental confidence in their ability to function analytically. It is as though music teachers, themselves entranced by the atonal, forgot to help beginners learn chords. But the profound appreciation of the atonal is possible only after having an acquaintance with the musical traditions that preceded it. I think that our neglect of the basics is not accidental. It feeds our own self esteem to identify ourselves with theories currently in vogue, that have cache. In short I think our challenge, as teachers, not unlike our challenge as clinicians, is to privilege a primarily non-narcissistic investment in candidates' growth.

I would also like to mention our insufficient preparation, in my judgment, for what it is like to age, as an analyst. Of course it says much about me, that I am thinking about this issue. Personally, I can't recall any mention of it in my own training. I think it might be incredibly helpful to talk about how dealing with erotic transference and countertransference, for example, changes as we age. I am sure these issues have somewhat different meanings for me now than they did when I was in my thirties. And yet, most often, transference and countertransference are discussed in training, at conferences, and in our literature as though we were ageless. What it is like to be desired, and to desire, or not to be desired and not to desire, must surely have a different coloring at various points in life. No matter how much we emphasize that in fantasy everything is possible, in reality we are all members of a culture that sees each phase of life as having its own set of privileges. I think it takes a fairly sturdy sense of self to bear what the wider culture communicates to us about how we should see ourselves, at each age. But it is even more complicated for me, as an analyst. In the transference, some patients may see me as thirty, or seventy, and my countertransferential wishes may match or greatly differ with these perceptions. What if my countertransference leads me to misperceive how old I seem to the patient?

How might discovering this affect my own self-esteem? Once again, while some training analysts and supervisors may address these issues, I feel when we graduate we are often left insufficiently equipped to deal with them. Training can't prepare us for everything we will face in our careers, but it should aim for a sturdy enough professional and personal self confidence to stay the course.

ACTIVELY DAMAGING CANDIDATES' SELF ESTEEM IN TRAINING

Thus far I have focused on what is all too absent from clinical training. In summary, I think we often fail to sufficiently nurture candidates' confidence and impart a way (note- not *the* way, but just *a* way) of working analytically. Now I will mention something all too present. By this I mean the actual damage we frequently do to the candidate's self esteem. By no means universally, but frequently, we make candidates feel like cowards, in several ways. First, our evaluative processes often imply that the candidate is insufficiently confronting with patients. The implication is that the candidate lacks sufficient courage. Second, the candidate is placed in the position that she is expected to show comfort when she may not feel comfortable. For example, at case conferences, where candidates presenting their work often feel quite anxious, they may be judged on their capacity to integrate criticism, or at least listen to it. Any difficulty with this can be understood by the candidate as evidence of her own insufficiency.

I have spoken and written before about some of the ways we shame candidates in training. I have suggested that if the process of becoming an analyst gratuitously shames, it certainly won't enhance the candidate's capacity to treat patients' self-esteem issues. If analytic education stifles the candidate's unique voice, it won't hone her ability to help her patients individuate. How we teach shapes what is learned. The medium is the message. In other words, how we treat candidates as human beings has at least as much impact as what we say to them. Here I will only list some of the ways we may actually inculcate shame.

First, there is the ever-present issue of what is, and what is not, considered "analytic." This question, important though it may be, has been used too often to humiliate candidates and other colleagues and to exclude some from the analytic fold. Regardless of our position on whether analysis and therapy differ qualitatively or quantitatively, it is often assumed that what is analytic is superior intellectually. This is a prejudice that breeds what prejudice always breeds: scapegoating. In analytic circles it tempts candidates to lie, distort, or otherwise misrepresent their clinical work in supervision, classes, and presentations. Of course, feeling compelled to lie is bound to create anger, shame, guilt, and, most especially, a lasting sense of having betrayed oneself. I think this is an important part of how we can fail to nurture clinical values, such as integrity and that fierce love for the truth that is, for me, the hallmark of the analyst.

Next, let me mention that gratuitous shaming can be especially harmful. If a candidate, or patient, or anyone else, feels that some shame was necessary, or inevitable, I think it feels different from situations where the shame seems gratuitous. When any part of the training process feels unnecessarily shaming, the candidate can feel something like, "You chose to shame me, when you could have made your point in another way. Maybe you like to see me squirm, or you enjoy feeling superior, or you revel in your power." If the candidate is silent about these feelings, the sense of having collaborated in being shamed can have an especially harmful impact.

Elsewhere (2008) I have come to the conclusion that shame about having shame can be especially deleterious. In training we are expected to want to know ourselves, and be known. Candidates are learning to do something intensely personal, and personally revealing. In architecture, when our progress is negatively assessed it might make us feel bad at our job as architects, but in analytic supervision when we feel our personal limitations have inhibited our work, we often feel deeply ashamed of ourselves as *human beings*. A senior analyst, a seasoned clinician, has found our interpersonal skills wanting, in some sense. No matter how carefully it is worded, a negative evaluation can read as highlighting a current shortcoming in the candidate as a human being. This, in itself, is likely to be quite painful. But if, in response, the candidate feels an urge to hide, that can add to the shame, since she knows she has entered a profession dedicated to self-knowledge.

I have also thought a good deal about the consequences of some built in secrecy in the training process. For example, negative evaluations during training can become hidden sources of shame, that the candidate may not share with anyone other than their training analyst, and, partially for that reason, the evaluation can be powerfully self-defining. Elsewhere (2008) I have compared this to the learning process in other professions. In any other field of study a student given a negative evaluation might challenge it, or might show it to friends, mentors, family members, and colleagues. Its impact might be balanced by other, perhaps more favorable reports or, at least, appraisals with a different emphasis. But the analytic candidate can feel that exposing a negative evaluation is, itself, evidence of a character flaw. To complain in any way, or even to question the judgment can seem like it proves the candidate is characterologically limited. It is assumed that if the candidate dares to complain the community's assessment will be something like, "He doesn't even see what is wrong with him," and "He is unable to take criticism." Thus the negative evaluation is often hidden in the emotional equivalent of the back of the closet, and becomes a secret source of shame, unmodulated by other feedback, unchallenged by other self-experience. Rarely discussed in public, I believe negative evaluations during training can have profound and permanent impact, often reverberating over the span of a long career and perhaps defining the perimeters of ambition. Can those who have been marked by this secret shame dare to aim high? Do they ever go on to realize the fullest expression of their talents?

SOME LONG TERM CONSEQUENCES OF SHAMING CANDIDATES

Essentially, I suggest that professional and personal self-esteem damage in training can set the stage for early burnout. Of course the candidate in training already has a character style, and strengths and vulnerabilities. And events with profound impact on the sense of competence can occur after training is completed. But I think experience in training can be crucial to the development of a sturdy, resilient professional self regard. I

72

am not suggesting that we would insure against burnout by plying candidates with compliments. A resilient analyst can be well aware of her limitations. But she needs to be highly capable of the relatively non-narcissistic investments in her patients that can preserve satisfaction over the long haul of an analytic career.

What exactly, is burnout? Some forms of it are immediately obvious, such as the middle aged analyst who leaves practice, admitting that the pressures became unbearable. But most of the ways burnout debilitates are more subtle, in my opinion. In order to be brief I will just name some forms of burnout, and other less drastic consequences of our narcissistic injuries and vulnerabilities.

Probably the most pervasive form of burnout is, simply, an increasingly obvious absence of interest in the work, and passion for treating people. Most of us enter our careers with enthusiasm. A fascination with the inner workings of mind and heart, and a wish to facilitate growth, clearly play roles in the choice of clinical training. Over the years, some analysts maintain bubbling curiosity about the endless permutations of the human psyche, and unflagging dedication to helping people create richer lives. They are able to get pleasure from the work itself, and not just from its outcome. They live their days, rather than merely survive them. Often, they are able to communicate their passion to supervisees, and others.

But if, in training, the candidate's capacity for non-narcissistic investments is not sufficiently nurtured, later on she may require immediate gratifications from her patients, and from other aspects of her career. Thus, for example, I believe we have inadvertently contributed to some analysts' problems terminating with patients. I am not suggesting that letting go of patients should be easy. But, I think, if we have made a relatively non-narcissistic investment, it is possible to privilege our patients' need to move on, at some point, over our own needs to be central to them, or to hold on to them. The analyst who holds onto patients, to fulfill her own needs, will miss out on the profound satisfactions of a genuine commitment to the growth of another human being. Baffled by these bungled terminations, the analyst may then get discouraged about doing treatment. For some it is easy to blame external conditions, such as managed care, a sagging economy, and a culture addicted to the quick fix. The analyst may tell herself that the string of one sided terminations, and her own lack of professional satisfaction, are both due to an inhospitable culture for analysts. I am not denying the existence of these external factors. But I believe we play a role in how they affect us.

Extreme pessimism about the future of analysis sometimes sounds to me like externalized despair, or burnout. For some, it may be easier to believe that the field is dying than to recognize why they have been unable to maintain their own passion about psychoanalysis. Again, I recognize that there are very serious issues, such as the shortage of candidates interested in entering the field. But, some of us pronounce psychoanalysis (like the theater) dead whenever it has to adapt to a changing world.

Using patients to meet our own self-esteem needs takes countless forms, as I am sure we can all imagine. Well before any recognizable burnout has occurred, we may, for example, take undue credit for patients' accomplishments, court adulation, or see ourselves as the only one who could really help the patient. As analysts there are many ways to play out the grandiosity and entitlement that form the other side of self-esteem deficits.

Our behavior as teachers, supervisors, and training analysts often reflects our own unmet narcissistic needs. Unfortunately, this point is probably too obvious to need elaboration. Thus we have a self-perpetuating cycle, with self-esteem damage in training (as well as before and after that point) leading to limitations in the capacity for non-narcissistic investments in patients and candidates, leading to increasing burnout and misuse of our roles to serve our own narcissism, leading to injuries to those in training with us, and so on. Our own damaged egos can be expressed in our need to find fault with candidates, dwell on their shortcomings, and create another generation of analysts with under-nourished self esteem.

And there are plenty of other outlets for our prideful demonstrations. Politics in institutes and other analytic organizations provide endless opportunities for narcissistic strutting. We create elitist hierarchies, and gain status (at least, in our own eyes) by keeping "undesirables" out of our clubs. It is not hard to see how pervasive, and how damaging, these antics can be. The resulting waste of time, effort, and spirit is mind boggling.

I want to emphasize three aspects of the negative consequences of self esteem damage in training.

1. It creates pressing need for immediate gratification from patients, candidates, and other colleagues. This can result in misuses of our roles.
2. It sows seeds of burnout, and despair about psychoanalysis.
3. Most especially, it delimits the capacity for non-narcissistic investment in life and growth which is, from my viewpoint, a truly sustaining foundation for an analyst.

SOME CLOSING THOUGHTS: TUNING UP THE INTERNAL CHORUS

I close with some thoughts about what can help us interrupt the cycle of damaged analysts damaging others. Elsewhere (2004, 2008) I have developed the idea of the internal chorus, a kind of professional ego ideal, that can be internalized during training and beyond. The voices of all our teachers can blend in this chorus. It can include those from our professional and personal lives who have lent us their egos, given us bits of their wisdom, mirrored us, and contributed to our sense of purpose.

My own chorus gets louder sometimes. I hear it most especially when I feel lonely in the room with a patient. During some endless stretches, when the work seems permanently stalled, I can hear my own training analyst, Rose Spiegel, M.D., telling me to hold on. She probably never actually said those words. But she lived them with me. Her investment in our work together was certainly palpable. Most often, it took the form of effort. She really tried to understand. And then she tried again. Of course she was, and continues to be, someone I learn from. But, more than that, she is someone I draw strength from.

I think we can break the cycle of narcissistic injury through how we act, and what we privilege, more than what we say, when we are involved in training, and in other professional roles. A strong effort, to teach, to reach, tells someone they matter. Their growth, the quality of their training and their life, matters. Passion about the work can't be faked, but, when it is there, it can make a lasting impact, most especially on those who are first trying to forge a professional identity.

Every hour, in treatment, supervision, and teaching, brings opportunities to prioritize out loud. We are always deciding what to focus on. If, with patients, I pay most attention to what makes me look effective, they will probably intuit something about my self esteem needs. This understanding may never be formulated, in Donnel Stern's (1997) sense of the term. But it will be known.

I think we would all agree that in treatment moments of blazing clarity are rare. But in every moment of every session we are making decisions about what is worth saying, and what should be left unsaid, at least for the moment. In a sense, leaving something unsaid is our most frequent interpretation and, often, I would argue, our most significant. It is the aggregate of these ordinary moments, these ubiquitous decisions, that determine what gets internalized by those we treat and teach. Our own primarily non-narcissistic investments can provide models but, even more importantly, can strengthen the sense of mattering, of those we train.

To conclude, I am suggesting that, as analytic educators, we can facilitate the candidate's development of a sense of professional adequacy and lasting commitment to the field by teaching basics clearly, by modeling the adventurous spirit of analytic inquiry, and by paying close attention to how we are affecting the candidate's self esteem. Each generation of analysts has an opportunity to prevent passing our own narcissistic vulnerabilities to the next generation. I believe that the best legacy we could leave would be to facilitate enough professional confidence in our candidates that they can set aside their own pride as they work toward a greater capacity to experience life, for their patients and for themselves. I would like to end with a poem that humorously captures putting pride in perspective. It is by Richard Wilbur (2009).

A RECKONING

At my age, one begins
To chalk up all his sins.
Hoping to wipe the slate
Before it is too late.
Therefore I call to mind
All memories of the kind
That make me wince and sweat
And tremble with regret.
What do these prove to be?
In every one, I see
Shocked faces that, alas,
Now know me for an ass.
Fatuities that I
Have uttered, drunk or dry,
Return now in a rush
And make my old cheek blush.
But how can I repent
From mere embarrassment?
Damn foolishness can't well
Entitle me to Hell.
Well, I shall put the blame
On the pride that's in my shame.
Of that I must be shriven
If I'm to be forgiven.

REFERENCES

Buechler, S. (2004). *Clinical Values: Emotions that Guide Psychoanalytic Treatment*. Hillsdale, NJ: The Analytic Press.

——— (2008). *Making a Difference in Patient's Lives: Emotional Experience in the Therapeutic Setting*. New York: Routledge.

Eliot, T.S. (1943). *Four Quartets*. New York: Harcourt, Inc.

Hoffman, I.Z. (1998). *Ritual and Spontaneity in the Psychoanalytic Process*. Hillsdale, NJ: The Analytic Press.

Maroda, K. (1999). *Seduction, Surrender, and Transformation*. Hillsdale, NJ: The Analytic Press.

Stern, D.B. (1997). Unformulated Experience: From Disassociation to Imagination in Psychoanalysis. Hillsdale, NJ: The Analytic Press.

Wilber, R. (2009). "A Reckoning." In: The New Yorker, August 31, 2009.

CHAPTER SEVEN

Fire in the Belly*

INTRODUCTION

This personal essay describes the phases of my own "love affair" with psychoanalysis, including experiences that initially sparked my interest in training. Like any relationship, my connection to psychoanalysis has altered over time. The paper reflects on feelings that can sustain our involvement in psychoanalysis, despite inevitable modifications in ourselves, as we age, and alterations in the field. I ask what can sustain motivation once the need to prove oneself has abated, and the novelty of being a clinician has diminished. Hardships, such as losing every treatment partner we ever have, facing scornful reactions from insurance companies, and many other challenges, can try our commitment to psychoanalysis. Can we keep our love for our profession alive long enough to retire proud and grateful for the work we have done?

FIRE IN THE BELLY

Let me not to the marriage of true minds
Admit impediments; love is not love

---

* Paper presented at the William Alanson White Psychoanalytic Society meeting, December 5, 2014

Which alters when it alteration finds,
Or bends with the remover to remove.
O no, it is an ever fixed mark
That looks on tempests and is never shaken;
It is the star to every wand'ring bark,
Whose worth's unknown, although his heighth be taken.
Love's not Time's fool, though rosy lips and cheeks
Within his bending sickle's compass come;
Love alters not with his brief hours and weeks,
But bears it out even to the edge of doom.
If this be error and upon me proved,
I never writ, nor no man ever loved.
—Sonnet 116, W. Shakespeare, in H. Vendler, 1997, p.487

This paper tells a love story. Although my own, I am hoping it resonates some with your story, too.

For me, it was love at first sight. Although the relationship has changed, and in a mid life crisis I mourned roads not taken, I still wake up each day glad about my choice. In forty five years I have never really attempted to break off the relationship. But with time alterations have occurred. Anxious bouts of insecurity have given way to a gentler but persistent sadness. Of course, all my limitations as a human being also limit the relationship. It couldn't have been otherwise.

By now it is probably clear that I am talking about my relationship with the clinical enterprise. In this paper I discuss its stages, from an initial halcyon honeymoon, through an early period of intense desire to please, and to "make it work," to more somber current times. I especially focus on the motivation to strive. What ignites fire in the belly, in each phase? What can keep passion for doing treatment alive, as the field itself alters, and as we, ourselves, undergo inevitable changes?

Growing up I assumed I would study English Literature and be a writer. It never even occurred to me to question this assumption, until the summer before I entered college. To qualify for a special course I had to complete an extensive writing project. As I wrote I began to question how I would financially support myself as an author. Then, in my sophomore year I happened to sit in on a class, taught by a substitute teacher that day, who was a clinical psychologist. As bored as we were by the textbook, he decided to tell us about some of his cases. I was fascinated. At that time I knew virtually nothing about treatment. I came up to him after class and shyly posed a question: Do you get paid for doing that? Looking back, I can only imagine how hard it must have been for him to stifle his amusement at this naïve, smitten youth. I was hooked. I set up a tutorial to read, you guessed it, Freud's (1900) *Interpretation of Dreams*. I changed my major to Psychology, and took every course in the department. Was this a kind of rebound? Did I love psychology because it offered the one thing missing from the life I had imagined as an author: a way to survive financially? Perhaps that was part of my new attachment. But in the almost fifty years since then, my fascination with psychological insights gathered from literature is unabated, as my most recent book (2015) testifies. I never actually gave up my first love, but, in a sense, found a way to sublimate it or, if you wish, to subsidize it.

PHASE ONE: BLINDED BY LOVE

Like many newly smitten, in the first phase of my relationship to clinical work I struggled to feel worthy and to be seen as worthy. I would say that, in those very early days, a passion to reach people, personal strong connections with some patients, and my own considerable anxiety about becoming competent supplied quite enough fire in my belly. For me, intense striving first took the form of blind obedience to rules. I complied with what I thought was expected of me, on some less than conscious level hoping that this attitude, combined with a strong work ethic and fierce dedication eventually would gain for me the acceptance I craved.

One story from my early, infatuated, days. Faced with one of my first child patients in the youth guidance clinic where I worked just after getting my doctorate, I was overwhelmed, having had no training in working with children. But I was determined to please. The night before the first session I "crammed." That is, I carefully read Virginia Axline's (1947) book, *Play Therapy*, cover to cover, memorizing parts of it. After bringing the child from the waiting room into my office, I mouthed some version of Axline's formulaic opening gambit. "This is your room, your time, your toys. You can play however you want." The child waited patiently for me to finish my speech and then asked, "And when do I get to talk about my problem?" I was so eager to do well, to make it, that I prioritized doing everything "right" over finding my own style and relating to the patient. I had a lot to learn. To prove our worth, especially early in our careers, I think many of us try too hard to supply the "right" answers to our patients' questions even though, on some level, we know that it is impossible. In my 2012 book, *Still Practicing* (p.109) I discussed some deleterious effects this can have on us and on our relationship to the field.

To anticipate comments I will make later, I would say that early in my career I was driven to work very hard, partially because of anxiety. In other words, going back to the analogy with relationships, in the very beginning I was very highly motivated to please. But later in my career, as my place became somewhat more secure, would I still keep my motivation high? Or, would I inevitably begin to take my profession for granted, and stop really trying to make the relationship work? What would happen to the fire in my belly?

PHASE TWO: RIPENING

Over the next years, as I gained experience, I became a little more secure as a clinician and felt somewhat better able to try new modalities, taking the chance that I could do well enough. I see those, still young years as a time of searching for resonances between my natural, spontaneous self and the many options offered by my profession. As in any relationship, I was finding ways we could be together successfully as well as what didn't work. I came to deeply appreciate how much space my field gave me. I could try out various forms of clinical work and research and academic interests. I could spread my wings. I could ripen.

This was an adventuresome period, a time of challenge. I still worked hard, but now it wasn't so much out of anxiety as out of excitement although, of course, insecurities still grip me sometimes, and anxiety never entirely disappears. But as I played with possibilities, I was more and more convinced that psychology and I were right for each other. In this period the task shifted from proving my worth to, at least some of the time, finding my voice. Memorizing other approaches gave way to thinking about my own. I think that this contributed to my passion for my work, spurring me on, as anxiety had in an earlier phase.

For me, this meant prioritizing emotions, instead of drives or cognitions, in the study of human motivations. For the next thirty five years I would elaborate the clinical consequences of this belief. Professionally ripening was a process of expanding the ways I could use my passionate focus on human passions, to teach, to write, and to treat.

PHASE THREE: MID LIFE CHALLENGES

Inevitably, my expansive feelings eventually clashed with a growing comprehension of my limitations, in terms of time and other factors. In mid career I realized that if I wanted to fulfill my longstanding goal of becoming a psychoanalyst, I would have to leave academia. I met a crossroad, with its unavoidable regrets for the path not taken. I comforted myself with the belief that analytic training would enhance my writing and teaching, so I wasn't really giving them up. But since that point my passion for my field has been clouded by some regret. I think this awareness has affected but not destroyed my love for my work. Another way to say this is that I have had to forgive this relationship for its limitations that, of course, are partially shaped by my own. So, in mid career, leaving academia and beginning analytic training, I had to deal with a sense of the loss of who I could have become, had I continued my research. In some ways training and private practice have augmented this sorrow, but they have also balanced it with many sources of gratification. Since a good deal of my writing has focused on shame, grief, and gratification in training and practice, I will not explore these topics here, except to comment on how these feelings can affect the fire in our bellies.

For example, what is the impact of losing every patient we treat, on our capacity for investing emotionally in the next treatment relationship? Our analytic culture encourages the illusion that we can emotionally "move on" every time the buzzer sounds. This is, of course, absurd, and yet we do have other patients, often with pressing needs and a legitimate expectation that we will be attentive to them in their session. Our workdays are lived in forty five minute segments, often organized without time to register emotional reverberations. For myself, I will say that the image that has often come to mind is that I am like the proprietor of a store in a time of shortage, giving out supplies all day, left empty by the time she goes home. Of course our feelings vary, depending on many personal and interpersonal factors. But whatever we feel in a session, we have to move on if the next patient is waiting. Another hardship is the frequent experience of loss of a patient, from one or another cause. Loss is always with us, a part of the human condition, and, therefore, part of the analytic situation. Can we find ways to bear it that don't erode our love for our work? Can its sadness do its essential task, which I believe is binding us more firmly to each other, and to life itself? Can loss remind us of the preciousness of connection? Can sadness be acknowledged, and stay with us as sadness, uncomplicated by intense shame or other emotions? Can we recognize that no one can bear a lifetime of losing every partner she has, in a process as intimate as analysis, without significant grief? Can we create some forum where grief can speak?

It should not surprise us that we are profoundly affected by years of confronting these and so many other emotional hazards. Our work faces us with all of life's most painful situations. No week goes by without hearing about struggles with life threatening illness, devastating losses, shattering traumas. I am suggesting that some loss of fire in the belly is often, at least in part, a consequence of the difficulties of our task. Of course, our individual character issues, our equipment for our role, is a key aspect of how we live it. But, at least for the moment, I am focusing on sorrows I think we all face, and inviting us to consider their impact on our passion for the work. For me regrets about professional roads not taken, the cumulative impact of losses of patients, the frequent feelings of being unable to help, the constant pressure to keep moving throughout the day, and disillusionment with analytic politics have combined to challenge the tremendous excitement I felt at the start of my career. As I move toward its conclusion, I also feel what I think members of many professions come to experience as we age. So much of the technology, the language, the customs, are foreign to us. How can we follow Shakespeare's counsel, to continue to love, regardless of these alterations?

KINDLING THERAPEUTIC PASSION

What do we each believe can keep our love for psychoanalysis alive?. Analysts are long distance runners, in many of the treatments we conduct, and over the span of our own careers. What can keep our stamina high?

In this paper I have described my own evolving relationship to the clinical task. I started my career love struck, anxious to please and belong. These beginner's yearnings ignited more than enough fire in my belly. Over the years my anxiety diminished, but the fire has continued to burn, kindled, in part, by the need to keep finding my own voice. Many feelings, including profound sadness, loss, shame, and regret have challenged my commitment. But love has prevailed.

I close by asking us each to consider what can keep the fire burning in our own bellies. For myself, I have had to challenge both classical conceptions of neutrality, and some post modern views of our role. For many excellent reasons, analysts have been leery of declaring our values as a profession. For years we felt obligated to strive toward a kind of "neutrality" that seemed to preclude manifesting values. We wanted to avoid being seen as indoctrinating, as a cult, or a religion. While this is understandable and laudable, I believe it has left a kind of spiritual vacuum. For me, at least, without seeing myself as fighting on behalf of life, for more life, for myself and my patients, I don't think I could keep passion alive.

REFERENCES

Axline, V.M. (1947). *Play Therapy.* New York: Ballantine Books.

Buechler, S. (2012). *Still Practicing: The Heartaches and Joys of a Clinical Career.* New York: Routledge.

———(2015). *Understanding and Treating Patients in Clinical Psychoanalysis: Lessons from Literature.* New York: Routledge.

Freud, S. (1900). The Interpretation of Dreams. *Standard Edition 4-5.*

Vendler, H. (1997). *The Art of Shakespeare's Sonnets.* Cambridge, MA: Harvard University Press.

CHAPTER EIGHT

Preparing Candidates for the Challenges
of a Globalized World[*]

INTRODUCTION

Should we have a standard way of preparing all candidates to be analysts, regardless of the society in which they will practice? In this contribution I discuss invariant aspects of psychoanalytic treatment, as well as some that are fundamentally products of a particular time and place. I suggest that in some cultures we may have to modify how we prepare candidates for an analytic career. I think of treatment as, in one sense, a dialogue about what it means to be a human being. That conversation is partially shaped by its cultural environment. For example, while all analytic approaches value truthfulness, cultures differ in what is considered "appropriate" or "inappropriate" to say, even in an analytic context. In this paper I argue that these cultural differences must be reflected in how we train candidates. While there are some invariant clinical values, candidates need to learn how they can be effectively applied in the context in which they will practice.

---

[*] Paper presented at the 2015 APCS Conference on "Border tensions: Troubling Psychoanalysis," Rutgers, New Jersey, Oct. 24, 2015.

PREPARING CANDIDATES FOR THE CHALLENGES OF A GLOBALIZED WORLD

However much analysts agree or disagree about the fundaments of our field, should we understand them in universal, or culturally specific terms? That is, if we see transference as key to a psychoanalytic vision, is transference more simply human than otherwise? Can we use the term in the same way in China and Portland, Oregon? What about the concepts of the frame, boundaries, resistance, defense, diagnosis, and, perhaps most importantly, the concept of treatment itself? If all of these, and many other concepts have different meanings in different cultural contexts how should this affect psychoanalytic training? Can we have a standard way of preparing all candidates to be analysts, regardless of the culture in which they will practice? As Horenstein (2015 p. 103)succinctly put it, "Wrong would it be for a discipline which considers the uniqueness of those who consult us its privileged quest, to deny the uniqueness of the context where it is practiced" (Horenstein, 2015).

In this contribution I discuss invariant aspects of psychoanalytic treatment and training as well as some that are fundamentally products of particular cultures.

NAMING EMOTIONS

What's universal and biologically encoded between cultures that we can postulate as an invariant element? I believe that the basic elements that can be placed as a foundation for an individual's psychic 'birth' and which are constantly found in all human cultures are the affects. Affects and emotions are something that characterize the human, in every culture, as the result of an evolutionary heritage that unites us, as Darwin has taught us...Affects organize perceptions, thoughts, memories representations, physiology, behavior and social interactions, and have the complex function of connecting not only body to mind, but even the bodies and minds among different individuals. (Bastianini, 2015, p. 75).

In the 1970's, with Carroll Izard, I studied facial expressions of the discrete or fundamental emotions. Our assumption was that these emotions were part of human experience, regardless of culture. Each fundamental emotion had a characteristic facial expression, with specific muscle movements associated to it. The discrete emotions we studied were: interest, (curiosity) joy, surprise, sadness, disgust, contempt, anger, fear, shame, and guilt. Let me emphasize that these emotions belonged in this category because each had a characteristic facial pattern and other features, and not because they were more significant than, for example, loneliness.

While the emotions are universal, culture plays a role in *what triggers an emotion and how it is experienced and expressed.* In fact, a very significant mentor of Izard's, Silvan Tomkins, (1962, 1963) developed a whole theory about the socialization of emotions, suggesting that each human being is partially a product of what we have been taught to feel about what we feel. As psychoanalysts we are trained to approach and prioritize the emotions differently, depending on our theoretical orientation. For example, some of us especially focus on anger, or anxiety, or shame. But I believe all analysts would advocate differentiating emotions and registering their intensity, in ourselves and our patients.

In a paper on the "right stuff" to be an analyst (1997) I suggested (p. 305) that the sensitivity to discern emotional nuance, and differentiate closely related emotions, can be cultivated in training, although candidates enter with differing degrees of aptitude. To be intensely aware of shifts in one's own feelings and the patient's "requires exquisite intra-and interpersonal sensitivity. All who are involved in the training process must actively cultivate the candidate's potential for this 'right stuff.' Like the conductor who hears each individual note, the analyst must be attuned to the nuances of major and minor emotional shifts in herself and her patient." While, of course, there are significant individual differences in awareness of emotional nuance, there may also be some emotions that are harder to track in some cultures. If, for example, a culture teaches that curiosity is impertinent, it may be harder for analysts and patients to become fully aware of its presence and shifts in its intensity. Because I believe so strongly in the universality of the need for emotional awareness, and the importance of differentiating seemingly similar emotions, such as shame and guilt, and because I assume that the emotions are universal, though their triggers are partially based in culture, I feel that analytic training should include helping candidates attain greater emotional self awareness.

I am suggesting that which emotions I privilege, and how I respond to them, are products of my analytic and non-analytic culture and, of course, my own character and personal history. The more any human being, analyst or lay person, can differentiate subtly different emotions, the better structured is their emotional experience, and the more clearly communicated it can be. All analysts cope with our own feelings and our patients' emotions. Therefore, I suggest that all training programs should privilege developing the candidate's facility in recognizing the verbal and non-verbal expressions of the emotions in themselves and their patients.

One thing I think we often do in treatment is name emotions, differentiating them from each other. For example, I was taught to help people differentiate anger from hate. Thus, my patient, Jim, collects moments that feel to him like "anger" and develops experience about coping with that feeling. This augments his self knowledge, in that he has access to a history of Jim angry. To me it seems that the need for an appreciation of emotional nuance exists regardless of culture. Bastianini, (pp.82-83) outlines several tasks she considers basic to working with emotions in treatment. By reading non-verbal cues we help the patient focus on his or her emotional experience and link it with previous moments. We also act as witnesses, enabling the patient to feel he is able to communicate his emotions to others. We "loan" the patient our own symbolizing capacity, which facilitates the development of a more structured internal world and a clearer sense of self. Finally, the patient's emotional experience may first take shape in the analyst's countertransference, eventually enabling it to reach the point where it can be verbalized.

Here is a clinical example of the value of naming and differentiating emotions in treatment. Many years ago I treated John, a young, male outpatient, shortly after his release from a state hospital. John presented a daunting array of symptoms for a novice to treat. He spoke in a stilted monotone, seemingly devoid of any emotion. In the most matter of fact tone possible he described a childhood of unbelievable neglect. John had been locked in a room most of his first years of life, with food left at the door sporadically. He was unaware of his own name until he went to school. The world of children's games and toys was unknown to him. Play of any kind still remained a mystery, even years later.

In a childhood devoid of much real human contact John developed an arsenal of protective rituals. There was a proper way to wash, involving avoidance of warm water. The proper way to sleep was to set the alarm clock to go off every few hours throughout the night. John spent most of his time and energy making sure he adhered to these guidelines. Although the rules were of his own making, they had acquired absolute power over him.

At least in his childhood, far from being the enemy, rituals were probably the companions that helped save John. They gave him an identity, a kind of name. He was the boy who washed his hair with cold water. He made sure not to let this tenuous sense of self get lost in dreams, by punctuating sleep with the startling buzz of the alarm clock. Rituals brought a sense of being in control to a child left adrift.

I didn't question this at the time, but now I wonder about how my own countertransference was shaped by my cultural background. I wanted to free John from ritual. If my own psychic development had occurred in another time or place, might I have been less eager, less intensely invested in that goal? Or would I have felt just as deeply committed to his having choice?

Looking back I think we must have found each other strange creatures, and, fortunately, curiosity was evoked in us both. For me, he was the edge of what I could bear. I now suspect the feeling was mutual- I was probably at, or sometimes over the limit of the intensity he could take from another person. His mechanical quality challenged me to understand the perimeters of aliveness. My emotionality was probably, for him, just at the rim of the bearably unpredictable. We were each the very edge of what the other could emotionally take, which spurred growth in us both. I could wonder enough about this stranger to want to make his strangeness more familiar, by using words I know, from my own experience, to try to describe his.

Without the benefit of any theoretical rationale I found myself using even more than my usual quota of words that refer to emotions. Whatever John told me, in his matter of fact monotone, I tried to imagine feelingfully. It was like watching a black and white movie and fantasizing colors. I was probably, in some (Bollas, 1999) unthought known way, simply trying to supply what I found missing, for my own sake, as much as for John's. Several years into our work John told me a story of something he had done, I can't remember what, and said, "You would say I felt X," naming an emotion. I still remember the joy I felt that day. I'm sure I could not have explained why, but I knew this to be progress.

But the treatment dialogue goes beyond naming discrete emotions. It passionately comments on what it means to be a human being and live a human life. I see some emotional challenges as built into the human condition, although, of course, culture shapes their meaning. Let us take the ability to bear loss as an example. While culture may dictate what events are experienced as significant losses, loss itself is ubiquitous. I believe that in treatment we live this issue together. We inevitably meet it in many ways, most especially at termination, but at other points as well. We have a dialogue that is, at times, spoken, about how being human entails bearing loss. We work something out about how we each can approach loss. Of course anything we work out involves the fundamental emotions that are core to human experience. Bearing loss well is an inescapable task. It is a high calling, often involving the whole system of discrete emotions. Loss is always with us, an inevitable part of the human condition. The only question is not whether it happens, but how we live it. The treatment dialogue explores the question of how to live loss. Sometimes this exploration is explicit, as it usually is at termination, if the treatment has been able to establish genuine connection. But more subtle, implicit conversations about loss occur throughout the work. In a paper entitled "Which geographies? Psychoanalytic anthropology of human diversity" (Preta, 2015, pp.45-53) Alfredo Lombardozzi suggests that the questions members of different cultures ask about the meaning of life and death are similar, but may be answered differently in different places. This way of thinking links the universal and the particular in us as people.

As human beings, we all can feel curious, sad, afraid, ashamed, and so on. But, for example, some of us grew up in a culture that blurred distinctions between shame and guilt. It may take an analyst to help us differentiate them. But once we do (as analysts or patients) we can build a "file" of experience with that feeling, and learn from it. Thus, for example, I know what I often feel when I am ashamed, and I bring that self awareness to every time I feel shame. This may help me remember ways of bearing shame that have been effective in the past. Even more important, it may remind me that I have been able to live through those experiences.

Furthermore, if I am aware of the sense of insufficiency that usually lies at the foundation of shame, I may be able to understand better what the present moment means to me. For example, if a friend decides to drop me, and picks up another friend, I am likely to feel some sense of shame. Connecting this with other, emotionally similar moments, I might understand that the question in my heart is something like, "Why wasn't I enough?" The analyst who is attuned to emotional nuance will help me differentiate insufficiency shame from, for example, guilt about paying too little attention to my friend.

LISTENING AND WITNESSING

While psychoanalytic orientations and the wider cultures shape what we privilege when we listen to a patient, listening itself is a universal aspect of analytic treatment. It is assumed that people need to be listened to, and traumas need to be witnessed. In other words psychoanalysis is an approach to the fundamental human experience of suffering. Preta (2015, p. 20) put it succinctly.

"...can psychoanalytical hypotheses have a universal value? Can they describe the same-or similar-psychic dynamic for any human, regardless of the historical, social, and cultural context?" ....."Can psychoanalysis help with mental suffering in different contexts? To try to answer we must establish some basic experiences that we recognize as human."

Elsewhere (2010) I explored three attitudes about human suffering and discussed how each influences the analyst's approach. When analyst and patient fundamentally differ in their understanding of the place of suffering in psychic life, potentially treatment destructive clashes can result. Our childhood cultures, our religious upbringing, as well as our professional cultures help shape our attitudes about dealing with pain in treatment, and, more generally, in life.

What do we each believe helps sufferers? While we all experience suffering we may not have fully formulated our attitude about its place in psychic life. When is suffering to be borne, rather than medicated, muted, or eradicated? When should it be taken as a sign of a full appreciation of the human condition, rather than a sign of pathology? Our personal and professional attitudes about suffering have significant impact on much of our behavior in a session, and our sensibility about treatment's goals.

I have always liked a passage by Lee Stringer (in Casey, 2001, p.112) that captures something about life, from one culturally shaped perspective.

One grows older and more knowing over time; life's more facile charms grow dim; the soul yearns, seeking more than could ever be had on this earth, more than could ever be wrought out of three dimensions and five senses. We, all of us, suffer some from the limits of living within the flesh. Our walk through this world is never entirely without pain. It lurks in the still, quiet hours which we, in our constant busyness, steadfastly avoid.

It seems to me that, whatever else training does, it needs to help the clinician hone the strength to accompany those struggling to face what it means to them to be human.

CONCEPTIONS OF PSYCHOLOGICAL HEALTH AND PATHOLOGY

'Sanity,' as a term, has had its uses, as we shall see; but it has always lived in the shadow of madness, as the weak antagonist. It has always found it difficult to match the infernal dramas and melodramas of madness; our torments have made us more imaginative than our consolations. (Phillips, 2005, p. 18)

In "*Going Sane,*" Adam Phillips questions why we hardly bother to define sanity, while we lavish attention on pathology. Declaring that our notions of health are always culturally shaped, Phillips sees sanity (p. 36) as "...harmonious organization, a state in which things are as they should be." But, of course, how things "should be" depends on how a culture wishes them to be.

Is this the best we can do? Is defining normal, sane, healthy psychic functioning hopelessly subjective, and inevitably culturally biased?

When we identify a patient as schizoid or hysteric what are we assuming about healthy emotional functioning? What personal and cultural factors affect our beliefs about normal intensities and qualities of affective experience and expression? How do these beliefs shape our diagnoses of patients as paranoid, borderline, or depressed?

For example, what expressions of grief qualify a person to be diagnosed depressed? Is it a matter of duration, so that grief lasting ten years is more likely to be called depressive? Or do we differentiate grief from depression based on the mode of its expression, the mix of emotions, their intensity, the quality of overall functioning, or other bases? I think cultures dictate the "normal" expression of sadness, as well as anxiety, anger, fear, and other emotions. In doing so, cultures are shaping practitioners' visions of health and pathology.

A while ago I attended a meeting of the American Psychological Association, where I met many very well intentioned people, striving to learn how to use behavioral, cognitive, and positive psychological "techniques" to cure people of their feelings. If we only said certain magic words to our patients, or re-framed their reality in accord with some newly discovered psychological principle, all of life's pain would be eradicated. Perhaps some fairy tales are harmless, and maybe it is beneficial to believe them for a while. But I don't think this one is harmless.

Can we have the strength to help the young put their trust in the hard work that so often precedes insight? Can we help them accept that frequently, in treatment, enlightenment only comes after years of pains-taking struggle in the dark? Can we, in this fast paced era of the sound-bite, embrace this truth ourselves?

Each culture has assumptions about independence, dependence, healthy expression of free will, the importance of family and, more generally interpersonal relatedness, and the concept of the unique, separate self, to name but a few issues. Culture communicates who we should be and, in treatment, who the patient should become.

Phillips (2005, pp. xx-xxi) gives us one answer.

> We need an alternative now to wealth, happiness, security and long life as the main constituents of a Good Life. To think about sanity as a different kind of prosperity, as a realistic hope rather than a merely bland or (austerely) grand alternative to madness, is an opportunity, I think, to include in our accounts of a Good Life for ourselves both the unpredictable effect on us of our histories- both what we have experienced ourselves and the illimitable experience of previous generations- and the urgencies and vulnerabilities of our biological destinies. It would be sane now to work out how we have become the only animals who can't bear themselves; and how, if at all, we might become the animals who can.

It seems clear to me that (analytic and non-analytic) culture helps shape our attitudes about pathology, health and, therefore, about the goals of treatment. We can only wonder whether Freud's patients heard something palatable to them when he famously promised

> ...you will be able to convince yourself that much will be gained if we succeed in transforming your hysterical misery into common unhappiness. With a mental life that has been restored to health you will be better armed against that unhappiness. (Breuer and Freud, 1895/1957, p. 305)

Perhaps in his time this prospect was enough, but it has always seemed lacking in motivational heft for me. I hear this as, essentially, defining health as the absence of pathology. It may be my personal or culturally driven optimism that says, that is just not enough. Psychological health is not merely the absence of illness. But what is it?

Sullivan (1956) defined health as the ability to profit from new experience. I find that an interesting approach and, like much in Sullivan, more complicated than it at first appears. To learn from new experience one must first recognize that it is new. This is where the analysis of transference can come in. That is, in order to be healthy, one must be able to differentiate the past from the present. Often a tall order, to be sure. But, from my point of view, not a bad definition. If someone can discern that an experience is new and learn from it, he or she is open to change which, I feel, is a clinically useful way to understand health. But is my feeling merely a product of my culture and character, and not universally applicable?

CLINICAL VALUES

Elsewhere (2004) I have written about a set of values that I assumed to be intrinsic to the clinical task, irrespective of cultural milieu. These included curiosity, hope, kindness, courage, integrity, a sense of purpose, the ability to bear loss, and emotional resilience. Also implicit was a privileging of truthfulness, for both treatment participants. I concluded that analytic programs should choose to train those applicants who seemed most able to embrace these universal clinical values. Admittedly, these attributes can be hard to assess, and even harder to teach. But I still think they have a place in the process of becoming an analyst.

However, it has become increasingly clear to me that the expression of these values (in treatment and in training) is quite variable, depending in part on the cultural milieu. My experience, and that of colleagues I have consulted, suggests that, while kindness and truthfulness are universally valued, their expression and degree of priority differs according to the mores of a particular time and place. For example, I have had lively debates with some of my Japanese colleagues about kindness and the analysis of defense. Much of my teaching and supervision takes for granted that, as analysts, part of our role is to foster the patient's awareness of defensive behavior. Ultimately, one of our goals is to facilitate the patient's decreasing need for defenses, thus freeing up energy for other uses. In my way of thinking, although, on the part of the clinician, addressing defensiveness can take courage,, integrity, and a sense of purpose, generally it is ultimately an act of kindness. But some of my Japanese colleagues have pointed out that we may have different ways of understanding kindness. In their culture, confronting defenses directly may be so shaming as to constitute an act of extreme unkindness only warranted when unavoidable. I hasten to add that many of my colleagues from the USA would agree with them. Like the wider culture, analytic orientations have their own heroes and heroines, outlaws, languages, and cultural assumptions. And even within an analytic institute, differences abound. But I do think culture affects the manifestation of the basic clinical values, and I believe in our obligation to convey to candidates both the fundamental values and their culturally, theoretically, and personally varying expressions.

Cultivating Cultural Curiosity in Analytic Training

> The place of the psychoanalyst,...that place out of place-requires in some way to be in their own language as a foreigner and all the exhausting process of training of a psychoanalyst could be seen in those terms: how to become a foreigner, even without having left your own city (pp.99-100). Mariano Horenstein, "Psychoanalysis in minor language," Preta, 2015, pp. 97-110.

I believe that the attitude clinical work requires is very similar to the attitude of the dilettante in the work of the Indologist, Heinrich Zimmer. Aside from his studies of Indian symbolism, Zimmer wrote a series of philosophical stories, drawn from both Eastern and Western literature, and published in the anthology, *The King and the Corpse* (1948). In Zimmer's introduction he described the dilettante as "one who takes delight (diletto) in something...The moment we abandon this dilettante attitude toward the images of folklore and myth and begin to feel certain about their proper interpretation (as professional comprehenders, handling the tool of an infallible method), we deprive ourselves of the quickening contact, the demonic and inspiring assault that is the effect of their intrinsic virtue." And later, "Delight, on the other hand, sets free in us the creative intuition, permits it to be stirred to life by contact with the fascinating script of the old symbolic tales and figures...The true dilettante will be always ready to begin anew. And it will be in him that the wonderful seeds from the past will strike their roots and marvelously grow" (pp. 2-6, italics in original). In my opinion, Zimmer captures the spirit of pleasurable curiosity that is the clinician's most positive emotional state. Of course we don't go through our days in continuous rapture. But I think the spark he describes is necessary, at least to my own survival. The "demonic and inspiring assault" that the patient's view of me might bring me tomorrow is part of what keeps me going. The "creative intuition" that is occasionally "stirred to life" in me helps to sustain me.

Both patient and clinician must be sufficiently interested in themselves and each other to turn ideas around out of curiosity. How is this curiosity cultivated, in the analyst in training, and in the patient, in treatment? I have often suggested to people in training that reading and writing poetry is one of the best ways I know to prepare for clinical work. Listening to poetry asks us to bear the ambiguity of the unfinished thought. We have to wade into a poem, letting it wash over us, feeling it out. If we demand that it immediately surrenders its meaning to our forces of reason we are likely to get no where. I would suggest that poems are not unlike dreams in this regard. A tight, military approach to their capture inevitable fails.

Nina Coltart (1993) was emphatic about liking entering the world of the other. "We enjoy the ever-new fascination of traveling deep into inner space, both ours and the patients." I suggest that in order to function clinically we must be able to sustain curiosity and some joy in the face of the tremendously difficult, painful life circumstances we encounter with our patients.

REFERENCES

Bastianini, T. (2015). The subject of the affect: How can the 'actual' be expresses in difference cultures? In: *Geographies of Psychoanalysis,* ed. L. Preta. Mimesis International.

Bollas, C. (1999). The *Mystery of Things.* New York: Routledge.

Breuer, J. & Freud, S. (1997). The right stuff. *Contemporary Psychoanalysis* 33:295–306.

Buechler, S. (2004). *Clinical Values: Emotions That Guide Psychoanalytic Treatment.* Hillsdale, NJ: Analytic Press.

——— (2010). No pain, no gain? Suffering and the analysis of defense. Contemporary Psychoanalysis 46:339–355.

Coltart, N. (1993). *How to Survive as a Psychotherapist.* London: Sheldon Press.

Horenstein, M. (2015). Psychoanalysis in a minor language. In: *Geographies of Psychoanalysis,* ed. L. Preta. Mimesis International.

Lombardozzi, A. (2015). Which geographies? In: *Geographies of Psychoanalysis,* ed. L. Preta. Mimesis International.

Phillips, A. (2005). *Going Sane: Maps of Happiness.* New York: HarperCollins.

Preta, L. (2015). *Geographies of Psychoanalysis.* Mimesis International.

Stringer, L. (2001). Fading to gray. In: N. Casey, ed. *Unholy Ghost: Writers on Depression.* New York: HarperCollins.

Sullivan, H.S. (1956). *Clinical Studies in Psychiatry.* New York: W.W. Norton.

Tomkins, S.S. (1962). *Affect, Imagery, and Consciousness: Vol I, The Positive Affects.* New York: Springer.

——— (1963). *Affect, Imagery, and Consciousness: Vol II, The Negative Affects.* New York: Springer.

Zimmer, H. (1948). *The King and the Corpse: Tales of the Soul's Conquest of Evil,* J. Campbell, ed. Washington, DC: The Bollinger Foundation.

II. Practice

INTRODUCTION

The papers in this section are my attempts to apply my clinical experience and theoretical allegiances to what I do in sessions with patients. Reading (among others) Freud, Sullivan, Fromm, Guntrip, and Winnicott, has permeated my thinking about being human, as has my reading of Dostoevsky and my work on the earliest facial expressions of the fundamental emotions. These papers reflect my belief that, at its fundament, psychoanalysis is an exchange between two people about what it means to be human. We bring to that conversation everything we have read that has moved and informed us, as well as everything we have ever experienced that has changed us.

This exchange is not usually an abstract theoretical discussion but, rather, an interaction infused with feeling. This section of *Psychoanalytic Reflections* looks at some of the emotions analysts and their patients are likely to experience in the course of treatment. In an early paper (1997) I ask what equipment an analyst needs, to plumb depths of feeling in herself and her patients. A few years later (1999) I begin a dialogue with the concept of neutrality. How can we retain some of the benefits of a neutral stance, while also harnessing the motivating power of an intense emotional exchange?

Because I believe that each emotion has its own unique qualities, I look at hope, (1995) loneliness, (1998) sadness, (2000 joy, (2002) and guilt (2009) in separate papers. Another thread is the question of how the analyst's attitudes (about the place of suffering in psychic life, 2010) about defensive strategies, (2002) about psychoanalytic theories, (2014) and about the phases of life (2015) affect the treatment process.

In the "Epilogue," I express my belief that, for me and for many others I have encountered, psychoanalysis is a vocation, a calling. We bring our whole selves to the task of trying to help others have richer psychic lives. However we define our task, it takes enormous stamina, courage, and personal integrity. The self exploration that accompanies our work with patients is never ending, often daunting, sometimes thoroughly surprising, and occasionally tremendously distressing. When we enter the field, and sign up for a lifetime of psychoanalytic reflections, we may have only a limited understanding of how our work and personal lives will affect each other.

Who must we be, to flourish with this much self scrutiny and profound interpersonal exchange? As is often the case for me, the poet, Rainer Maria Rilke (1934, p. 90) expressed it most succinctly. "...only someone who is ready for everything, who doesn't exclude any experience, even the most incomprehensible, will live the relationship with another person as something alive and will himself sound the depths of his own being."

Rilke, R.M. (1934), *Letters to a young poet*. New York: Norton.

CHAPTER ONE

Hope as Inspiration in Psychoanalysis*

INTRODUCTION

This paper, which is about analytic inspiration, was itself inspired by the insight and generosity of Stephen A. Mitchell. Mitchell gave his time, his wisdom, his playful wit, and his unquenchable curiosity to a generation of colleagues. His classic, *Hope and Dread in Psychoanalysis*, (1993) set a standard for scholarship, straightforward language, and heart.

For both participants in psychoanalysis, hope can be a motivating force. Many have written of the patient's and the analyst's hopes in terms of their expectations of the benefits treatment can confer. It is my belief that this emphasizes the cognitive aspect of hope, at the expense of its more emotional component. This paper addresses the question of how hope can inspire analytic participants to sustain the strength and stamina the work requires.

I can now view this paper as my first attempt to grapple with the question of how the analyst and patient can sustain passionate faith in a process that proclaims its subjectivity. Our literature abounds with contradictions about the most basic issues: What is health? What are reasonable goals for an analytic treatment? How does analysis work? We ask our patients (and ourselves) to devote years of our lives to a process

---

* *Psychoanalytic Dialogues*, 1995, 5:1, 63–74.

rife with controversy. This paper began my search for hope inducing ways to live the challenges.

ABSTRACT

In this paper, hope is explored as a motivating force in analysis. To see the patient's and the analyst's hopes in terms of changes they expect the treatment to accomplish emphasizes the cognitive aspect of hope. While touching on these cognitive expectations, this paper focuses on the emotional, rather than the cognitive, function of hope in treatment. It addresses the question of how hope can inspire analytic participants to have the strength and stamina that analysis requires.

HOPE AS INSPIRATION IN PSYCHOANALYSIS

How many times have you attended an analytic conference that proceeded with due gravity until a venerable older member offered a pithy, utterly direct comment that sent the group into gales of relieved laughter? Why do her words, delivered with the straightforwardness of a child, carry the authority of an oracle? Amusement aside, why do we also feel stirred?

I believe it is partially because the older analyst has spoken passionately, without doubt, without equivocation, as though it were obvious that some things are right and others wrong, that some things matter and others don't. This spirited relationship with good and bad is something that we all have as children but, particularly in the current climate, come to question as adults. We live in "a universe in which truths are replaced by opinions," a universe in which, as the literary theorist and professor of law Stanley Fish (Quoted in *The New York Times*, January, 28, 1994), suggested, the death of objectivity "relieves me of the obligation to be right" and "demands only that I be interesting." Some of us seem, in our last years, to recapture the simplicity of earlier convictions.

Emotional investment in *a* truth isn't just comforting, it's inspiring. It elicits acts of courage and fortitude. In war, in illness, in distress, if we feel we're fighting for life, for something that is indubitably right, good, and worth it, we can go on fighting.

In *Hope and Dread in Psychoanalysis* (Mitchell, 1993) asks what can inspire both participants in the analytic dyad in this perspectivist age. How do we sustain our own passionate engagement and elicit it in our patients, in a process shorn of its 19th-century certainties? As Mitchell succinctly states the problem:

> The shift from the view that the analyst knows the Truth to the view that the analyst knows one (or more) among various possible truths about the patient's experience has created a crisis of confidence in psychoanalytic theorizing and a crisis of authority in the psychoanalyst's self-image. The certainty and its consequent hopefulness that pervaded traditional psychoanalytic theorizing have become inaccessible to contemporary analytic theorists or clinicians. Is this a problem? Is uncertainty a cause for nihilism and dread, or the basis for a different sort of knowledge? If the content of what analysts know is not the Truth, is the authority that analysts can claim diminished? [pp. 47–48].

Freud's clear convictions about what the patient needs, and what the analyst knows, are impossible to recapture in this age of theoretical diversity. The eye of the beholder significantly affects what the patient seems to need. Political and intellectual allegiances shape what the analyst thinks he can contribute to the process of the patient's growth.

The traditional analyst had a clear sense that what needed to be achieved in treatment was the patient's overcoming of the force of infantile, instinctual pulls. What the patient needed was this increasing mastery; what the analyst provided was a clarity of goals and a method for their attainment.

Contrast this with our current diversity of opinion about the goals and methods of treatment. In *The Actor's Nightmare*, Christopher Durang (1980), that puckish escapee from Catholic dogma, created the perfect expression of what the unmoored modern analyst may feel. Durang's play has the protagonist caught in a script whose plot he can't quite fathom, desperately trying to figure out his lines as he goes. Hopeless muddles result from his efforts to take his cues from the other players, since the protagonist's sense of where the script is headed keeps evolving.

These observations raise fundamental questions about the psychoanalytic endeavor and, even more broadly, about human nature. If hope is an emotion, what gives it its motivating force? Is hope equivalent to the strength of an expectation? Is it a product of certainty about the value and attainability of a goal? How are these (cognitive) qualities related to the emotional experience of being inspired by hope? Can we sustain emotional hope without cognitive certainty? Is such hopefulness contagious in psychoanalysis? How is hopefulness in one partner communicated, or engendered, in the other? How do we understand hope's absence and its sometimes unfortunate coalescence in the lives of some psychoanalyses?

A survey may astound the reader with our vast neglect of these topics. We have yet to achieve clarity about the nature of emotion (Spiegel, 1980; Buechler, 1993a) and its relationship to cognition (Barnett, 1968, 1980) in treatment. The literature on emotions in psychoanalysis is curiously consistent in its attention to feelings that disrupt the work, such as anxiety, but its relative silence about what can sustain the effort. Recent contributions (Stern, 1989, 1990) have suggested the importance of curiosity in keeping the inquiry alive. Along with curiosity, hope must surely be among the motivating forces that propel the participants in an analysis.

Defining the psychiatric interview, Sullivan (1954p. 4) considers it essential that the patient expect to derive benefit from revealing his characteristic patterns of living. Bion's oft-quoted injunction to the analyst to enter every session without memory or desire is not usually prescribed as a goal for the *patient*. The patient enters each session, one hopes, with increasingly elaborated memory and an unquenchable desire to lead, as a result of the process, an enriched life.

In addressing the nature of hope in psychoanalysis, we must ask how what goes on in our heads affects what happens in our hearts, and vice versa. If hope is seen as an expectation, with a particular degree of certainty or uncertainty, its cognitive aspect is emphasized, but this understanding of hope does not, I believe, fully account for its motivational power. When we refer to what the patient expects to derive from treatment, or what the analyst expects to offer, we are focusing on an appraisal that is the cognitive aspect of hope. We are explaining only part of the phenomenon of hope. We are not yet comprehending what it is about an expectation that sometimes gives it the emotional force to drive us forward.

Schachtel (1959) supplies a framework for the study of hope as an emotion. As background, Schachtel distinguishes all affects into two categories: the embeddedness affects, which have as their goal the discharge of tension, and the activity affects, which are our eager, directed strivings. Hope, in his view, can be either an embeddedness affect or an activity affect. As the former, it is wishful expectations that things will change for the better in the future. Tomorrow someone, or an event, or time itself will bring happy fulfillment. In contrast, in the activity affect of realistic hope,

> the present is not experienced as a desert through which one has to wander in order to arrive at the future. It receives significance from the activities which make one's life meaningful and/or through which one tries to help bring about hoped-for change. While realistic hope, too, is directed towards the future it does not shift the emphasis from the present to anticipation of the future [p. 39].

Thus we have a contrast between an essentially passive expectation of something in the future and an active striving that gratifies in the present, as it prepares for the future. Behavior that is motivated by hope as an activity affect should be gratifying both as means to an end and as an end in itself.

If we apply this distinction to analytic participants, we can see that their expectations might not result in a galvanizing activity affect, no matter the degree of certainty with which they are held. Our 19th-century Freudian's certainty about the Truth may not be enough to give him *mobilizing* hope, though it would provide an expectation of success, under the right circumstances (with an analyzable patient). To provide the power to propel, his hopefulness would have to embody an active attitude, a focus on the process as well as its intended results, an eagerness to expend effort. The same can be said of his patient, whose hope would have to include these attitudinal factors to sustain his active engagement.

In a similar vein, writing of hopeful expectations for a fuller life, Fromm (1968) says, "Indeed this kind of expectation could be hope; but it is non-hope if it has the quality of passiveness, and 'waiting for'—until the hope becomes, in fact, a cover for resignation, a mere ideology" (p. 6).

It should be clear that, like all other human emotions, hope cannot be understood outside the context of the other emotions it joins (Buechler, 1992, 1993b). The emotions form a system in the human being (Izard, 1977) with the experience and expression of each modified by the levels of all the others. We cannot speak of the hope of the analyst and patient without reference to what is, or is not giving them joy, and what is, or is not, creating anxiety, anger, shame. Their hope is shaped, partially, by their capacity to be surprised and by their eager curiosity. As an emotion, hope is modified by the other motivating forces it accompanies.

Thus, in Schachtel's (1959) language, we could probably predict the strength of the embeddedness affect of hope from knowing the degree of certainty of the individual's expectations, for this type of hope is close to a cognitive appraisal. But to understand the motivating, activity-inspiring power of hope, we need to look beyond expectations, regardless of their certainty, to a complex array of other emotions and attitudes that shape these forces.

In the realm of expectations, the hopes of the two participants may diverge significantly, creating discords familiar to any clinician. Mitchell (1993) underscores difficulties we all face when he writes of the neurotic patient who enters treatment with an agenda that for the therapist amounts to a perfection of the neurosis rather than an overcoming of it. He raises other clinically complex issues, such as the difficult judgment calls we make in assessing whether what the patient wants from us is a legitimate need, which should be granted, or a regressive wish, which should be denied. He also cites instances when the patient hopes the treatment will not result in real change or resolution and prefers instead to use the therapy in the service of stasis.

In all these situations, the clinician is called on to wear the mantle of the expert, in some sense equipped to bring to the treatment a separate vision of what would be good for the patient. These situations remind us that we are not mere facilitators of a naturally unfolding process in the patient. We actively contribute to the process by lending our own vision of what is potential for the human being we are treating. As analytic instruments, we have more to offer than a method for the patient's self-examination. We must bring more to the table than a knowledge of the "how" of analytic exploration. We must provide more than merely a self-observant "other" available to the patient for mutually reflective interactions. We need a map of the territory, not just a knowledge of how to drive the car. We cannot fully operate without the theories that lend us a sense of where we should be going.

Theory can provide the cognitive aspect of hope, the expectations the analyst brings to the interaction. This is a type of hope that guides, but it is not enough to inspire. It is necessary, but not sufficient. It can tell us much about where we are going *after* we have mobilized the strength to continue our efforts. For both patient and analyst, something else, closer to the essence of hope as an emotion, or in Schachtel's (1959) phrase, an activity affect, is also needed. Though difficult to define, the presence of this active hope may sometimes differentiate the analyst from the patient and form a significant aspect of the analyst's contribution to the process. I suspect that, although the expectations patient and analyst bring have changed from Freud's time to ours, cultural shifts may not have altered what inspires.

For some analysts, treatment must address specific unmet developmental needs. Others, believing that if the patient can profit from all that life can teach, healing will occur, focus more on the patient's capacity for new experience. If only the patient could fully experience what is now "inattended," the patient would progress. A strong belief in either of these paradigms, or in any other conception of growth, will give analysts a sense of what their mission is. But will it make us the long-distance runners we all need to be? Will it carry us through the bleak, lifeless periods where no movement seems possible, let alone evident?

This is not meant to devalue the importance of theory. Clarity of purpose is a vital ingredient of hope. As Viktor Frankl often repeats, in his moving autobiographical tale of survival during the Holocaust, Nietzsche captured an essential truth when he said that "he who has a *why* to live can bear with almost any*how*" (Frankl, 1985p. 97). It would be difficult to mobilize the emotion of hope without a sense of conviction about the purposes of analytic effort.

I feel that Mitchell (1993) may be alluding to the gap between expectation and inspiration when he says, "Analytically useful forms of meaning and hope do not lie preformed in the patient; they are generated when the analyst has found a way to inspire personally meaningful forms of growth and expansion from the inside out" (p. 225). It is, I believe, as difficult to define this gap as it is to fill it, although in my attempts to define hope as a component of the emotion system and in what follows, I try to do so.

In an effort to apply Frankl's insight to analytic participants, it may be useful to look, again, at the "why" of their efforts, that is, the purposes analysis is currently thought to serve, so that we may understand what inspires analysands to bear with the "how" of analysis. These purposes of analytic effort are inextricably interwoven with our current understanding of the nature of the self, the ultimate subject of the analytic process. In Mitchell's (1993) vision, treatment strives toward the goal of continuity and diversity of self-experience. While I need an ongoing sense of "I," my growth is equally dependent on an expansion of what can consciously constitute "myself." I must come to hear the theme, and recognize its variations. I am reminded of a definition of the creative process that describes it as a method of "making the strange familiar" and "making the familiar strange" (Gordon, 1966). The growth of a sense of self entails recognition of personal consistencies in my approach to life. I must contact a familiar "me" in my seemingly strange moments. Reciprocally, I must recognize and tolerate my own diversity, appreciating nuances of difference in who I become in varying contexts.

In contrast to a drive-centered understanding of self-experience, Mitchell suggests ". . . psychoanalytic theorizing will have more to contribute to our understanding of personal individuality if we can get away from a search for presocial or extrasocial roots of the core or true self and focus on what it means at any particular moment to be experiencing and using oneself more or less authentically" [p. 150].

The search for a bodily based core comes to naught, since the meaning of any experience is always inextricably interwoven with its interpersonal functions.

Thus, the issue, "What is the purpose of psychoanalysis?" leads to the question, "Who is the self we are trying to affect?" To know this "self" requires us to raise, once again, the thorny issue of the nature of human motivations and, in particular, aggression and how it arises as part of self-experience. Is aggression a prewired drive, an inborn push seeking an outlet regardless of interpersonal contexts? Is it something I can, therefore, recognize has always been a part of me, no matter what the circumstances? If so, does that lend it the quality of "depth," or a sense of being "true" and basic to who I am? Did I enter this world "leading with my chin," looking for a fight? If so, I am motivated to *impose* an aggression-releasing meaning on some of my experience, and the recognition of this ongoing aspect of my motives would enhance my acquaintance with myself. The contrasting position holds that aggression is a response that is within our capacity but that its expression is not an inner yearning. I would know myself better if I understood what *evokes* an aggressive response from me.

Rejecting the idea of an aggressive drive, Mitchell's (1993) vision takes from the traditionalists their sense of the centrality of aggression in human experience, but focuses on aggression as a response to an endangered sense of self, rather than as an inborn push. For me, this perspective raises two questions:

1. Are aggression and assertion as separable as this point of view suggests? If they are not, as, for example, Thompson (1950) indicates, it will be more difficult to exclude the possibility of a prewired assertive/aggressive push.

2. Do we bring prewired emotions (rather than drives) with us into the world? On the theory that all that is prewired strives for expression, this would suggest that each fundamental emotion, each of the universally experienced human feelings *is* a bodily and interpersonally based given and crystallizes an aspect of self. That is, I come into the world with some

propensity to experience, for example, fear. I develop a history of who I am as a fearing person. This history, of course, is interpersonally and contextually shaped. But it is inevitable that I have some fear-inspired experiences, and these form part of who I am to myself. I do come into this world with a tendency, a pull, toward fearing, and this imposes meaning on some of what happens to me. I feel fear, anger, shame; therefore, I am. I would not be me, to me, without my sense of who I am as a fearing person. A long history of empirical/developmental, and cross-cultural research (Izard, 1971; Buechler and Izard, 1983) supports such a view. Notions such as Tomkins (Izard and Tomkins's, 1966) belief in the "socialization" of emotions suggest that each fundamental emotion is both catalyst and organizer of self-experience.

To add to the complexity, we might see Kernberg's (1992) more recent contributions as suggesting that prewired emotion components are the constitutionally based constituents of the drives. Here emotions are seen as the primary building blocks of the drives. This view retains body-based, constitutional imperatives, but, with the emotions rather than the drives in the primary place, it leaves room for more possibilities of individual differences in makeup.

What difference would these viewpoints make in what is hoped for from treatment? I am reminded of the prayer that is so central to the tenets of Alcoholics Anonymous, asking for the ability to accept what cannot be changed, to change what can be changed, and to have the wisdom to distinguish the two. We cannot hope to change bodily based givens. Patients entering treatment often ask to be made less angry, or fearful, or ashamed. It is certainly not that these hopes are unreasonable. Just because we, as human beings, are born with propensities to feel these emotions does not mean we should passively accept whatever comes to be our experience of them. But the simple recalibration often implicit in the patient's hopes is impossible. We as analysts cannot, directly, make anybody less anything. Emotions cannot be turned up or down, like a thermostat.

The question is, rather, what kind of interchange in treatment can result in the patient's enjoying a healthier emotional life, given that some experience with each of the fundamental emotions is essential to being human. The patient may well leave treatment more curious, hopeful, and joyful, and less angry, fearful, or ashamed; but I don't believe these changes can be approached directly as goals. Like happiness, these emotion-system changes are, I would suggest, by-products of healthy relating.

This theoretical position has implications for how hope, as an active emotional motivator, evolves in treatment. Is it contagious (in Sullivan's sense of early experiences of anxiety as passed from mother to child)? Is it modeled, learned by example? Does the analyst's hope for the patient, or for himself, somehow communicate itself to the patient, infecting or instructing him?

I don't believe it is, specifically, the analyst's hope that engenders hope in the patient, but the analyst's whole relationship to life. The patient observes the analyst's struggle to make sense of things, keep going in the face of seemingly insurmountable obstacles, retain humor and courage in situations that seem to inspire neither. The analyst stumbles, reacts without self-hate, works to recover. The analyst is willing to work hard. She is honest without being crippled by shame. She wants to live even the most difficult moments. She doesn't shrink from what is ugly in herself or the other. She is more interested in growth than in being right, more curious than self-protective. She can be wounded but refuses to be made dead. While in part this attitude may provide a model, and it may be contagious, I think that what mainly creates hope is the patient's experience of finding a way to relate to such a person. For many, this task requires substantive changes, alterations in all components of the emotion system. The deepened curiosity and joy, the lightened envy and hate that results engenders hope.

Mitchell's (1993) title also refers to "dread," an emotion I feel may have an important anxiety component. It is difficult to say whether dread is merely hope's absence or a more complicated array of emotions. It is surely true that trying to face life without much hope should engender anxiety. The patient who does not retain, or gain, an active sense of hope in treatment may leave more damaged than helped.

To return to our venerable, show-stopping analyst, her power derives from the commitment to life that is the palpable context of her expectations. As Fromm (1968) suggested, hope may be defined as "a psychic commitment to life and growth" (p. 13).

The aspect of active hope that affirms a commitment to life is probably not generally communicated in the content of what is said but, rather, in the fervor of the tone, in the strength of conviction that may be signaled by directness and forcefulness of speech. In analysis, this is probably conveyed to the patient more fully by personal and professional attitudes the analyst reveals unwittingly. Love of the work, a passion for promoting life and growth, an empathic stance toward herself and others, a willingness to struggle, joy in the humor and challenge of life are some of the intangibles that make themselves known in the subtle timing and gestures of the music, rather than in the words. What the analyst focuses on, responds to, is willing to break the frame for, lets pass in silence, meets with passion, expresses in the first person, tires about, is willing to fight, says a great deal. The same can be said in supervision, where the supervisor's and the supervisee's attitudes about treatment and life are often explicitly, as well as implicitly, studied.

The relationship between author and reader also provides avenues for the inspiration of hope. We probably absorb more from who the author is, in front of us, and how we are treated than from what is said to us. For example, in his last pages, Mitchell (1993) expresses his hope that his work will be "valued without being sanctified" (p. 230). As his readers, we have been allowed access to the personal and professional experience of a profoundly thoughtful analyst. We have watched him work hard to make sense of his treatment experiences. We have heard about how his struggles as a father inform his analytic understanding. We have witnessed the cross-fertilization of his private and public lives. We have experientially understood the values essential to his clinical work, partially by living with his approach to us as a writer. We have sensed his passion about growth and life. We have had the opportunity to gather hope.

REFERENCES

Barnett, J. (1968). Cognition, thought and affect in the organization of experience. In: *Science and Psychoanalysis, Vol. 12*, ed. J. Masserman. New York: Grune & Stratton, pp. 237–247.

Barnett, J. (1980). Cognitive repair in the treatment of the neuroses. *Journal of the American Academy Psychoanalysis* 8:39–55.

Buechler, S. (1992). Hatred: The strength of the sensitive. Discussion of paper by Otto Kernberg, presented at William Alanson White Scientific Meeting, New York City, October.

——— (1993a). Clinical applications of an interpersonal view of the emotions. *Contemporary Psychoanalysis* 29:219–236. http://www.pep-web.org/document.php?id'cps.029.0219a

——— (1993b). The analyst's experience of loneliness. Presented at William Alanson White Clinical Conference, New York City, October. http://www.pep-web.org/document.php?id'cps.034.0091a

——— & Izard, C. (1983). On the emergence, functions, and regulation of some emotion expressions in infancy. In: *Emotion: Theory. Research, and Experience, Vol. 2*, ed. R. Plutchik & H. Kellerman. New York: Academic Press, pp. 293–313.

Durang, C. (1980). The Actor's Nightmare. New York: Samuel French.

Frankl, V. (1985). Man's Search for Meaning. New York: Washington Square Press.

Fromm, E. (1968). *The Revolution of Hope*, New York: Harper & Row.

Gordon, W.J.J. (1966). *The Metaphorical Way of Learning and Knowing*. Cambridge, MA: Synectics Education Systems.

Izard, C.E. (1971). *The Face of Emotion*. New York: Appleton-Century-Crofts.

——— (1977) *Human Emotions*. New York: Plenum. http://www.pep-web.org/document.php?id'aop.012.0415a

——— & Tomkin, S.S. (1966). Affect and behavior: anxiety as a negative affect. In: *Anxiety and Behavior*, ed. C. D. Spielberger. New York: Academic Press.

Kernberg, O. F. (1992). The psychopathology of hatred. Presented at the William Alanson White Scientific Meeting, New York City, October. http://www.pep-web.org/document.php?id'apa.039s.0209a

Mitchell, S.A. (1993). *Hope and Dread in Psychoanalysis.* New York: Basic Books.

Schachtel, E. (1959). *Metamorphosis.* New York: Basic Books.

Spiegel, R. (1980). Cognitive aspects of affect and other feeling states with clinical applications. *Journal of the American Academy Psychoanalysis* 8: 591–614. www.pep-web.org/document.php?id'jaa.008.0591a

Stern, D.B. (1989). Discussion of G. Friedman, "Keeping the analysis alive and creative." *Contemporary Psychoanalysis* 25 346–355. http://www.pep-web.org/document.php?id'cps.025.0346a

Stern, D.B. (1990). Courting surprise. *Contemporary Psychoanalysis* 26: 425–478. http://www.pep-web.org/document.php?id'cps.026.0452a

Sullivan, H.S. (1954). *The Psychiatric Interview.* New York: Norton.

Thompson, C. (1950). *Psychoanalysis.* New York: Hermitage House.

CHAPTER TWO

The Right Stuff: The Analyst's Sensitivity to Emotional Nuance[*]

INTRODUCTION

What does it take to be an analyst? In this paper I focus on the emotional "right stuff." What kind of relationship with our own emotions is conducive to conducting an analytic practice? How can the clinician cultivate it?

Before my analytic training I wrote about the "discrete" emotions (Izard, 1977). Cal Izard, my mentor and co-principal investigator on a National Science Foundation grant, taught me a way of thinking about the contribution each emotion plays in our motivational lives. Together we explored the first expressions of each of a series of emotions, in the first two years of life. I became familiar with anger's squared mouth, the subtle nuances of fear, and the open smile of joy, among other facial expressions.

It took many years for me to find ways to integrate this background with my roles as an analyst and supervisor. Intuitively, I knew that it was clinically immensely helpful to be in touch with gradations of feelings. But how could I marry that sensibility to a way of working informed by

---

* *Contemporary Psychoanalysis*, 1997. 33:2, 295–306

the interpersonal/relational analytic schools of thought? What part does recognizing our own subtly shifting emotions play, in developing the "right stuff" to be an analyst?

THE RIGHT STUFF: THE ANALYST'S SENSITIVITY TO EMOTIONAL NUANCE

To be sensitive to the subjective experience of others and of ourselves requires our increased sensitivity to the range of feeling states. We tend to be simplistic and think only of the major, or what may be called the massive, states of feeling, such as depression, despair, resentment, anger, rage. Most of these the patient can tell us about, can verbalize. But at times a far wider range of feeling states is present than we psychoanalysts and psychologists are prone to consider. Our compass of emotion tends to include love, hate, resentment, ambivalence, anger/rage, depression/despair/grief, elation/mania, anxiety, shame, and guilt. This list omits many more terms, often with nuances that we are tempted to homogenize away, thus closing off our awareness of the related experience. Some closing off of exploration unfortunately lies at our door. We need the poet's range! (Spiegel, 1980)

Rose Spiegel's statement issues a challenge to us as analysts. We must become attuned to the subtle shadings of emotional experiences in ourselves and our patients. Awareness of major shifts is insufficient. Like the poet who can capture fine gradations of meaning in apt phrases, we must be able to catch hold of minute degrees of our own and others' emotions just as they make their appearance, so that we may search for adequate words to embody them. We sense the subtle appearance of a feeling in ourselves or our patients, and we must apprehend—later, perhaps, comprehend—its quality. Well-chosen words may help us move from apprehension to comprehension, but the whole process depends on that initial *noticing* of a subtle emotional experience.

Think of how many ways noticing minor emotional shifts serves us as analysts. Awareness of a slight boredom in ourselves, for example, can alert us to examine our countertransference. Further, Sullivan (1953, 1954) advised us to pay attention to the effect of our interventions on the patient's level of anxiety. This requires great sensitivity to emotional nuances. Every analytic hour is an exercise in observing a richly patterned, intricate interplay of emotions in ourselves as well as in the patient. For example, at a particular moment when we are clearly saddened, presumably by what we are hearing, is there *also* an ache of loneliness? Might that, rather than any considerations of technique, be what is prompting our unusually active analytic stance? Awareness of the faint tinge of loneliness could lead us to this understanding.

Are analysts who can make such observations of self and patient made or born? The training analysis presumably increases the candidate's awareness of his own defensive maneuvers, but is this sufficient to ensure that our graduates will be able to call upon their sensitivity to emotional experience as a resource? Or is it in supervision that candidates are *taught* to notice subtle shadings of emotion in themselves and their patients? Or is it largely in the selection process that we must choose applicants who have, or have the potential to develop, the "right" emotional "stuff"?

Just what is the "stuff" that enables the analyst to register barely noticeable emotional nuances? Some might suggest we consult the vast literature on empathy to examine the question of the analyst's sensitivity to the patient's emotions. As for the analyst's understanding of his own feelings, we could study the voluminous work on counter-transference. Others would have a different approach. Since it could be argued that any interference with the analyst's perception of subtle emotions would result from his own defenses, we might peruse the analytic literature devoted to the processes of defense.

Each of these avenues of inquiry is relevant and fascinating. But what I have argued elsewhere (Buechler, 1993) and will further elaborate here is that the analyst, like any other human being, has a lifelong relationship with each of the fundamental emotions. She comes to her work as an analyst with a previously formed, deeply ingrained set of attitudes about what constitutes healthy and pathological emotionality. These attitudes are to a great extent emotion-specific. For example, she has beliefs, often unexamined, about how intensely anger "ought" to be expressed, about the proper mode of showing curiosity, and about what can be constructive in shame and guilt. During training, the candidate is exposed to the attitudes in her institute's variant of the psychoanalytic culture (Buechler, 1988) toward how emotions should be handled in treatment. She "picks up" mores about expressing love for patients, about experiencing contempt or disgust for them, and about conveying hope. She is "taught" (often outside the awareness of both teacher-supervisor-training analyst and candidate) what emotional experiences and expressions are "appropriate" for analysts, and "healthy" for patients. She learns what she is supposed to do with her own and the patient's aggression in treatment. She senses the degree to which she is supposed to feel (and to show) surprise. She probably intuits without direct communication what place courage should have in her work and how much loneliness she is expected to bear. Her pretraining, personal orientation toward each of the fundamental emotions (Izard & Buechler, 1978) undergoes some modification in training, but remains reflective of her lifelong patterns. Some of us enter training as intense people, prone to extreme responses and convinced that highly charged emotionality is healthy. There might be some exceptions to this belief, so that, for example, we might feel that extreme anxiety is maladaptive. But in general we might be unusually comfortable with intense emotionality and bring this attitude to our training process, in which we learn the assessment of emotional pathology in patients and the expressions appropriate to the role of the analyst. The institute's cultural beliefs about emotions will modify our personal attitudes, but only to some extent. Some enter and leave training comfortable only with low-intensity emotionality in themselves and their patients, and in experience as well as expression. For still others, their attitudes are extremely emotion-specific, in that they have very different feelings about, for example, strong anger and intense fear. In short, everyone enters training with attitudes toward emotionality in general and emotion-specific beliefs. Training alters these patterns to some degree, but like any other deeply ingrained aspect of personality, these lifelong patterns retain some of their original shape.

The "right stuff" for the analyst allows him access to awareness of emotions, at low levels of intensity, in himself and his patients. Each of us has a threshold that an emotion would have to reach to be recognized. But, as suggested above, the threshold differs according to the emotion, our attitudes about it, and especially, our comfort with it. Perhaps before training I had to be very ashamed to be aware of my shame, but I could be easily in touch with low levels of anger. If my training emphasized the importance of knowing about shame as an aspect of health in general, and as an important piece of equipment for the analyst, I may have become better able to recognize minute feelings of shame in myself. I may also have improved in recognizing these feelings in my patients. But I may never become as able to sense slight shame as my colleague, who entered training very comfortable with this emotion. On the other hand, I might be especially adept at spotting anger at its lowest intensity levels in myself and others.

While analysts differ in their approach to the handling of countertransference, none would argue against access to knowing about their own emotional reactions. Similarly, we might disagree about the proper technique in responding to the patient's emotional shifts, but we would all be in favor of our awareness of them. The "right stuff" for an analyst enables him not to "homogenize away" important nuances of experience, to use the expression from Spiegel's work that introduces this essay. In the following pages, some examples are given of situations in which important nuances of experience are "homogenized away" by analysts, with extremely negative consequences for the treatment.

A TREATMENT DEADLOCK

Any list of the vital tools of our trade must include the analyst's curiosity (Stern, 1989, 1990). While some might not include curiosity among the emotions, many emotion theorists do include it, because it so clearly plays a key role in motivating active behavior from the beginning of life (Izard, 1977). In a previous work (Buechler, 1996b) I suggested that curiosity is crucial to the candidate's bearing of the inevitable shame and anxiety experiences in training. But what if access to genuine, alive, creative curiosity is blocked? What if defensive maneuvers and strong emotions grossly limit access to curiosity? What if one intense emotion takes over the analyst's experience, so that all nuances of curiosity and other feelings are "homogenized away"? The following vignette illustrates the dead, going-through-the-motions quality that can result in the treatment.

The analyst in training has extensive experience and is intensely motivated to learn. The patient is a thirty-five-year-old man, clearly chronically depressed, with marked schizoid and obsessional tendencies. Although he is relatively successful in his career, both his work and social relationships are extremely limited. He has never been involved with a woman for more than a few months. This patient's awkward, silent, stubborn withdrawal in the treatment hour is occasionally punctuated by highly detailed elaborations of his work problems. A challenge for his therapist is to genuinely engage him in an active effort to notice his own defensive behavior and understand its functions.

The therapist, while clear about this goal, often finds herself enacting a painful parody of analytic neutrality that takes the treatment nowhere. While she is generally an enthusiastic learner and an alive presence, in this treatment she is silent and passive with nothing to ask. Often she gets engaged in the patient's overly detailed detours into his professional quandaries, though she is aware at these times that she is acting out of a desperation to engage him in a dialogue of any kind. The therapist is acutely aware of her own mounting anxiety before and during these sessions. She can sometimes contact the anger that contributes to her matching the patient's stubborn withdrawal with her own. But anxiety, and occasionally anger or frustration, are all she is aware of feeling. She is unable to sense increasing anxiety or any other feeling in the patient. She can only engage in a silent Mexican standoff, or parrot what the patient has last said, or ask obvious questions, such as "How did that make you feel?" The patient's contempt, distrust, and hopelessness mount with each of these "interventions." Sensing that the patient may be about to withdraw into silence, the therapist feels increased anxiety, and she becomes even more obediently bland, following the patient wherever his obsessional defenses carry them, until they are both quite lost. Listening to tapes of these sessions, I, as the supervisor, sometimes imagine that the fog Sullivan suggested engulfs obsessionals (1956) is about to descend on both patient and therapist, so that by the end of some sessions they actually have no idea what they are talking about.

This unfortunate situation can be worked with in several ways. Depending on her view of supervision as primarily didactic or primarily therapeutic (Levenson, 1982), the supervisor might engage the therapist in a thorough personal exploration of her feelings and defenses, or suggest she take this up in her training analysis. In either case, I think the supervisor should help the therapist become more aware of the patient's anxiety as it escalates, as well as each shift in her own anxiety and its effect on her natural curiosity. This therapist, who is such an avid learner, can't let herself wonder what is going on with her patient at the time it is happening. She can only do so after the fact, in the supervision. Her lifelong experience of anxiety, her defensive maneuvers to avoid awareness of it, her own threshold for obliterating curiosity in the face of anxiety, and many other factors contribute to this deadened treatment.

The therapist's anxiety affects her access to more than just her own curiosity and the patient's emotional shifts. It has also decreased her *capacity to be surprised* by what happens in the treatment, another vital tool (Stern, 1990). Without this ability, we tend to trot out tired theories and use them as Procrustean beds for our patients. We fit the patient to the preformulated theory. We use what happens in the hour as an illustration of something previously memorized. In this supervision, the therapist seemed so anxious to prove herself an able student that she used the material in the treatment to try to display her knowledge of theory. I considered my job as her supervisor to entail more than merely pointing out her anxiety and its effects. I felt I had to help her connect with her loneliness in this treatment, with the deadness of it, the lack of hope and joy, the lifelessness of stultified curiosity. I had to help her be aware of nuances of shame and guilt she felt about failing the patient, and of the lack of courage she felt in trying to "pass," rather than grow, in supervision.

Thus I felt my work was to help her connect with the more subtle shadings of her feelings, not just the obvious anxiety and anger. That

125

which was so clearly present, the anger and anxiety, blocked awareness of other emotions that could be important elements in the treatment. What was absent was at least as important as what was present. Whether these matters should be merely mentioned in supervision or be more fully explored depends on supervisory style and is a subject for debate. I see it as my supervisory function, at the very least, to comment on the therapist's missing resources, to help her wonder why she is so unable to use her full self in her work with this patent. I am trying to awaken her curiosity about what is going on in this treatment. I am also trying to model the use of curiosity by giving full reign to my own. My goal in the supervision is to facilitate the supervisee's awareness of every emotional resource that she normally has, but is unable to use in this deadened treatment. If I bring to the supervision my own curiosity, hope, capacity for surprise, and sensitivity to nuance, I will not engage with the supervisee in a deadened, damaging parallel process that "homogenizes away" most of the feelings she needs to access in order to break the deadlock in the treatment.

MOBILIZING THE ANALYST'S AGGRESSION

This second vignette has elements in common with the first, but important differences as well. The therapist is also an analyst in training with extensive experience. She is also a "good" and eager student. Her patient is a thirty-seven-year-old artist who came to treatment jaded by his previous therapy experiences, expecting little from this work, but needing help to deal with the recent death of a close friend. From their first session this patient threatened to leave the treatment if the therapist didn't accord him special privileges. He couldn't trust her unless he had access to her personal life. The frame of treatment, with its rigid time and payment schedule, was dehumanizing and insulting. He had to know the therapist's thoughts as they occurred, or else it would be useless to reveal his own. He doubted she had the experience or intelligence to be of any real help.

Barraged by his demands, the therapist felt cornered. In a previous publication (Buechler, 1996b) I described the bind experienced by the candidate subjected simultaneously to the demands of certain patients for extra-analytic contact and their supervisor's expectations that they maintain the frame. This candidate was immediately enmeshed in this bind from the first session of her work with this patient. She would sometimes give in to his demands, revealing aspects of her personal life, but feeling very uncomfortable in the treatment and guilty in the supervision. At other times she would refuse to respond to the patient's inquiry, but would feel anxious that he might follow through with his threats to leave the treatment. Whatever she did, the therapist felt "off her game," unable to keep the patient rather than herself the focus of the work.

As in the first vignette, a Mexican standoff resulted, but this was a much noisier affair. The treatment hours were filled with the patient's dramatic bargaining, including suicidal threats. Like the therapist in the first example, this candidate felt mounting anxiety before and during the treatment sessions. But unlike the first, this candidate remained in touch with a range of feelings in herself and her patient. She was acutely aware of his desperation, his fear that he couldn't find a way to trust her, his terror of dependency, his rage at being so often disappointed, his humiliation at needing help. She remained in touch with her own deep desire to succeed as his therapist and as an analyst in training. She felt her own humiliation at being so "successfully" bullied by the patient. Yet she remained genuinely eager to be of help to him and sensitive to his real pain and fear. At times she could be curious about what was going on in the treatment and use her curiosity to try to enlist the patient's.

What was, however, not fully available to this candidate was an adequate degree of assertion or, perhaps, mobilized aggression during the sessions. She frequently became passive and unable to withstand his assaults.

This suggests to me an addition to what Epstein (1986) has so usefully described as the therapist's need to feel like a good therapist. In the work with the borderline patient this need for "good therapist" feelings can stymie the work when the treatment requires that the therapist be able to contain the patient's toxic rage. I would add that, at least in the vignette I am reporting, the therapist also needed her own anger available to her as a resource to mobilize her active, rather than passive, involvement in the session—to help her act rather than be acted on. Thus I suggest that being able to contain the patient's projected rage is not enough. Even the ability to maintain a sense of competence, despite having extremely negative feelings about the patient, is not sufficient, although it is necessary. Using these capacities allows the therapist to contain the potentially damaging effects of the patient's anger and her own. This addresses only the *dangers* of anger and the therapist's role in damage control and detoxification.

A belief that each fundamental emotion has important functions in psychic life (Izard, 1971), and that anger in particular has important mobilizing functions (Buechler, 1992a), requires even more of the therapist. In addition to containing and detoxifying the patient's anger and her own, she must also mine the anger as a vital resource.

This view of the positive functions of anger was proposed by analyst Clara Thompson (1950) as well as by some emotion theorists (Izard, 1971, 1972, 1977). My own previous work on the positive functions of hatred and related emotions (Buechler, 1992a) suggests that these emotions perform vital functions, especially in our efforts to avoid immobilizing depression. Anger can be a tremendous mobilizing force, enabling us to fight for what we believe in. Rage, for example, at the desecration of our environment, energizes the battle to save it.

To return to the vignette, this therapist needed to be able to draw upon her anger at the patient's bullying tactics. Perhaps at a deeper level, she had to connect with her own rage at the aspect of him that was willing to forfeit his treatment and even his life in the service of his pride. The therapist had to be equipped to fight for life, her patient's life, and in a more general sense, the sanctity of life. She had to take an unequivocal position that his life was more important than their power struggles. She had to show him this belief, this commitment, in her behavior. To do this, I feel, requires mobilized aggression. An aspect of the therapist's health is her readiness to fight for the patient's life against any forces that oppose it. Some patients will repeatedly test the firmness of this stance. The therapist can not maintain the required position without the force of mobilized aggression.

My sense is that this does not substantially differ from Ferenczi's (1929) position, when he disagreed with Freud's belief that we are born equipped with enough life force. Ferenczi suggested that we must be called into life through the caregiver's active concern. Ferenczi was postulating an interpersonal rather than an intrapsychic source for the impulse toward life. In this regard, I would stress the active nature of what is required of both caregiver and therapist. In the vignette presented here, the therapist had to use her own mobilized aggression to fight for the preeminence of the life of the treatment. She had to act in its interest, putting its survival first. She had to verbalize her belief in its importance, in the meaningfulness of the work that she and the patient had to do together. She had to tell the patient that they both needed to search for ways to keep the treatment going, despite urges to the contrary.

Of course courage, tact, hope, and love for life, or what Fromm (1964) might call "biophilia," were necessary ingredients in this affirmative therapeutic stance. But without the conscious intention to fight for something she believes in, I feel it would be impossible for the therapist to maintain this position. Eventually this therapist was able to connect with enough healthy aggression to create the required milieu.

CONCLUSIONS

Ours has been called the "impossible profession," an expression which, I suggest, reinforces the skepticism and pessimism about treatment rampant in the current climate. We cannot measure the damage this does to the newest members of the profession, who have as yet to prove themselves. Several years ago I tried to outline some of the stresses on the beginning analyst (Buechler, 1992c), emphasizing how hard it can be to depend on interpersonal relations for a professional, as well as a personal, life. Today's climate adds to the strain. Performing any task well requires a sense of its meaningfulness (Buechler, 1996a). The erosion of belief in the effectiveness and significance of our work will most adversely affect those who are young and idealistic. They have as yet to establish a full practice. They must find a way to earn their livelihoods as analysts, so they must deal with the practical obstacles in this managed-care, bottom-line-driven world. But more importantly, they must find faith in the meaningfulness of the life's work they have taken up. Paradoxically, this faith is required *before* they have had a chance to see the positive impact of their efforts.

I would like to call ours the "passionate" instead of the "impossible" profession. It requires the full presence of the analyst every working moment. It asks that all of his emotional resources be at the ready. The analyst cannot afford to "homogenize away" any of his feelings. He must be in touch with each one and careful to distinguish one from the other. Their full, active use requires their painstaking recognition. Accordingly, the analyst's training must acquaint him with his history and attitudes toward each of the fundamental emotions and the defensive maneuvers he may employ to block awareness of them.

Analytic work is inherently difficult, but without full emotional awareness the analyst would lose his greatest sources of information, as well as the forces that propel the work forward. The analyst must remain in touch with minute shifts in all of his emotions, not merely the overshadowing, predominant ones. He must understand that his emotions form a delicate system, with slight shifts in one affecting the intensity of all the others. I believe it is often the analyst's less prominent emotional responses that provide key countertransferential information.

Equally important is the analyst's sensitivity to minute shifts in all of the patient's emotions. Late in his career, Freud discovered the importance of awareness of signal anxiety (1926). Sullivan (1953) also accorded it a central role in the learning process. We can expand this to suggest that signal levels of *all* the emotions must be attended to. Health requires their use as information, and as protection against alienation. The alienated person has lost vital connection with his own emotional life. He can neither know himself nor propel himself forward. He has lost a sense of wholeness, centeredness, and meaningfulness. He is likely to be depressed (Buechler, 1995). Since each of the fundamental emotions performs crucial functions in psychic life, being fully alive requires access to them all, and not just to the few that predominate.

The analyst must allow full reign to her curiosity, be prepared to be surprised, be ready to mobilize healthy aggression to promote the life of the treatment. She must be able to tolerate her own anger, anxiety, shame, and guilt at her moments of seeming failure. She must often bear the loneliness of being the only one actively fighting for the patient's life.

At the same time, the analyst needs sufficient hope and love to keep working despite setbacks and long periods of seeming stasis. She must have faith in the worth of her work and belief in its long-term effectiveness. She must focus some of her attention on the present moment, but much of it on the far horizon, on the potential of this patient for fuller living.

To accomplish this requires exquisite intra- and interpersonal sensitivity. All who are involved in the training process must actively cultivate the candidate's potential for this "right stuff." Like the conductor who hears each individual note, the analyst must be attuned to the nuances of major and minor emotional shifts in herself and her patient. Analysis requires our whole presence as self-aware and responsive human beings. The fully passionate analyst can sustain the strength, the courage required of her to persuasively call her patient to life.

REFERENCES

Buechler, S. (1988). Joining the psychoanalytic culture. *Contemporary Psychoanalysis* 24:462–470.

——— (1992a). Hatred: The strength of the sensitive. Discussion of paper by Otto Kernberg, presented at William Alanson White Scientific Meeting, New York City, October.

——— (1992b). Shame and anxiety in psychoanalytic training. Presented at the International Federation for Psychoanalytic Education, Denver, November.

——— (1992c). Stress in the personal and professional development of a psychoanalyst. *Journal of the American Academy of Psychoanalysis*, 20:183–191. http://www.pep-web.org/document.php?id'jaa.020.0183a

——— (1993). Clinical applications of an interpersonal view of the emotions. *Contemporary Psychoanalysis* 29:219–236. http://www.pep-web.org /document.php?id'cps.029.0219a

——— (1995). Emotion. In: *Handbook of interpersonal psychoanalysis*, ed. M. Lionells, J. Fiscalini, C. H. Mann & D. B. Stern. Hillsdale, NJ: The Analytic Press, pp. 165–188.

——— (1996a), A commentary. In: *A Prophetic Analyst: Erich Fromm's Contribution to Psychoanalysis*, ed. M. Cortina & M. Maccoby. Northvale, NJ: Jason Aronson, Inc., pp. 402–412.

——— (1996b). Supervision of the treatment of borderline patients. *Contemporary Psychoanalysis* 32:86–92. http://www.pep-web.org /document.php?id'cps.032.0086a

Epstein, L. (1986). Collusive selective inattention to the negative impact of the supervisory interaction *Contemporary Psychoanalysis* 22:389–409. http://www.pep-web.org/document.php?id'cps.022.0389a

Ferenczi, S. (1929). The unwelcome child and his death instinct. In: *The Final Contributions to the Problems and Methods of Psychoanalysis*. London: The Hogarth Press. http://www.pep-web.org/document.php ?id'ijp.010.0125a

Freud, S. (1926). Inhibitions, symptoms and anxiety. *Standard Edition*, 20:87–175. http://www.pep-web.org/document.php?id'se.020.0075a

Fromm, E. (1964). *The Heart of Man: Its Genius for Good and Evil*. New York: Harper and Row.

Izard, C. E. (1971). *The Face of Emotion*. New York: Appleton-Century-Crofts.

——— (1972). *Patterns of Emotion*. New York: Academic Press.

——— (1977). *Human Emotions*. New York: Plenum Press.

——— & Buechler, S. (1978). Emotion expression and personality integration in infancy. In: *Emotions in Personality and Psychopathology*, ed. C.E. Izard. New York: Plenum Press.

Levenson, E. (1982). Follow the fox. *Contemporary Psychoanalysis* 18:1–15. http://www.pep-web.org/document.php?id'cps.018.0001a

Spiegel, R. (1980). Cognitive aspects of affects and other feeling states with clinical applications. *Journal of the American Academy of Psychoanalysis*, 8:591–614.http://www.pep-web.org/document.php?id'jaa.008.0591a

Stern, D.B. (1989). Discussion of G. Freedman. Keeping the analysis alive and creative. *Contemporary Psychoanalysis* 25:346–355. http://www.pep-web.org/document.php?id'cps.025.0346a

Stern, D.B. (1990). Courting surprise. *Contemporary Psychoanalysis* 26:426–478. http://www.pep-web.org/document.php?id'cps.026.0452a

Sullivan, H. S. (1953). *The Interpersonal Theory of Psychiatry.* New York: W. W. Norton.

——— (1954). *The Psychiatric Interview.* New York: W. W. Norton.

——— (1956). *Clinical Studies in Psychiatry.* New York: W. W. Norton.

Thompson, C. (1950). *Psychoanalysis; Evolution and Development.* New York: Hermitage House.

CHAPTER THREE

The Analyst's Experience of Loneliness[*]

INTRODUCTION

We are each in solitary confinement, in the sense that no one sees the world entirely from our perspective. Nowhere is this more apparent than in an analytic relationship, where examining these differences is part of the everyday fabric.

During sessions we are not alone, but we can often feel lonely. This paper first describes some of the ways loneliness has been understood by psychoanalysts. It suggests that the quality of the analyst's experience of loneliness may differ, depending, in part, on the patient's character structure. The paper also considers what aspects of our own character and theoretical orientation can exacerbate our loneliness.

In the "loneliness" paper I anticipate my later work on "The ordinary tragedies of an analytic life" (in *Still Practicing: The Heartaches and Joys of a Clinical Career*, 2012, chapter 8, pp. 157–179). Patients' difficulties adhering to the analytic frame are well documented, but what of the loneliness it can induce in us? Our ongoing feelings often crystallize at termination, when loneliness takes solid shape. In the 2012 book I wrote of my own experience, when a patient left, that (p.178) "Some of my selves are gone. Persons I was becoming may never exist." When I wrote

---

[*] *Contemporary Psychoanalysis,*1998, 34:1, 91–115.

the 1998 paper I was just beginning to understand how my loneliness can stem from losing touch with aspects of myself.

THE ANALYST'S EXPERIENCE OF LONELINESS

In her classic, posthumously published article on loneliness, Fromm-Reichmann (1959) cites A. Courtauld's observations of isolation in a Greenland weather station. Courtauld (1932) recommends that "only persons with active, imaginative minds, who do not suffer from a nervous disposition and are not given to brooding, and who can occupy themselves by such means as reading, should go on polar expeditions." It is the thesis of this article that the habits of mind required to bear the loneliness of analytic exploration are remarkably similar. It is in the realm of the imagination, relatively protected from brooding and anxiety, nurtured and stimulated by selected reading, that the context for withstanding the loneliness of analytic inquiry can be created.

Fromm-Reichmann is clear about the necessity for the analyst to be aware of his or her own loneliness and the anxiety it may engender.

> The psychiatrist's specific problem in treating lonely patients seems to be that he has to be alert for and recognize traces of his own loneliness or fear of loneliness, lest it interfere with his fearless acceptance of manifestations of the patient's loneliness. This holds true, for example, when the psychiatrist, hard as he may try, cannot understand the meaning of a psychotic communication. He may then feel excluded from a "we-experience" with his patient; and this exclusion may evoke a sense of loneliness or fear of loneliness in the doctor, which makes him anxious. (p. 329)

But despite this unequivocal indication of the importance of investigating the loneliness of the analyst, this territory has scarcely been explored. Perhaps a general confusion between "aloneness" and "loneliness" is, in part, responsible. Fromm-Reichmann (1959), Mendelson (1990), and others have emphasized the importance of carefully distinguishing aloneness from loneliness. Many of us, however, may blur their meanings, assuming that analysts who spend most of their time in intimate conversations with others do not suffer from loneliness. Rarely alone, we analysts are in a superb position to define the difference between "alone" and "lonely." Although some attention has been given to the loneliness of the analytic patient (Fromm-Reichmann, 1959; Satran, 1978), the analyst's experience of loneliness has been too long neglected.

In this article I attempt to describe the loneliness of the analyst as it is shaped by four factors: the loneliness of the patient, the patient's prevailing way of relating, the analyst's stance regarding countertransference, and the nature of the other emotions recruited in the analyst by working with this patient. I suggest that the analyst's loneliness contributes to various forms of work-related stress and certain frequently observed treatment impasses. Finally, I explore some approaches to dealing with the analyst's loneliness.

THE NATURE OF LONELINESS

What makes loneliness painful? A review of this question has already been undertaken (Buechler, 1995), hence only some of the essential points are summarized here.

Perhaps Sullivan (1953) most clearly articulated how hard it is to define loneliness: "I, in common apparently with all denizens of the English-speaking world, feel inadequate to communicate a really clear impression of the experience of loneliness in its quintessential force" (pp. 260–261). One way to differentiate how various analysts view the pain of loneliness is to consider what, for each, the lonely person has lost. Although it is not always expressed in these terms, it seems that loneliness always involves some type of painful loss. Thus Rollo May (1953pp. 23–30) writes of loneliness as a threat to the sense of self. Because we need human relations in order to orient and know ourselves, loneliness endangers our relationship with ourselves.

The loss that loneliness entails is given a different slant by Fromm-Reichmann (1959). Her writings emphasize the lack of hope of human connectedness in the profoundly lonely person. She focuses on the importance of hope of future interactions and the subjective meaning of the loneliness in explaining its effect. She explores possible antidotes to loneliness, such as a feeling that the loneliness has a purpose, that it is, for example, in the service of a cause. She also suggests that mental stimulation may somewhat relieve the feeling. Thus for Fromm-Reichmann, the most profound loneliness would entail the loss of hope, purpose, and stimulation.

For Sullivan (1953), the need for contact is so essential to being human that loneliness would have to involve a profound deprivation. It could mean no less than the loss of that which sustains human life. We are, at our core, interpersonal.

> From a consideration of these three principles, it is possible to think of man as distinguished from plants and animals by the fact that human life—in a very real and not only a purely literary or imaginary sense—requires interchange with an environment which includes culture. When I say that man is distinguished very conspicuously from other members of the biological universe by requiring interchange with a universe of culture, this means, in actual fact, since culture is an abstraction pertaining to people, that man requires interpersonal relationships, or interchange with others. (p. 32)

This would imply that loneliness greatly endangers security.

Whether we pivot our understanding of the pain of loneliness around the loss of the sense of self, hope, stimulation, security, or some other factor, it is clear that a painful loss is involved. But what can turn this pain to good account? The poet Rilke (1934) suggests that

> you should not let yourself be confused in your solitude by the fact that there is something in you that wants to break out of it. This very wish will help you, if you use it quietly, and deliberately and like a tool, to spread out your solitude over wide country. (p. 53)

The poet's answer is to embrace the inevitable. When we use our solitude as a tool, when we *will* it, we can bear it. Thus, it seems that what is most painful about profound loneliness for Rilke is that it is an experience our will rejects. This suggests that the loss involves the sense of personal control. Loneliness is an inevitable part of life, made profoundly painful by setting one's will against it.

No one has written the last word on loneliness. It has preoccupied poets and analysts, Biblical scholars and portrait painters. Job, forsaken by his God, Dostoevsky's Underground Man, alienated from his society, and so many others cry out against what they have lost. What can be of comfort, until the sense of connection is restored?

THE LONELINESS OF THE ANALYTIC PATIENT

Although there has been some attention given to the experience of loneliness in the analytic patient, I suggest that loneliness may play an unnamed part in many familiar treatment phenomena, such as resistance to the couch and difficulties with the frame. Thus, loneliness may play a greater role in the patient's experience than has been recognized.

Satran (1978) suggested that some of the patient's loneliness in treatment may result from a defective therapeutic alliance, and hence may be, in a sense, an iatrogenic neurosis. Satran's thinking supports the notion of an optimal degree of loneliness in treatment, just as there may be an optimal degree of anxiety. Some loneliness may be an inevitable, or perhaps even a useful, aspect of the experience, while a too intense loneliness may be destructive.

In a series of discussions of Fromm-Reichmann's essay on loneliness, Mendelson, Rosen, Hegeman, Mohacsy, and Satran contributed thoughts on the emotion of loneliness in general, and the patient's loneliness experiences in particular. Among the many evocative observations of these writers, I highlight just a few of their thoughts. Mendelson (1990) cautions that

> Even though the exact place of loneliness in the causal sequence or network of events is not always ascertainable, there is a practical sense in which the suffering of loneliness, and not just of the most

severe kind emphasized by Fromm-Reichmann, calls for recognition and attention by the psychotherapist or psychoanalyst. Whether this attention can produce durable relief or something approaching cure is not predictable. (pp. 350–351)

Mendelson goes on to differentiate various causes of the patient's loneliness, including some that he suggests are relatively likely to be accessible to psychotherapy, because they are mainly a function of the patient's character. Mendelson concludes with this description of the goals of treatment with regard to the patient's loneliness.

> Both connection and solitude being part of the human condition, each offers its pleasures and pains. A function of psychotherapy in this broader context, may be to free the person to discover the optimal mix for him of relatedness and solitude, and to cope self-respectingly with the sorrows that accompany solitude and that attend connection. (p. 354) 1

Mohacsy (1990) cites Winnicott's thinking on the capacity to be alone, as it is normally developed through experiences of playing alone while near the mother. Mohacsy suggests that the holding environment we provide for patients

> mimics this childhood process and may compensate for it when it has been inadequate. This is not a "corrective experience" in the more primitive sense of Alexander and Ferenczi. As my patient complained, the analyst cannot do breast-feeding. However the analyst can possibly supply the good introject when the mother has failed in this respect. (p. 363)

To amplify this notion a bit, one might view the patient playing with ideas, lying on the couch, near but not in sight of the analyst, as quite literally analogous to the situation provided by Winnicott's good enough mother, who offers proximity without intrusion. This implies another rationale for the idea of an optimal level of loneliness in treatment: it may be an experience, when digested, that contributes to the patient's growing capacity to be alone.

I would suggest that we, perhaps ironically, have focused more attention on the loneliness the patient brings to the treatment than on the loneliness we may create for him in the way we treat him. The patient's experience of loneliness in treatment may be a product of the nexus of these two contributing factors. There may be times when, without our awareness, we are asking an acutely lonely patient to endure a loneliness-engendering process that he has not yet developed the tools to bear. The patient, then, may balk at the use of the couch, or the analyst's unavailability between sessions, or his unwillingness to reveal his own reactions, and we label this patient as resistive to the frame, or borderline. As descriptions, these labels may be true, but they do not comprehensively explain, in that they do not fully take into account the interaction between who the patient is and what our treatment context is asking him to do. What I suggest is a more interactional definition of the patient's loneliness; rather than see it as residing within him, we can view it as an occurrence in an interpersonal context that is a product of intrapsychic and interpersonal factors.

Although I don't believe we have a great deal of data on the experience of loneliness in treatment, we might search patients' first-hand accounts of their treatments to study whether they describe themselves as lonely, and if so, how they coped. I have not attempted the project of looking through the literature of patients' accounts of their treatment to obtain this data, but I think this would be a worthwhile study. What I have read, however, coincides with my own experiences, as a patient, analyst, and supervisor, which suggest to me that if a sense of collaborative inquiry is established in the treatment, this can go a long way in assuaging loneliness on the part of both participants or, at least, in making the inevitable loneliness tolerable by imbuing it with a sense of purpose. A brief quotation from the recollections of the patient known as the "Wolf-Man" illustrates this: "in my analysis with Freud I felt myself less as a patient than as a co-worker, the younger comrade of an experienced explorer setting out to study a new, recently discovered land" (Gardiner, 1971p. 140). Although one might see this as the expression of a patient unwilling to fully embrace the patient role, resistant to the frame, another viewpoint is that this patient developed the collaborative potential of the treatment relationship in a constructive attempt to bear its inevitable loneliness. A patient and analyst able to create such a team may subject each other to less debilitating loneliness.

THE ANALYST'S LONELINESS
ON BEING THE ANALYST OF A NARCISSIST

Turning from the patient's experience of loneliness, we now look at the analyst's loneliness as it is shaped by the patient's predominant way of relating. For example, a patient whose treatment I supervise is a waitress and graduate student in her thirties. Her sessions often center on how unfairly she is being treated by the current man in her life. He is not sufficiently appreciative of her intelligence and beauty, or he is not sufficiently faithful or involved in the relationship. With no apparent recognition of the inconsistency, she can recite instances of her own affairs outside the relationship and, moments later, complain about his unfaithful behavior. In a voice filled with righteous indignation, she can demand to know how *she* could be treated so poorly! What nerve he has! Can't he even see who he is with? How dare he make her feel so unappreciated! The patient waits expectantly for her therapist to indicate how outrageous her boyfriend's behavior has been, how indignant she deserves to be, and that his infidelity is purely a function of his own neuroses, and no reflection on her.

The supervisory session begins with a sigh of relief on the part of the therapist. "Thank God I can tell you about this." The supervisee was quite aware that the patient's double standard has to be pointed out and interpreted. She is not particularly fearful of confrontations and has, in the past, been perfectly capable of saying hard things for a patient to hear. But it was her judgment, in this instance, that she had to approach this situation with some care not to intensely narcissistically injure this patient. She felt that helping the patient connect with her entitlement, helping her to be aware of the narrowness of her vision, was an important therapeutic goal that could not be achieved in one session. To confront the patient too directly might well reproduce, in the treatment, the injury incurred by the patient in her life, without producing any greater insight, because the patient might become tremendously defensive.

Winnicott (1949) writes of how we must let a patient know, before the end of treatment, what we have borne in their interest. Otherwise, he suggests, the treatment is not complete; but the timing is all-important. The patient has to be able to hear what it is like to be with him, without experiencing it as global, obliterating criticism. With the narcissist, it may be that some foundation needs to be laid in the treatment, before some of this work is possible. Bromberg (1983) suggests that the analyst of the narcissist must move from a more mirroring toward a more interpretive stance. Whereas interpretive activity should be tried from the onset of the work, the proportion of interpretation increases as the patient and the therapeutic relationship strengthen.

Leaving aside, for the moment, whether or not one agrees with this therapeutic approach, it seems likely that at least at the onset of the treatment, the therapist is alone with his or her vision of the patient's way of relating. Initially, some of the therapist's real reactions to the patient probably cannot be communicated to the patient. Of course, much about these reactions depends on who the therapist is, but certain feelings are probably highly likely to occur. The therapist may well feel anger that the patient is so blind to, and apparently uninterested in, her own impact. We devote so much energy to studying and improving *our* interpersonal impact. How dare this woman so blithely ignore hers! How dare she expect her therapist to collude in such a limited and one-sided vision!

The therapist in this situation may well feel like he or she is in a difficult and frustrating position. To confront is to injure, to fail to confront is to collude.

The loneliness of the therapist, under these circumstances, has many components; some are largely a product of the therapist's life experience and character, but others (Winnicott, 1949) are essentially expectable reactions to what is presented by this patient. Like all countertransference, the mix of the idiosyncratic and expectable responses of the therapist is unique to each treatment dyad.

143

The therapist may bring a variety of life experiences of double standards, entitled individuals, infidelities, to the session. Perhaps even more decisive is the quality of the therapist's narcissism, and the degree to which it is in conscious awareness.

Regardless of these factors, though, I suggest that there is an inevitable loneliness in the therapist's position in this situation. The loss in this loneliness may be seen as the absence of the sense that we two, therapist and patient, can see something similarly, can express what we each feel about it, can tell the whole truth as we know it at this moment; or the loss might be seen as the absence of empathy for the patient, a painful inability to identify sufficiently with the patient to sustain full motivation to help. Perhaps the loss involves the absence of hope, because the therapist may see the patient as so profoundly interpersonally damaged that a good therapeutic outcome seems unlikely or, at best, uncertain and far into the future. Again, depending on who the therapist is, the greatest loss might be the loss of unambivalence toward the patient, toward this treatment, or for the moment, perhaps, toward practicing in this field. Another possibility is that the greatest loss for the therapist is a momentary loss of a sense of integrity, or even of personal identity, if the therapist feels that he can't be his whole self with this patient at this time and still remain effective.

Of course, some therapists would take a more confronting stance, reveal more of the countertransference, and thus avoid at least some of these losses—but, I suggest, not all of them. There still may well be the absence of the sense of having a partner in the patient, in the exploratory search that is treatment. Perhaps, as the analyst of a narcissist, the sense of having a real partner is a long-sought-after therapeutic goal that when reached, may be particularly exhilarating.

ON BEING THE ANALYST OF A SCHIZOID PATIENT

There is, I suggest, a qualitative difference in the loneliness of working with a schizoid patient. My supervision of the treatment of a seventeen-year-old, depressed, withdrawn young man comes to mind. The patient's favorite words are "it doesn't matter." His feelings don't matter, how people treat him doesn't matter, how he does in school doesn't matter, what the therapist thinks doesn't matter, whether he comes to the session doesn't matter, whether he lives doesn't matter. Needless to say, all of these things matter very much to his therapist.

I often feel that from the point of view of the schizoid, less is more. That is, less involvement, less feeling, less expenditure of energy, less investment in life, all feel safer and better. The therapist often feels in the position of trying to get the patient to care about something. To be the one who cares, when the other doesn't, can be a terribly lonely position.

To contrast, for a moment, work with the narcissist and work with the schizoid, it may be that each condition profoundly challenges some of the basic tools of treatment. The narcissist has trouble bearing self-reflection, with its potential for shame and narcissistic injury, yet, of course, self-reflection is at the heart of the talking cure. The schizoid, in treatment, resists anything mattering enough to look at. Treatment requires some active investment on the part of both participants. Like the bride left at the altar, the therapist is often the only partner truly willing to make the necessary commitment.

Working with the schizoid person, the analyst often feels uncomfortable with his own impulse to actively engage the patient. The analyst may find himself or herself calling the patient if a session is missed, or making unusually structuring suggestions about how the patient might use the hour that come close to telling the patient what to talk about, in order to avoid prolonged silences in which both participants might wonder why they are there. The analyst, at such times, may lose his own sense of the meaning and purpose of the work.

Emotion expressions help human beings read each other's experience and communicate with one another (Izard, 1971, 1977; Buechler & Izard, 1983). They might be seen as the "glue" of the interpersonal interchange. The schizoid patient, perhaps rather like the unresponsive infant or caregiver, doesn't give his partner something to react to, and provides little feedback about how the therapist's interventions were received. The therapist may have images of trying to work in a vacuum, of sending messages in bottles into an expanse of sea, or of trying to play tennis when the ball doesn't come back. The loneliness with the schizoid may be particularly disorienting, since we use human responsiveness to know, literally and figuratively, where we are with each other. The absence of emotional response may make us wonder if there is any hope we can penetrate the patient's facade. Our own loneliness, under these conditions, would be tinged with whatever extreme separateness and isolation may mean to us. We each may have a different degree of need for human responsiveness. The analyst of the schizoid patient is bound to find out, more vividly than usual, just how much of that need he has.

ON BEING THE ANALYST OF A BORDERLINE PATIENT

Searles (1979) has written movingly of the loss of personal identity in the analyst of the borderline. Accused of being someone else, the analyst may (temporarily) not remember who he is. Even more painfully, the analyst may find himself or herself acting in ways that seem unfamiliar, or even alien.

Thus, I suggest that central to the loneliness of working with the borderline patient is the analyst's loss of the sense of being himself, and a hopelessness about communicating who he is to the patient.

In supervision, a highly sensitive, empathic therapist tells me how his borderline patient experiences him as sadistically uncaring. Any attention to the frame of the treatment on his part is felt as deliberate cruelty, an effort to "rub in" the fact that she is the patient. The therapist is aware of responding with hostile impulses toward the patient. To what, for him, is an unusual degree, he feels like *making* her conform to therapy's limits, *forcing* her to look at herself rather than dwell on an analysis of his shortcomings. He sometimes feels provoked into being more rigid about the "rules" than he would be with any other patient. Thus, he can't even feel that her vision of him is distorted and that some day she will see him for the empathic, caring person he is. He has no hope of such resolution. With her, he isn't who he (most of the time) feels he is. With her, he is someone he wouldn't like to be.

The loneliness of working with the borderline patient may be even more profound than any other, in the sense that even in supervision the therapist may feel deeply misunderstood, though differently misunderstood by his supervisor than he is by his patient. In a previous paper on the supervision of the treatment of borderline patients (Buechler, 1992d) I suggest that

> It is typical, I believe, for the supervisee to feel incompatible pressures from the supervisor and the borderline patient. In the treatment, he feels he is not helping the patient feel better. Analysis is not improving the quality of the patient's life experience. The patient's troubles are urgent, and require immediate relief. What the treatment provides is too slow, abstract, intellectualized, removed from the patient's day-to-day crises to be of any help. With the supervisor, however, the supervisee feels equally inadequate, but for an entirely contradictory set of reasons. He feels he has been *too* concerned with the patient's life, and not sufficiently focused on the patient's analysis. (p. 8)

In working with the borderline patient, the analyst will find some of his or her crucial tools challenged. Whereas the narcissist balked at self-reflection, and the schizoid opposed attributing meaning and importance to the treatment and to investing energy, the borderline patient, as has been amply illustrated (Kernberg, 1967,1975; Meissner, 1988), has great difficulty with the frame. This cornerstone of the work comes under fire. The analyst may be alone with the knowledge that the frame is an essential part of the process, designed to create a viable therapeutic space, rather than to torture, humiliate, or deprive the patient.

Another problem faced by the borderline's analyst is finding a way to constructively use countertransference feelings. With these patients, it is often unusually difficult to respond to one's countertransference as information, rather than as evidence of one's unfitness to be a therapist (or, in the more extreme cases, as evidence of one's unfitness to be a sensate human being). Borderline patients are known for their ability to get under our skin and their uncanny insight into our weaknesses (Epstein, 1981).

It can be terribly lonely to work with borderline patients because, in more than one sense, the therapist doesn't even have himself with him. That is, one doesn't feel like oneself in this work. One isn't working as well as usual, is easily caught off guard, makes laughable mistakes, engages in petty power struggles. The therapist may not even like himself or herself very much while with this patient. It is an uncomfortably big relief to have the hour over. Winnicott (1949) indicated that the analyst's hate is appropriately conveyed with the closing of the door after the session, but this is not much reassurance to the analyst counting the minutes until the end of the hour and struggling not to race to the door and slam it shut. With other patients, the idea of "hate" in the countertransference seems like an extreme reaction. After all, hatred can be defined as an emotion, beyond anger, that includes a wish to destroy or eliminate the object (Buechler, 1992a). But often with the borderline patient, hate in the countertransference is no exaggeration; it is an accurate description of the analyst's feelings.

Whereas it has been said that we most often need to talk about our work with the borderline (Sherby, 1989), we are frequently ashamed of this work (Buechler, 1992b) because it seems to exaggerate and advertise our weak points as analysts. Thus, we are in the position of needing to talk, to hear a response from a colleague that indicates that he, too, has his troubles with such patients. But if the work induces too much shame and self-doubt, we may not be able to bring it up for discussion with colleagues, or we may even be reluctant to reveal it in supervision. If so, the analyst is indeed in a lonely spot, without a partner in the patient, who is outraged at the frame, without a good sense of self or professional competence, without an avenue for sharing his or her experience with colleagues. In this loneliness experience we can discern all of the elements hypothesized to constitute loneliness in the first section of this article: the loss of self, the loss of security, the loss of hope.

THE ANALYST'S STANCE ABOUT SHARING COUNTERTRANSFERENCE

The loneliest therapist might seem to be the traditional, classical, blank-screen analyst, who would agree with Freud (1910) that countertransference arises

in the physician as a result of the patient's influence on his unconscious feelings, and (we) have nearly come to the point of
requiring the physician to recognize and overcome this countertransference in himself ... every analyst's achievement is limited
by what his own complexes and resistances permit. (p. 289)

Or is one's stance about the proper use of countertransference unrelated to the degree of loneliness in doing the work?

It is possible to order various theoretical positions on a continuum
from more to less conservative in their approach to the use of countertransference. At the most conservative end, as has already been
indicated, would be those analysts for whom the countertransference is
an unfortunate obstacle. At the next "station" we might have analysts
who consider countertransference as containing useful information that
may help in informing interpretations. Further along, we have analysts
who share countertransference if it is, in Winnicott's (1949) phrase,
"objective," that is, if it is the kind of response that just about any analyst
would have to this patient, rather than a more idiosyncratic response.
Still further are those analysts (Blechner, 1992) for whom the sharing of
a range of countertransference responses is a central aspect of the work.

The literature on the use of countertransference is too vast to summarize here, but the question of whether the analyst's position on this
continuum affects his loneliness must be raised. Although I know of no
data on this issue, I suggest that one's stance about countertransference
does have an impact on loneliness, but the relationship is far from
simple. My belief is that regardless of one's orientation, if one is able to
carry it out with this patient, to act according to one's convictions,
loneliness is less prominent. Thus, if the most traditional analyst, while
not sharing countertransference reactions with the patient, is able to
maintain what for him is a comfortable stance, with countertransference
"interference" kept at a minimum, he will probably not be terribly
lonely. He will have many "supervisors," past, and perhaps present, to
whom he can inwardly relate. He will feel connected, most likely, with
his own analyst while doing this work. He will feel like himself, and
professionally competent, thus experiencing no loss of a sense of self. He

will have sufficient hope that this analysis will be successful. He will feel secure, and not particularly anxious.

The same could be said for analysts at each point in the continuum, if, in the work with a particular patient, they are able to use their countertransference in a familiar, personally and professionally acceptable manner. Remembering the various ways we earlier distinguished between aloneness and loneliness, the more "conservative" analyst *is* more alone with his countertransference reactions, but he is not necessarily more lonely. As was suggested by Fromm-Reichmann, the sense of hope, the sense of purpose, of acting in the service of a cause, and mental stimulation mitigate potential loneliness in the alone individual.

This would suggest that the analyst's loneliness is, at least in part, a product of the mix of the particular patient and the analyst's stance about countertransference. When, with a patient, the analyst's most comfortable stance doesn't "fit," when the analyst is, so to speak, "off his game," then he is likely to be lonely. This may not be unlike the finding, in the infancy literature (Stern, 1985), that what creates a bond is the synchrony between attributes of infant and caregiver, not the qualities of either one.

VARIETIES OF LONELINESS

The quality of experience of an emotion greatly depends on other emotions concurrently being experienced (Izard & Buechler, 1978a). The emotions form a system (Izard, 1971), in which any alteration in one affects the experience of all others. For this reason, for example, if curiosity can be evoked, it will change the experience of fear or anxiety (Buechler & Izard, 1980). Infants whose curiosity is aroused actually seem to feel less physical pain, in pain-inducing situations (Izard & Buechler, 1978b). Similarly, it may be that the analytic patient who becomes curious enough may more easily bear the expectable anxiety, shame, and loneliness of the analytic situation (Buechler, 1993).

We may suppose, too, that the quality of loneliness is at least partially shaped by the other emotions it joins. In a sense, Fromm-Reichmann's (1959) suggestions about what mitigates loneliness anticipated this point. Writing of the experience of a World War II prisoner kept in solitary confinement, Fromm-Reichmann explains how he survived his ordeal.

> I believe that his unquestioning, matter-of-fact belief in the spiritual validity of the political convictions which were the cause of his imprisonment may have been an additional factor which helped him to survive his ordeal without becoming mentally ill.... The delinquent prisoner is not likely to have the determination and devotion to a cause which helped Burney to stay mentally sound, even though he was deprived of the opportunity to work or to receive stimulation through reading—which for many others seem to have been the two most effective antidotes or remedies for the humiliation of confinement and the rise of disintegrating loneliness. (p. 324)

A loneliness exacerbated by shame will be different from one mitigated by a sense of purpose. Where intense curiosity is evoked by mental stimulation, loneliness will be a different experience. Where hope is alive, loneliness will have a different cast.

To bring this to the experience of the analyst, it seems to make sense that the quality of his loneliness will be partially shaped by the other emotions he predominantly feels working with this patient. Of course, emotions vary within a session and, perhaps, within a moment. But if we ask an analyst what it is like to work with a particular patient, I suggest that most analysts could answer the question easily, and the response would imply certain emotions as more prominent in their experience than others. Sherby (1989), for example, writes about her work with borderline patients: "For me, the work with borderlines is a constant struggle around issues of love and hate, the patient's and the therapist's" (pp. 574–575). Sherby suggests that she feels more intense emotional reactions when working with this group of people. Similarly, Paolino (1981) advocates choosing whether to work with a patient partially on the basis of what emotions the patient immediately evokes in the analyst, on the premise that these emotions will predominate in their work and affect its quality. It may also be seen as analogous that Epstein (1981) encourages the analyst of the borderline patient to accept his or her "bad feelings," in order to be able to work effectively with this population. From my perspective, this suggests that if the analyst is not also experiencing guilt, the other negative emotions he may feel working with the patient will be tolerable.

Thus, certain patients often evoke in us specific emotions. Since I am assuming that loneliness is also part of the analyst's experience at times, with every patient, with some we might most often have a loneliness tinged with anxiety, while with others, for example, our loneliness might usually be mitigated by hope and curiosity.

So far, we have seen that the quality of the analyst's loneliness with a patient is probably affected by

1. The patient's loneliness and potential for collaboration
2. The patient's diagnostic type
3. The analyst's stance about countertransference, or more accurately, whether his most comfortable stance can be effective with this patient
4. The other emotions predominantly evoked in this analyst by working with this patient.

One way to study the varieties of loneliness in the experience of doing analysis would be to examine the writings of analysts about their work. Consider, for example, this statement by Helene Deutsch about what certain patients could be like for her.

Sitting for hours on end behind someone whose talk is so empty and barren because one has heard it so many times before; immobility with inner restlessness;... So I shut myself off, I don't listen, I stare incessantly at the clock, etc. (Roazen, 1985p. 297)

Certainly, many factors may have contributed to this experience, but the lack of connection between analyst and patient is prominent. Here, the analyst sounds bored and frustrated, as well as isolated and lonely.

She seems to be deliberately cutting herself off. Here the emotions that seem to be joining in the analyst sound likely to exacerbate each other, and there is no mitigating force, such as hope, curiosity, or perhaps not even the appearance of a negative emotion, such as fear about the patient's state, to break through the stalemate.

LONELINESS AND STRESS IN THE ANALYST

In a previous article on stress in the experience of being an analyst, I discussed various sources of the strain inherent in maintaining the analytic role (Buechler, 1992c). Among these are culturally and personally induced pressures to be above human frailties. The analyst is the target, first of all, of the patient's often unrealistic, transferentially induced expectations. Our psychoanalytic culture, in expecting the analyst to put aside thoughts of his or her own human physical and emotional needs while at the analytic task, may add to the pressures and demands the patient is making of us. Thus we may join our patients in expecting a selflessness of ourselves that is hard to achieve, "especially since the therapist is engaged in helping patients legitimize concern about the quality of *their* lives. The therapist's failure to put self-concern aside may result in a sense of fraudulence or, perhaps, envy of the latitude accorded his or her patient" (p. 189). While many other pressures add to the burden of analytic work, I single out the strain of putting aside personal concerns during the session, because I suggest that this, perhaps more than most other factors, may contribute to the analyst's loneliness. I have often felt that what makes analysis such hard work is the quality of attention, or intensity of focus, that is required. While listening to a patient, we must delicately balance attunement to the emotional nuances of the patient's words, openness to our countertransferential reactions, understanding of this patient's historical background, awareness of theoretical concepts that might help us therapeutically use this moment effectively, and a grasp of where we are in the process of our work with this person, among many other possible claims on our attention. Writers have tried to describe the process of attending analytically with phrases such as "evenly hovering attention" (Freud) or "listening with the third ear" (Reik). However it is described, I think all would agree it is hard work, requiring energy, stamina, and concentration. Just to maintain a balance between minutely focused attention on the patient and freely wandering observations of our own inner experiences is a difficult task. I think of it as analogous to what a pianist or ballet dancer asks of his or her muscles—that combination of tautness with fluidity, that supremely shaped suppleness that combines discipline and art.

This task brings certain aspects of our humanness to the forefront but, I suggest, it requires of us that we temporarily neglect focusing on others, and this, I feel, is one source of our loneliness. For example, a patient may describe an experience that reminds us of something from our own past. We begin to follow our associations, remembering the feelings we endured in what sounds like similar circumstances. Although it may be that different analysts would take these private associations further or cut them off sooner, and some might share them with the patient and others would not, I suggest that most or all would feel some pressure to continue to hear and respond to the patient, remaining aware of the analytic context. Like our patients, we are only partially alone, having some of the benefits of solitude, but not all of them. Like the patient, we are balancing aloneness and connectedness; but unlike the patient, we are involved in a task whose principal goal is the healing of someone else. So we are in the position of connecting with feelings, memories, experiences that may be quite painful, at a moment when, at best, they can be incompletely shared or even explored and when our focus must, at best, be divided. My point is that I think we are lonely as analysts, in part, because during emotion and pain-inducing moments, we can't have enough of ourselves with us to be of comfort.

THE LONELY ANALYST ACTS OUT

A supervisee reports a session with a schizoid patient, in which the therapist tried interpretation after interpretation of a highly evocative, emotionally significant-sounding dream. After each of the therapist's efforts to explore the meaning of the dream, the patient remained unresponsive and unconvinced. Aware of what felt like his overactivity, the therapist nevertheless felt driven to continue, offering the patient personal experiences in order to try to connect with him, all to no apparent avail. At the end of the session the therapist felt dejected, with something having gone wrong. I suggested to him that it might have been easier on him had he *wanted* a response from the patient, without *needing* one. The dream was, I thought, a gift from this unusually psychologically hoarding individual, who was probably hoping the gift would be gratefully accepted, perhaps, unopened, with just an acknowledgment of its probable cost.

What made such a stance unavailable to the therapist was, I believe, his loneliness. Whether or not one agrees that the more self-contained stance I suggested would have been helpful, it seems clear to me that loneliness drove this therapist to act in a way that, to him, felt unconstructive. It is true that just because it *felt* unconstructive doesn't mean it *was* unconstructive, and some might feel that my supervisee's stance was precisely what was required, and could be beneficially mutually explored in their further work. I agree that this may be a valid approach, but suggest that however one might proceed clinically, the therapist's loneliness must be recognized in this situation, and he must find a way to cope with it that allows him to feel competent.

What feels to the therapist like overactivity is only one of the behaviors that I suggest are often responses to his loneliness. Others may include the overuse of jargon, in which the lonely analyst may be attempting to relate to the patient as a professional colleague. Our loneliness may, at times, drive us to deny or ignore evidence of negative transference, because we are in need of a sense of unambivalent comradery from the patient. Out of loneliness, we may overemphasize the patient's likeness to ourselves, selectively inattending to differences that could make the patient feel more like a stranger. Thus, I suggest that our loneliness may drive us to focus, perceive, and behave in ways that limit the full use of our faculties with the patient. More specifically, I argue that our loneliness may drive us toward impatience with the patient's pathology, because we may experience that pathology as the obstacle that keeps us from being able to connect more fully with the patient. Thus, the schizoidness of the schizoid, the narcissism of the narcissist, the obsessionalism of the obsessional, each may feel like the thing that is driving us apart, that is keeping us from a more satisfying collaboration. Of course, in a sense, that is exactly the case. But the patient's pathology is the subject matter of the work, not a personal enemy of the therapist. We, however, in what I suggest could be our own paranoia, may experience it as an obstacle, deliberately thwarting our therapeutic efforts. Thus, while the patient may be busy merely being himself, we are seeing him as intentionally resisting us, because, out of loneliness, we *need* him to be someone who can relate to us better. We are in the position of not merely *wanting* the patient's pathology to diminish, but of *needing* it to do so. Hence, I suggest there is a world of wisdom in Bion's oft-quoted injunction to approach every session without memory or desire. It is, I think, our own loneliness that can make the patient's interpersonal handicaps into targets of our impatience, or sometimes, of our contempt. We must be able to bear without malice whatever currently stops the patient from full collaboration with our efforts.

THE ANALYST'S CAPACITY TO BE ALONE

> The relationship of the individual to his or her internal objects, along with confidence in regard to internal relationships, provides of itself a sufficiency of living, so that temporarily he or she is able to rest contented even in the absence of external objects and stimuli. (Winnicott, 1958p. 32)

It might be argued that the analyst's capacity to be alone is no different from anyone else's and entirely depends on the analyst's maturational level. While this may be so, I suggest that as analysts we go through a second process of development in our training, with phases not unlike the first (Buechler, 1988, 1992c). That is, our training recapitulates the earlier processes of separation-individuation and identity formation. As a result of training we are partially identified with an analytic family, but also have our own separate identities. Our training can be seen as the gradual development of an understanding of the ways in which we each put our unique, personal stamp on an analytic tradition. We have a strong need to belong to some group (Schafer, 1979) but also to develop a separate voice.

Thus, it might be suggested that during training we internalize relationships to our analyst, supervisors, and teachers, and that for each of us, these internalizations form an important foundation. Each analyst brings his or her own private, internal "chorus" to every session. Assuming a good enough training experience, what allows the analyst to retain a capacity to be alone with a specific patient?

First, as has already been suggested, the analyst (and his or her internal chorus) must be satisfied with the stance about countertransference required for work with this patient. But I believe that this point must be broadened, to help explain the analyst's capacity to be alone. There must exist, I suggest, a *general* absence of persecutory feelings in the analyst to retain the ability to be alone with the patient. That is, the analyst must not consistently feel overly harsh feelings, toward himself or the patient. This will allow for the possibility of some creative uses of the aloneness.

Although it is necessary, this relatively benign inner atmosphere in itself is not sufficient. In order to be able to play alone, I believe the analyst needs a play room and some toys. That is, when left alone by the patient, the analyst must have a context in which to fit the experience, and some conceptual frameworks to tentatively explore as explanations. Like Fromm-Reichmann's World War II prisoner, the isolated analyst must be able to find meaning in his experience, hope, and mental stimulation, to survive intact. Here is where theory can provide meaningful context, conceptual framework, and the stimulation of curiosity.

The analyst is often alone when with the patient, but not necessarily lonely. Loneliness with a patient, I suggest, stems from a sense of permanent, rather than temporary, isolation. If the analyst feels cut off from the patient in some unalterable way, a deepening loneliness can develop. The patient's diagnostic type or predominant way of relating, the comfort level of the analyst with countertransference stances available with this patient, and the other emotions this patient evokes in the analyst, all play a role in creating the emotional climate for the analyst. They contribute to the analyst's sense of how much he can be himself with this patient, or rather, how much he can be the competent, skilled self that the internal chorus of his own analyst and supervisors helped to mold. If the analyst finds it impossible to be this self with a particular patient, he may feel cut off from his internal chorus. He may experience a need to blame someone, and either become impatient toward the patient's pathology, treating it as a personal enemy (the more paranoid reaction), or feel incompetent (the more depressive reaction), or both. Either way, a deepening loneliness can result.

Looked at from an emotion-systems point of view, loneliness, in this situation, may be joined by anxiety, shame, guilt, and anger. Perhaps what is most important, the analyst with this deepening loneliness will not have available any of the antidotes we have previously discussed, such as hope, the sense of purpose, the stimulation of curiosity.

How can we analysts, long-distance runners that we all must be, avoid at least some of this loneliness? Of course, our own character types and early experiences play a significant role in our vulnerability to loneliness when alone. How able we are to retain a sense of self in the absence of confirmation or in the presence of disconfirmation depends on *both* of our developmental histories: our early, childhood separation-individuation and identity formation experiences, and our later, analytic separation-individuation and identity formation experiences. These histories are, I suggest, equally important.

The internal chorus we bring into our offices every day must be of comfort, and must be sufficiently stimulating, to encourage the creative use of aloneness. The feeling the chorus must give us is that whatever may go on today, with this particular patient, does not define us as analysts, for we have already been defined and have defined ourselves, through our analytic identifications and identity formation. We are not personally and professionally at stake with each new interaction with a patient. With this foundation, we can experience aloneness with a patient as information, rather than as judgment. We can turn the aloneness over in our minds, wonder what it is about, become curious about it, see it as meaningful, as something to understand, but not as an obstacle or an indictment. An aloneness that doesn't cost us a good connection with ourselves, with our chorus, or with the patient can be used creatively. A creatively used aloneness is not loneliness.

To be alone while with a patient is not painful, so long as we can retain a connection with a good sense of self, and a nonpersecutory sense of the patient. Theoretical concepts can aid this process, by providing something to play with during alone times with the patient. A good, supportive internal chorus and enough to play with can, I believe, allow the analyst creative possibilities for the productive use of aloneness.

REFERENCES

Blechner, M.J. (1992). Working in the countertransference. *Psychoanalytic Dialogues* 2:161–179.

Bromberg, P.M. (1983). The mirror and the mask: On narcissism and psychoanalytic growth. *Contemporary Psychoanalysis* 19:359–387. http://www.pep-web.org/document.php?id'cps.019.0359a

Buechler, S. (1988). Joining the psychoanalytic culture. *Contemporary Psychoanalysis* 24: 462–470. www.pep-web.org/document.php?id'cps.024.0462a

——— (1992a). Hatred: The strength of the sensitive. Discussion of paper by Otto Kernberg, M.D., presented at the William Alanson White Scientific Meeting, October.

——— (1992b). Shame and anxiety in psychoanalytic training. Paper presented at the International Federation for Psychoanalytic Education, November.

——— (1992c). Stress in the personal and professional development of a psychoanalyst. *Journal of the American Academy of Psychoanalysis* 20:183–191. http://www.pep-web.org/document.php?id'jaa.020.0183a

——— (1992d). Supervision of the treatment of borderline patients. Panel discussion, presented at Division 39, American Psychoanalytical Association. http://www.pep-web.org/document.php?id'cps.032.0086a

——— (1993). Clinical applications of an interpersonal view of the emotions. *Contemporary Psychoanalysis* 29:219–236. http://www.pep-web.org/document.php?id'cps.029.0219a

——— (1995). Emotion. In: *Handbook of Interpersonal Psychoanalysis*, ed. M. Lionells, J. Fiscalini, C. Mann & D. Stern. Hillsdale, NJ: The

Analytic Press, pp. 165–188.

——— & Izard, C. E. (1980). Anxiety in childhood and adolescence. In: *Pressure Point: Perspectives in Stress and Anxiety*, ed. I. Kutash & L. Schlesinger. New York: Jossey-Bass, pp. 285–297.

——— ——— (1983). On the emergence, functions, and regulation of some emotion expressions in infancy. In: *Emotions: Theory, Research and Experience, vol. 2*, ed. R. Plutchik & H. Kellerman. New York. Academic Press, pp. 293–313.

Courtauld, A. (1932). Living alone under polar conditions. *The Polar Record*, No. 4, July 1932. Cambridge: The University Press.

Epstein, L. (1981). Countertransference and judgments of fitness for analysis. *Contemporary Psychoanalysis* 17: 55–68. http://www.pep-web.org/document.php?id'cps.017.0055a

Freud, S. (1910). The future prospects of psycho-analytic therapy. *Standard Edition* 11: 139–151. http://www.pep-web.org/document.php?id'se.011.0139a

Fromm-Reichmann (1990). Loneliness. *Contemporary Psychoanalysis* 26: 305–330. http://www.pep-web.org/document.php?id'cps.026.0305a

Gardiner, M. (1971). *The Wolf-Man*. New York: Basic Books.

Izard, C.E. (1971). *The Face Of Emotion*. New York: Appleton-Century-Croft.

——— (1977). *Human Emotions*. New York: Plenum Press. http://www.pep-web.org/document.php?id'aop.012.0415a

——— & Buechler, S. (1978a). Emotion expressions and personality integration in infancy. In: *Emotions in Personality and Psychopathology*, ed. C. E. Izard. New York: Plenum Press, pp. 10–61.

Izard, C. E. & Buechler, S. (1978b). Emotion expression ontogeny and cognitive attainments. Grant application, received funding by National Science Foundation.

Kernberg, O. (1967). Borderline personality organization. In: *Borderline Conditions and Pathological Narcissism*. New York: Aronson, 1975, pp. 3–47. http://www.pep-web.org/document.php?id'apa.015.0641a

——— (1975). *Borderline Conditions and Pathological Narcissism*. New York: Jason Aronson. http://www.pep-web.org/document.php?id'ijp.089.0299a

May, R. (1953). *Man's Search For Himself*. New York: W.W. Norton and Co.

Meissner, W. W. (1988). *Treatment of Patients in the Borderline Spectrum.* Northvale, NJ: Aronson. www.pep-web.org/document.php ?id'pi.008.0305a

Mendelson, M.D. (1990). Reflections on loneliness. *Contemporary Psychoanalysis* 26:330–355. www.pep-web.org/document.php?id'cps.026.0330a

Mohacsy, I. (1990). Solitude in a changing society: A discussion of Fromm-Reichmann's "loneliness." *Contemporary Psychoanalysis* 26:360–364. http://www.pep-web.org/document.php?id'cps.026.0360a

Paolino, T. J. (1981). Analyzability: Some categories for assessment. *Contemporary Psychoanalysis* 17:321–340. http://www.pep-web.org/document.php?id'cps.017.0321a

Rilke, R. M. (1934). Letters to a young poet. New York: W. W. Norton.

Roazen, P. (1985). Helene Deutsch: A psychoanalyst's life. New York: Doubleday. http://www.pep-web.org/document.php?id'ppsy.021.0622a

Satran, G. (1978). Notes on loneliness. *Journal of the American Academy of Psychoanalysis,* 6:281–300. http://www.pep-web.org/document.php ?id'jaa.006.0281a

Schafer, R. (1979). On becoming a psychoanalyst of one persuasion or another. *Contemporary Psychoanalysis* 15:345–360. http://www.pep-web.org/document.php?id'cps.015.0345a

Searles, H. (1979). The countertransference with the borderline patient. In: *Essential papers on borderline disorders,* ed. M. Stone. New York: New York University Press. 1986, pp. 498–526.

Sherby, L. B. (1989). Love and hate in the treatment of borderline patients. . *Contemporary Psychoanalysis* 25:574–591. http://www.pep-web.org/document.php?id'cps.025.0574a

Stern, D. N. (1985). The interpersonal world of the infant. New York: Basic Books. http://www.pep-web.org/document.php ?id'zbk.016.0001a

Sullivan, H. S. (1953). The interpersonal theory of psychiatry. New York: W.W. Norton. http://www.pep-web.org/document.php?id'apa.003.0149a

Winncott, D.W. (1949). Hate in the countertransference. *International Journal of Psycho-Analysis* 30: 69–75. http://www.pep-web.org /document.php?id'ijp.030.0069a

——— (1958). The capacity to be alone. In: *The maturational process and the facilitating environment*. New York: International Universities Press, 1965, pp. 29–36. http://www.pep-web.org/document.php?id'ipl.064.0001a

[1]*Contemporary Psychoanalysis*, 26:330–369. Fromm-Reichmann's 1959 essay is reprinted therein (pp. 305–330).

CHAPTER FOUR

Searching for a Passionate Neutrality[*]

INTRODUCTION

My indebtedness to the work of Erich Fromm first began to make itself fully known to me in this paper. The debt took the form of a challenge. How could I integrate the values I learned from Fromm with the neutrality that gave patients the luxury of uncommonly uncluttered space? From Fromm I took a belief that it is impossible (and unacceptable) to divorce concern for society from concern for one's patients. I learned that promoting patients' and my own full self realization is part of my job as an analyst. Fromm taught me that health had to be practiced, that hope had to be active, that courage and integrity were not optional for the psychoanalyst.

In this context, what are some of the difficulties that the concept of neutrality poses? In this paper I ask how the analyst can adequately support the patient's emergence from depression, while also facilitating the patient's full expression of self destructive urges. For my patients' sakes I want to offer them the chance to create themselves, without my imposing my own values. But I naturally incline toward Fromm's "biophilic," life loving attitudes. I am persuaded when Fromm (1941, p. 8) says "...we believe that ideals like truth, justice, freedom, although

---

* *Contemporary Psychoanalysis*, 1999, 35:2, 213-227.

they are frequently mere phrases or rationalizations, can be genuine strivings, and that any analysis which does not deal with these strivings as dynamic factors is fallacious." I believe that my strong personal investments in these values show themselves in what I hear, remember, and respond to in sessions, whether or not I am aware of it. This is not the evenly hovering attention Anna Freud (1936) famously recommended for the neutral analyst.

A year after this paper was published I began working on my first book (*Clinical Values: Emotions that Guide Psychoanalytic Treatment*, 2004), which explores more fully the integration of passion and neutrality.

SEARCHING FOR A PASSIONATE NEUTRALITY

Everything about her announced her reluctance to leave childhood behind. Her thin, insubstantial body, her waiflike stare and stubborn pout made this young woman seem early adolescent. With little emotion she described more than a decade of internal warfare over eating enough to live. The struggle with her eating disorder had already taken her life, in that there was room for little else. I found myself immediately, deeply concerned. Every fiber of me wanted to wrestle with the self-destructive forces in her. I wanted the vibrant young woman I saw as her potential to emerge.

For me this is not an unusual clinical moment, although perhaps more vivid than most. I often feel, even with patients who would be considered more traditionally analytic, that treatment involves me in a life-and-death struggle. Fromm (1973) might describe it as the pitting of biophilic, or life-loving, forces against the necrophilic, death-loving pull. A central challenge for the analyst, I believe, is how to integrate her countertransferential responses to this struggle with an appropriately neutral analytic stance.

What follows is an attempt to delineate some of the difficulties neutrality poses. First, I ask how the analyst can express her concern for the quality of the patient's current life, and still retain the benefits of analytic neutrality. How can I actively encourage growth, but still facilitate the patient's exploration of her self-destructive, regressive, self-limiting urges? Next, I focus on the analyst's use of his passion as a tool in the treatment. Finally, after a note on the difficulties in training analysts to integrate concern and passion into their work, I describe passionate neutrality, and how it may be achieved.

CONCERN AND THE NEUTRAL ANALYST

I assume that all analysts hope their patients will develop fuller, richer lives, although they may or may not label this a goal of the treatment. Where we differ is in how we feel we ought to integrate concern for the quality of the patient's current life into a neutral stance. In what follows, several ways of defining analytic neutrality are examined to see how they can be integrated with concern for the patient's life. To be more specific, I believe that four aspects of the concerned analyst's role pose differing, though related challenges to her neutrality: her need to help the patient develop interpersonal skills; her need to facilitate the fight against depression; her need to convey a sense of urgency about change; and her need to inspire active hope.

DEVELOPING INTERPERSONAL EFFECTIVENESS

Presumably we would all like to facilitate interpersonal growth, but some analysts see the process differently from others. For some clinicians, fostering interpersonal growth requires them to confront the patient with his here-and-now impact on the analyst (this is amply illustrated in the work of Ehrenberg, 1992). It is in the encounter with how he affects a *particular* analyst that the patient develops interpersonally. This type of interchange, vital to the treatment process for some analysts, for others would be impossible to integrate with their conception of analytic neutrality.

The use of the analyst's reactions to confront the patient with his impact is described by Szalita in an interview in which she discussed her beliefs about effective analytic work (Issacharoff, 1997). Szalita tells of using her own reactions to a patient to help him learn the difference between his intentions and his actual interpersonal effect.

Several aspects of neutrality, as it has traditionally been defined, may be difficult to integrate with this technique. The concept of analytic neutrality has generally included some or all of the following components:

1. The analyst should maintain an even focus on material coming from the patient's id, ego, and superego (see, for example, A. Freud, 1936; Jacobs, 1986).

2. The analyst's countertransferential passions should be held in check, because his effort is to create an atmosphere that fosters the unhampered observation of all aspects of the patient's psychic functioning.

3. The analyst should not impose his own values or attempt to sway the patient toward certain kinds of changes.

4. The analyst should refrain from a "helpfulness" with the patient's current struggles that may be at the expense of long-term structural change (see, for example, Poland, 1984).

5. The analyst follows the unfolding material, rather than actively directing the course of the material.

6. The analyst's posture is unhurried, recognizing that profound change may take a great deal of time.

7. Because a goal is to help the patient become more consciously aware of his transferential patterns, the patient's impact on the analyst is used as information about these patterns, but not to "teach" the patient to behave more adaptively.

Szalita's stance differs from this conception of neutrality, first, in permitting herself to *share* her countertransferential responses, not just to mine them as information about herself and the patient. Second, in that she points the patient's attention to the gap between his intentions and his effect, she is directing the process, not just facilitating its unfolding. She is swaying the patient toward a certain kind of change that she believes to be desirable. Finally, she is valuing helping the patient in the present, rather than maintaining a focus on long-term change.

Poland (1984) provides a view that contrasts sharply with Szalita's. In his review of the concept of neutrality, Poland emphasizes that the analyst's neutrality protects the process from unwarranted intrusions by the analyst's intrapsychic forces. He suggests that a crucial consequence of the principle of neutrality is that the analyst does not direct the course of the work, but, rather, lets the material unfold. He also states that "The substantial long-term analytic goal of insight and structural change demands inhibition of short-term helpfulness" (p. 286). Elaborating on this, he implies that transference gratification could interfere in the patient's achieving the regression that is essential to the work.

Poland struggles with how to integrate a neutral stance with the fact that the analyst *does* have goals for the treatment, is invested in its success, and, inevitably, has a vision, not just of who the patient is, but also who the patient might become. In other words, the analyst would like to see the patient develop his potential for a richer life. Wondering how, given this, the analyst can listen with evenly distributed attention to the material, Poland asks, "Can an analyst truly interpret without trivializing unless he selects some issues as more related to anxiety, to defense, to inhibition, than others? Can an analyst in practice truly deal with a perversion as if it were not a constricted and symptomatic compromise formation?" (p. 297). I find this a poignant testament to how difficult it is, in the actual clinical interchange, to integrate real concern for the patient's interpersonal growth with the ideal of a neutral stance. If neutrality implies evenness of focus, how can the analyst avoid selectively attending to aspects of the material that seem most directly related to the patient's pathology?

These questions highlight some important differences between analysts in how they understand insight to develop. For Poland, the patient's regression to deeper transferential levels is crucial and must not be short-circuited by short-term helpfulness. For Szalita, the patient's deeper understanding of his behavior follows from realizing its impact on the analyst. The patient has to be informed of the analyst's responses and see his impact before he can move toward deeper understanding of his behavior. For Poland, the analyst blocks regression crucial to insight by helpfully sharing her reactions; for Szalita, this interpersonal exchange is the *basis* for the development of deeper insight. Thus, what for one analyst is necessary to the process of self-discovery, for another would block the process.

FACILITATING FIGHTING DEPRESSION

My experience tells me that what Bonime (1982) has called "the practice of depression" has to be actively fought. The depressed patient must be encouraged to combat his depression, to actively exert effort to emerge from it. When the analyst takes a position that fosters this effort, the patient understands that we are not facilitating his self-understanding entirely for its own sake, but we are fighting together to improve the quality of the patient's life. If neutrality is taken to mean nonalignment in relation to conflict, as an analyst I do not believe I can afford to be completely neutral toward the inevitable conflict, in my patient, between the forces within him that would prize expansion of his life versus the forces that would constrict it (or what Fromm, 1973, would call biophilia versus necrophilia).

The analyst may have difficulty integrating this position with several aspects of analytic neutrality as it is outlined in the preceding section. If the analyst believes he must be more invested in the patient's long-term structural change than in the quality of the patient's present life experience, it may be hard to convey to the patient the necessity that he actively oppose depressive forces now. Also, if the analyst feels he must follow the material, and not set an agenda, he may find it difficult to direct the patient's emergence from depression. The analyst's effort to encourage the patient's full self-expression, by making no value judgments and giving equal attention to all facets of the material, may hamper taking the relatively active role that I believe the treatment of some depressions requires.

Ferenczi (1929) offered us a theoretical basis for this more active position. Differing from the Freudian belief that we are all born equipped with sufficient life force, Ferenczi believed we must be welcomed into cherishing our lives by someone (most often the mother) who first values and protects us. I believe that many of our patients have yet to receive that welcome.

This raises a question. How do we adequately encourage the active emergence from depression without, as Greenberg (1991) warns, engaging in a therapeutic zeal that is

> detrimental to the goal of self-knowledge because it encourages the dissociation of crucial aspects of the patient's personality—aspects that may be regressive, masochistic, destructive, or rebellious. If the analyst clearly values a particular sort of change, the patient can come to feel that acceptance by the analyst is contingent upon the patient's being collaborative and making progress. The analyst can inadvertently become a kind of critical observing self, creating an atmosphere in which important aspects of the transference may be irretrievably lost. In contrast, the atmosphere embodied in the concept of neutrality is one in which the analyst is distinctly on the side of the patient, but not on the side of one aspect of the patient's personality at the expense of others. [pp. 214–215]

Without doubt, this asks the analyst to achieve a delicate balance between the support of life forces and the neutral invitation to the patient to express *all* the forces within him, regardless of whether they are biophilic or necrophilic in Fromm's terms. Cooper (1986) once described part of the strain of the analytic role as coming from its paradoxical injunctions. Especially, I feel, with the depressive patient, the analyst may have difficulty integrating enough active encouragement to battle the depression with an appropriately neutral stance that fosters the patient's increasing awareness of all the forces within him. To the extent that there are depressive features in other character types, this is an issue that is relevant in much of our work. It is further discussed in the final section of this article.

CONVEYING A SENSE OF URGENCY

Striving to adopt what he thinks of as a neutral stance, the analyst may not sufficiently convey the preciousness of time. In his unhurried approach, in his investment in future structural change, he may not create a sense of urgency about living life more fully *now*. But this urgency about his current life is, I believe, a crucial ingredient in the patient's motivation to work hard in the treatment.

This sense of urgency may be expressed, I believe, through the bluntness of the analyst's interpretations. By not "beating around the bush," the analyst conveys, perhaps more vividly than any other way, that we have no time to waste on niceties. We are aiming straight for the truth.

It is a temptation, I believe, for analysts to dismiss patients' objections to the length of analytic treatment in such a way as to leave the *mistaken* impression that we feel today shouldn't be as important as tomorrow. With much justification, we can feel the patient must be "educated" to take a less hurried approach, tolerate the frustration of aiming for long-term gains rather than short-term gratifications. But, especially in these managed-care-clouded times, a strident manner on the part of the analyst can convey an attitude easily misunderstood by the patient as contemptuous of his concern with his immediate needs. The patient's urgent need for his life to be better, his great investment in the quality of his current life experience, is a powerful source of his motivation for treatment. I don't feel we can afford to allow ourselves to be misunderstood as having a dismissive attitude toward its meaningfulness.

On the other hand, as analysts we do understand that long-term structural change is the lasting resolution of conflict. I believe that our task is to convey, with our blunt, direct *manner,* an urgency that promotes motivation for rapid change, balanced with interpretations whose *content* expresses a potent vision of the patient's long-term potential growth. More is said about this in the concluding section.

INSPIRING ACTIVE HOPE

I have come to believe that psychological treatment of any kind requires that the patient be inspired to develop a more active form of hopefulness. Aspiring to fulfill some conceptions of neutrality might block the analyst's communication of the passionate commitment to life and growth that I feel is essential for the inspiration of hope. As I have argued elsewhere (Buechler, 1995), the emotion of hope is not a passive expectation but an active striving. Many analysts (Sullivan, 1954; Fromm, 1968; Mitchell (1993) have considered some form of hopefulness a necessary ingredient of therapeutic progress. What kind of behavior on the part of the analyst can facilitate the patient's development of active hope? In an article on inspiring hopefulness in patients (1995), I described the process.

> I don't believe it is, specifically, the analyst's hope that engenders hope in the patient, but the analyst's whole relationship to life. The patient observes the analyst's struggle to make sense of things, keep going in the face of seemingly insurmountable obstacles, retain humor and courage in situations that seem to inspire neither. The analyst stumbles, reacts without self-hate, works to recover. The analyst is willing to work hard. She is honest without being crippled by shame. She wants to live even the most difficult moments. She doesn't shrink from what is ugly in herself or the other. She is more interested in growth than in being right, more curious than self-protective. She can be wounded but refuses to be made dead. While in part this attitude may provide a model, and it may be contagious, I think that what mainly creates hope is the patient's experience of finding a way to relate to such a person. For many, this task requires substantive changes, alterations in all components of the emotion system. The deepened curiosity and joy, the lightened envy and hate that results engenders hope. [p. 72]

In some sense, this requires the analyst to be a *new* object to the patient, thus circumscribing the patient's ability to transfer old relational patterns onto the analyst. As Greenberg (1991) suggests, the ideal analytic stance may require a tension between the analyst as an old object and as a new object. Perhaps the analyst must find, with each patient, an optimal balance between being neutral enough to serve as a transference object and vividly new enough, as an object, to inspire sufficient hope.

PASSION AND THE NEUTRAL ANALYST

I read the following words, from an interview of Dr. Alberta Szalita by Dr. Ammon Issacharoff (1997), while in the midst of my own reappraisal of the meaning of analytic neutrality.

> It's not that I considered myself not good before, but now I feel that I am more what I am supposed to be, including the way I see neutrality as part of my work. It is clear that one cannot be completely neutral. But now I am much more responsive and less involved. [p. 617]
>
> It requires, first of all, an emotional engagement between the participants. Therapy consists of the patient's engagement with his therapist; the therapist has to offer empathic understanding to the patient. To this the therapist brings all his life experience, which is forcibly eclectic, for it had many teachers. [p. 630]

How can we understand a neutrality that affords us an empathic emotional engagement with the patient that utilizes all that life has taught us? What does it mean to be (as Szalita suggests in the first quotation above) more responsive, yet less involved, in this emotional engagement?

Historically, neutrality has often been described as though the analyst could function dispassionately, without biasing emotions or subjective reactions. In a review of psychoanalytic paradigms, Cooper (1985) discusses the classical conception of the neutral analyst as a reflecting mirror, in which the patient could see himself objectively. The analyst should keep any of his own particular personal qualities and subjective reactions from affecting the picture the patient gets of himself from the experience of the treatment.

Jacobs (1986) gives us a rather clear description of the outer manifestations of the analyst's neutrality, as well as the inner state this behavior requires.

> The analytic idea of neutrality is a highly complex one. It involves not only a way of listening that receives with impartiality material

deriving from each of the psychic agencies and a technical approach that eschews the resolution of conflict through influence in favor of interpretations, but it implies in the analyst a state of receptivity that can accomplish these goals. The proper use of neutrality as a technical measure requires a considerable degree of inner "neutrality," that is, a state of mind in which ego functions necessary for analytic work are not impaired by conflict. [p. 297]

This understanding of neutrality suggests the absence of partisan favoring of, for example, the patient's superego-driven behavior. Freedom from personal conflicts about the material enables the analyst to outwardly show proper analytic neutrality, in this sense. The analyst should not be so invested in a particular outcome of the patient's conflicts, or so influenced by his own personal feelings about such situations, that his hearing of the material is affected by these feelings.

Discussions of analytic neutrality have often included assessments of the proper use of the analyst's inevitable countertransference reactions. Is countertransference an interference in the establishment of the appropriate neutral stance or an integral and vital aspect of the analytic dialogue? Abend (1989) reviews the movement from the first position to the second and, although largely approving the trend, issues cautions. Quoting a colleague, he suggests that "countertransference has become analysts' rationalization for indulging themselves in their own self-absorption" (p. 393). In this framework, the ideal of neutrality is a safeguard against the excesses that may result from taking the position that countertransferential reactions are useful data, rather than distorting influences.

I would like to make two points about the analyst's emotions and their impact. First, the analyst's emotional reactions and beliefs about emotions inevitably affect which material he hears, focuses on, and responds to. The analyst's passionate *perceiving* precedes, and to some extent dictates, his passionate responding. Second, this passionate response is not only inevitable but, as I will illustrate, clinically desirable. Especially when dealing with certain life-and-death issues, it makes possible a crucial form of engagement between the analyst and patient.

PASSIONATE PERCEPTION

Inasmuch as discussions of neutrality generally include even, impartial focusing as an objective, I would like to call attention to one particular influence on what the analyst focuses on, and responds to, in the material presented by the patient. As I have suggested elsewhere (Buechler, 1993, 1997), I believe that the analyst's attitudes about appropriate emotionality play a major role in how he hears and responds to the material. This, in turn, affects the *patient's* focus and self-presentation. The analyst, like every other human being, has a set of (conscious and unconscious) beliefs about what constitutes appropriate emotional expression (Izard, 1977; Buechler, 1993). For example, he has some sense, however formulated or unformulated, of what constitutes normal expression of anger toward a child, of grief after a significant loss, of anxiety about illness. In a session the analyst will focus differently on the patient's emotional reaction to an event if, to that analyst, the patient's response was inappropriate, too intense or too mild to fit the circumstances. Assumptions about normal emotionality may reflect relatively unprocessed amalgamations of analytic readings, personal experiences, and the analyst's basic character formation. Beliefs about appropriate emotionality influence whether we listen to the patient looking for, and inquiring into, the other causes for the intensity level of the response that we assume must exist if, for example, we have deemed his high intensity unwarranted by the present circumstances. Similarly, we look for what blocked his emotional response if we deem it too mild for the situation. The patient, seeing that his emotional response evokes analytic inquiry, may become defensive (e.g., arguing that others would feel similarly) or self-doubting (e.g., wondering why this *did* bother him so much). Both patient and analyst are assuming emotions work the way certain bodily signals operate. For example, for body temperature, there is an average ("normal") reading (98.6°) and a normal range of readings slightly different for each of us. But there are readings (e.g., 105°) that almost certainly indicate serious pathology. Body temperature may be measured objectively and varies relatively predictably, but human emotions are far more complex, far less easily quantified, and impossible to evaluate with anything like objectivity.

The fact that the analyst's emotion "theory" (however formulated or unformulated it may be)affects his focus in a session, his response to the material, and influences the patient's self-presentation reinforces our already established conviction that the analyst can never claim total objectivity. His personal slant about emotionality shapes how and what he hears and how and what the patient tells him. This slant will influence what the analyst sees as the goals of the treatment, how he assesses progress, when he chooses to interpret, and every other facet of the work (Buechler, 1993).

Because most conceptions of neutrality generally do include some notion of an even focus on the material, neutrality would seem impossible to achieve, given the influence of the analyst's emotion "theory." For example, when a patient recounts her argument with her husband, my "theory" about appropriate emotional expression will influence how I hear the story, *what I may not retain because, for me, it may be too commonplace to remember,* and what I inquire into because, for me, it is out of the ordinary enough to be worth pursuing.

In addition to the analyst's (more or less formulated) "theories" about emotions, his momentary feelings also shape his focus on the material. Emotion's affect cognitive functioning (Izard, 1977), so that when in a state of rage, for example, we hear differently from when we are in a state of intense curiosity. Discussions of countertransference too often begin with the analyst's reactions to the material, not taking into account how his emotions may have shaped what he could hear and therefore respond to.

It might comfort us, as analysts, to believe we hear our patients objectively, listening evenly to all the material, giving it all equal focus and an unbiased response. To accept that we can't even take in the material in a neutral manner, much less respond without bias and without our own slant on life shaping the patient's subsequent material, may be particularly threatening to our sense of professionalism, or scientific rigor, or egalitarianism. Whereas I may be able to withhold an overtly judgmental response to my patient's story, and may vigorously question the basis for private judgments I make about her "borderline rage" or "impulsivity," and so forth, I believe that I cannot, through vigilant self-

observation or through self-knowledge, eradicate the differential focusing that results, inevitably, from my emotional reactions and my
particular vision of appropriate emotional functioning.

PASSIONATE ENGAGEMENT

To return to the clinical moment that began this article, I believe that my
own feelings about life, about the preciousness of time, and about health
have deeply affected how I experienced my eating-disordered patient.
Some might consider what was mobilized within me as maternal; others
would see my yearning for her to embrace life as biophilic; still others
might see my response as an excess of therapeutic zeal, a distorting,
dangerous countertransference. Some would see this countertransference as potentially choking off the patient's exploration of her self-
destructive urges. She will sense what I feel from my focus on the material, if no other way. Will she repress or dissociate the self-hurtful and
self-limiting aspects of herself in response to my passion? Will a therapeutically needed regression fail to occur? Will her transference be
harmfully constricted?

What I believe is that these are serious dangers, but we will have to
contend with them. Furthermore, I believe that this situation exists in
the treatment of the less disturbed patient as well. In such a patient there
are still struggles between self-destructive and self-enhancing forces. In
all cases, I must maintain an alertness for evidence that the patient is
tailoring herself to my specifications, or that her experience in the
treatment is detrimentally limited. I feel it is my absolute, unequivocal
position in favor of life, growth, and self-expansion that will engage this
patient in the profound struggle that must be at the heart of this treatment. While verbally inviting her to express every facet of her
conflicting feelings, my tone, my fervor must leave no doubt how much
I want to help her emerge from her conflicts. It is in response to my
taking this passionate position that her deepest conflicts will be more
clearly expressed. For a time, she will, I imagine, fight me rather than
herself. *Her reluctance to live will become a resistance to treatment.* I must
convey that I am open to hearing about that resistance, in its many

forms, but that I believe in a life for her that lies beyond it. Even the first time we met, I could picture her in the future, grown stronger. I have to be the faithful repository of that picture until she can share it with me.

TRAINING PASSIONATE ANALYSTS

My sense is that because it is so difficult to derive from the general principle of neutrality what the analyst should and shouldn't do in the actual clinical interchange, analytic training may impart more of an impression of the neutral stance than a clear formulation of what it proscribes and prescribes. The candidate develops his formulation of what analytic neutrality entails, and feels impelled to try to live up to this standard. Of course, the various analytic schools of thought view neutrality differently. (See Greenberg, 1991pp. 209–225 for a discussion of these differences and a formulation of analytic neutrality that shifts away from preformed rules of technique.) Although conceptions of analytic neutrality differ from institute to institute, and from supervisor to supervisor, my reading and supervisory experience suggests to me that candidates often come to believe they should aspire to a state of neutrality they fear they cannot achieve in practice. To the extent that they have passionate, particular responses to individual patients, they feel they are failing as analysts. Some try to hide their responses while in training, hoping to "get through" without their feelings being noticed. Others admit their emotional reactions, but mount an argument as to why this particularly difficult patient evoked such an extreme response. They may imply that they have learned from this training experience, and would not react so strongly in the future.

I hope that candidates could be helped to create, in each treatment they conduct under supervision, an analytic stance, shaped for this particular analyst-patient dyad, that utilizes the candidate's emotional resources without sacrificing the patient's freedom of expression. The candidate must not be intimidated by a generalized, vague, authority-invested notion of neutrality to either stifle or pretend to stifle passion.

To encourage this passion, the supervisor should be affectively expressive and elicit the candidate's full emotional engagement in the supervisory work. Supervision should not be a dry recitation, but an alive interchange between two human beings who care deeply about promoting health. This allows the supervisor to model a stance the candidate can use to actively, emotionally engage the patient. Each supervision, like each treatment, is a unique interaction, shaped by the feelings of both participants, made more effective if the full range of their emotions can emerge.

TOWARD A PASSIONATE NEUTRALITY

To summarize, a neutrality I could embrace would have to leave me free to encourage the patient's active efforts to fight depression. It would have to allow me to present enough of a new relational challenge to foster hope. It would have to include a valuing of urgency about not wasting time. And it would have to leave me free to describe the patient's impact on me, so that I can help him understand the differences between his intentions and his effect.

How can I more concretely define a neutrality that will help me avoid the pitfalls of closing off the patient's fullest self-exploration, without robbing me of the immediacy and power of passionate engagement? It is, I believe, an important part of our task to accept that as analysts we will never have a set of rules that can guide our work with precision. We will never know, with blessed certainty, that we have been the best we could be. It will always be difficult to clearly define the proper analytic neutrality, and hard to judge whether, in any particular case, it was achieved. Rules that try to simplify it through blanket prescriptions or by starkly limiting the analyst's expressiveness are false comforts for the analyst. They attempt to reassure her she is altogether "correct" in a profession in which such certainties don't exist.

When asked how she has changed as an analyst over time, and, more specifically, what allows her now to feel free in her self-expression, Szalita (Issacharoff, 1997) said, "I'm not thinking about whether it's analytical to say it or not analytical to say it, and I'm not bound by it" (p. 627). I would like to believe that time will similarly affect me. But I don't think this freedom comes from the mere passage of time.

Earlier in the interview, Szalita said something else that, I feel, helps to clarify what frees her to speak her mind openly. "It boils down to one thing: to what degree you are concerned with yourself and to what degree you are, as a therapist, concerned with the other person" (p. 627). This, for me, helps to define a neutrality I can embrace. I should strive to be neutral in the sense of non-narcissistically invested in the work. Perhaps this is what Szalita meant by being "more responsive" yet "less involved." She is responsive to the needs and feelings of the patient, but she doesn't have a personal stake in the patient's lifestyle choices or how the treatment makes the analyst look to herself.

One hopes that the experienced analyst already knows he is competent. He doesn't need a "success" with this patient to prove it to himself or to anyone else. He is, therefore, *from a narcissistic point of view* not invested in whether the patient makes a good life for himself, or even whether the patient has a life at all. But from a human point of view this cannot be a matter of indifference. Passionate engagement in treatment is a genuine investment in life itself. It is communicated in the "music" of the treatment—in the analyst's tone, manner, directness, allegiance to the truth, and the deeply felt conviction about the meaningfulness of the work. *The passion is felt; the neutrality is spoken.* The analyst's *words* invite the patient to express all that is within him, even the most self-destructive and sadistic pulls. But, without consciously shaping it, the analyst's *manner* conveys an abiding commitment to life and growth.

I think this is how we can understand the changes over time that Szalita notes in her analytic stance. She has, and knows she has, "an intention to be useful to the patient" (p. 626). Her secure knowledge of this non-narcissistic intention lends conviction to her tone. This allows her to *embody* passionate engagement, while still conveying a neutral invitation to the patient to reveal all that lies within him.

REFERENCES

Abend, S. M. (1989). Countertransference and psychoanalytic technique. *Psychoanalytic Quarterly* 58:374–395.

Bonime, W. (1982). Psychotherapy of the depressed patient. *Contemporary Psychoanalytic* 18:173–189. http://www.pep-web.org/document.php?id=cps.018.0173a

Buechler, S. (1993). Clinical applications of an interpersonal view of the emotions. *Contemporary Psychoanalytic* 29:219–236. http://www.pep-web.org/document.php?id'cps.029.0219a

———— (1995). Hope as inspiration in psychoanalysis *Psychoanalytic Dialogues* 5:63–74. http://www.pep-web.org/document.php?id'pd.005.0063a

————. (1997). The right stuff. *Contemporary Psychoanalytic* 33:295–306. http://www.pep-web.org/document.php?id'cps.033.0295a

Cooper, A. (1985), A historical review of psychoanalytic paradigms. In: *Models of the Mind*, ed. A Rothstein. New York: International Universities Press. http://www.pep-web.org/document.php?id'zbk.081.0005a

———— (1986). Some limitations on therapeutic effectiveness: The "burnout syndrome" in psychoanalysts. *Psychoanalytic Quarterly* 55:576–598. http://www.pep-web.org/document.php?id'paq.055.0576a

Ehrenberg, D. B. (1992), *The Intimate Edge: Extending the Reach of Psychoanalytic Interaction*. New York: W.W. Norton. http://www.pep-web.org/document.php?id'pd.004.0303a

Ferenczi, S. (1929), The unwelcome child and his death instinct. In: *The Final Contributions to the Problems and Methods of Psychoanalysis*. London: Hogarth Press. http://www.pep-web.org/document.php?id'ijp.010.0125a

Freud, A. (1936), *The Ego and the Mechanisms of Defense*. New York: International Universities Press.

Fromm, E. (1941). *Escape from Freedom*. New York: Farrar & Rinehart.

———— (1968), *The Revolution of Hope*. New York: Harper & Row.

———— (1973), *The Anatomy of Human Destructiveness*. New York: Holt, Rinehart & Winston.

Greenberg, J. (1991), *Oedipus and Beyond: A Clinical Theory*. Cambridge: Harvard University Press.

Issacharoff, A. (1997). A conversation with Dr. Alberta Szalita. *Contemporary Psychoanalysis* 33:615–632. http://www.pep-web.org/document.php?id'cps.033.0615a

Izard, C. E. (1977), *Human Emotions*. New York: Plenum Press.

Jacobs, T. J. (1986). On countertransference enactments. *Journal of the American Psychoanalytic Association* 34:289–307.http://www.pep-web.org/document.php?id'apa.034.0289a

Mitchell, S. A. (1993), *Hope and Dread in Psychoanalysis.* New York: Basic Books.

Poland, W. S. (1984). On the analyst's neutrality. *Journal of the American Psychoanalytic Association* 32:283–299. http://www.pep-web.org /document.php?id'apa.032.0283a

Sullivan, H. S. (1954), *The Psychiatric Interview.* New York: Norton.

CHAPTER FIVE

Necessary and Unnecessary Losses:
The Analyst's Mourning*

INTRODUCTION

There is at least one chapter on grief in each of my four previous books (2004, 2008, 2012, 2015). Obviously, the subject has great personal resonance. But that is not the only reason for my many returns to this topic. I believe that my views about grief, which have evolved over the years, are an important aspect of my interpersonal analytic perspective.

This paper is an early attempt to define what grieving entails, from my point of view. Re-reading it, I still hear ideas carried over from my days as an emotion theorist. I apply some theoretical concepts, drawn from emotion theories, to the situation of the analyst bearing losses of patients.

What are the avoidable and unavoidable losses an analyst sustains? After a review of various conceptions of mourning, I suggest some specific complications in the analyst's mourning process, depending on how the loss occurs. I then describe my own experience of the death of a patient, including aspects of my mourning that are ongoing. Writing this paper helped me understand what knowing her did for me, as an analyst

---

* *Contemporary Psychoanalysis*, 2000, 36:1, 77-90.

and human being. This somewhat modified the experience of losing her. "Every time remembering her helps me in some way the balance of what I gained from her vs. what I suffered changes."

But it would take several more years (2008, p.150) for me to develop my interpersonally slanted view of mourning's most painful aspects. "I think it can be tempting to create a sanitized version of mourning that tames its agonies and fails to do justice to our need for palpable living, embodied, unpredictable others, and not just notions of others...a true grasp of our interpersonal natures forces us to conclude that the loss of actual, specific, intimately known others is irreplaceable. We need to feel their breath, to hold their hand, to watch them laugh, to experience them in the living moment, through every sense, and not just in memory...No matter how mature and well developed our inner life, there is no object relational substitute for an alive partner when you want to go dancing."

Necessary and Unnecessary Losses: The Analyst's Mourning

We were in what seemed to me to be a particularly productive phase of the treatment. At long last (from my point of view) the patient was recognizing narcissistic aspects of her character that had hampered her in developing an enduring relationship. At thirty-five she was, I felt, really ready, for the first time, to engage in a deepening intimacy. Her whole life had been a momentous, courageous struggle with physical disabilities. Now she seemed ready to emerge more fully from the constraints of her psychological limitations. It was over the weekend that I got the message that she had suddenly died.

My experience of losing this patient was extremely painful, but I know I am hardly unique in having sustained such a loss. How do we bear these losses? What effects do they have over time, on our personal and professional lives?

Of course, the loss of a patient is usually less dramatic than this example. Patients terminate treatment, sometimes abruptly, sometimes with measured preparation. What is the accumulated impact on us, over the years, of living through so many endings? How can we best bear the sorrows that accompany a life in this rather peculiar profession?

Describing some peculiarities of the analytic relationship, especially in its termination phase, Nina Coltart (1996) writes,

> The totality of the ending, which seems to go against the grain of all our work on love, loyalty, object-constancy, and intimacy, is reinforced by the austere prescription of no social contact thereafter. Thus we create an arbitrary situation that has much in common with a death. [p. 151]

This description is no less apt for the analyst than for the patient. We take it for granted that over the years we will suffer the loss of countless people who have been our partners in an intimate emotional exchange. However we lose contact with these people, the loss is usually total and final.

In an attempt to separate the unavoidable from the avoidable pain of these experiences. I suggest that the negative impact is exacerbated by:

(1) Inhibitions (implicit in how we conceive of our roles) against full acknowledgment of the depth of some of the losses.
(2) Obstacles, intrinsic to the nature of the analytic relationship, to our benefiting from the normal mourning process.
(3) Other, more subtle forms of loss that are also frequent occurrences in the professional life of the analyst.

Our training does not adequately prepare us for dealing with these losses. Part of the reason is that the treatments we conduct under supervision are generally in their beginning phases, so intensive study of the termination phase is limited. This rational reason, however, does not entirely explain how ill-equipped many of us are to explore our repetitive losses usefully. Once again I agree with Coltart, who suggests that analysts are reluctant to examine the similarity between treatment, termination and death because

> even a mature, level-headed, and commonsensical person may have an almost superstitious fear of talking about death, and this

would certainly include any comparative reference to death in connection with such a frequent phenomenon as ending a treatment in our own professional lives. [p. 148]

I begin this essay on our loss experiences with some comments on the situation for the analyst when the patient dies during the course of the treatment, either through suicide or natural causes. Of course, analysts are not alone in experiencing deaths, but here I suggest some of the ways the death of a patient in analysis is an unusual situation. In order to delineate some of the obstacles to healthy mourning for the analyst, I describe what I believe normal mourning requires.

Deaths comprise a small portion of the losses the analyst sustains. I discuss the analyst's experience of planned and abrupt terminations, and why we often fail to register their impact fully.

More subtle, pervasive losses than the actual death or departure of a patient abound in our work lives and, I believe greatly exacerbate our acute grief experiences. These chronic demoralizers include losses of dignity, integrity, and conviction, due to the impact of aspects of the wider culture, such as cynicism about analysis, managed care, and an overemphasis on pharmaceutical solutions to emotional problems. Eventually this can lead to a loss of involvement in analytic work or "burnout." This extremely painful condition, I argue, is not unlike severe depression in its effects on self-esteem, energy level, creativity, attitudes about the future, and the experience of leading a meaningful life.

Although much of this discussion could be considered under the rubric of countertransference reactions, I suggest that some of the difficulty for the analyst in the situations I describe derives from how he has been taught to conceive of his role. Thus, these unnecessarily prolonged, painful experiences are partly a product of the culture of analysis (Buechler, 1988, 1992) as well, of course, as a product of the particular character issues and life experiences of each analyst.

In a final section of this essay I offer some ideas about how we can best bear our inevitable, necessary losses, and limit the frequency and impact of the unnecessary ones.

THE DEATH OF A PATIENT

Each death, of course, carries its own very personal, individual meaning; but I feel there are some experiences that analysts often have following the death of a patient by suicide or natural causes. These experiences can be extremely painful and, in some ways, bizarre.

If he attends a funeral, the analyst may come in contact, most likely for the first time, with the patient's closest relatives. It can be very hard to find words that feel at all appropriate, and yet we may be expected, and may expect ourselves, to be especially interpersonally adept at handling this sensitive situation. The analyst has the sense of intimately, profoundly knowing all the parties involved, and yet they may never have met or spoken before. The relatives and friends, dealing with their grief, may be discomforted by the presence of the analyst, whose role in the patient's life they may have long resented. They may blame the analyst in some way for the death, or they may feel that for years they have been judged by the analyst, without any opportunity to defend or explain themselves. The relatives and the analyst may all be carrying an enormous load of conflicting feelings, without any store of positive memories of relating to each other to draw upon.

The patient I mentioned earlier comes vividly to mind. She was an unforgettable woman who touched many lives with her determination and lively spirit, and I know that my sense of loss was more than matched by many others. But I'm not sure they understood, as I felt I did, how hard she had recently been fighting for a better life. To see her die at such a young age caused me indescribable pain. Unlike others who mourned her, I had no one I could really talk to about these feelings. Her relatives and friends were not mine, and I would have felt it inappropriate for me to discuss the treatment with them. Some of the mourning of an analyst proceeds in solitude.[†]

[†] For many years of lessening that solitude I would like to thank the members of my peer supervision group: Drs. Mark Blechner, Richard Gartner, John O'Leary, Allison Stern Rosen, and Robert Watson.

HEALTHY MOURNING

Before further discussion of the experience of the analyst whose patient dies, I would like to comment on the nature of the mourning process. Freud, of course, in "Mourning and Melancholia" (1917), strove to discriminate the emotions that normally accompany loss from the pathological, depressive state. In so doing he defined normal mourning as a process of adjusting to loss by gradually shifting cathexis from the lost object onto new, available objects.

From another perspective, emotion theorists (Izard, 1971, 1972, 1977) have defined sadness as a universal part of human experience in response to loss. It is contrasted with depression, which is considered a complex rather than a fundamental emotion, in that depression includes sadness as a component but has other emotional aspects as well, depending on the life experience of the person. Sadness is the emotional pain it is temporarily natural to feel when a meaningful loss or blow is incurred. Depression, on the other hand, generally involves a loss of self-esteem, a narrowing of the range of other emotions, and an overall constriction in living.

Not all theoreticians conceptualize sadness as a healthy, functional, self-limited response to loss and depression as its pathological alternative. Some (e.g., Bonime, 1982) see the core of depression as anger rather than sadness, and envision the "practice" of depression as a characterologically based, destructive way of life. Spiegel's work (1960, 1965, 1967, 1968, 1980) suggests that the specific emotions contained in any particular individual's depression may differ, so it is always important clinically to make no assumptions about what depression "is," and to carefully inquire into the nature of each patient's depressive experience.

But for those interpersonal psychoanalysts who see depression as an unhealthy version of sadness, the two states can most easily be distinguished by looking at their effects over time, because sadness heals and passes, whereas depression repeatedly disrupts functioning. The difference between sadness and depression is well captured by Arieti (1978).

Common is the sorrow that visits the human being when an adverse event hits his precarious existence or when the discrepancy between the way life is and the way it possibly could be becomes the center of his fervid reflection. In some people this sorrow comes and goes repeatedly, and in some others, only from time to time. It is painful, delays actions, and generally heals, often but not always after deepening its host's understanding and hastening his maturation.

Less common—but frequent enough to constitute major psychiatric concern—is the sorrow that does not abate with the passage of time, that seems exaggerated in relation to the supposed precipitating event, or inappropriate, or unrelated to any discernible cause, or replacing a more congruous emotion. This sorrow slows down, interrupts, or disrupts one's actions; it spreads a sense of anguish which may become difficult to contain; at times it tends to expand relentlessly into a psyche which seems endless in its capacity to experience mental pain; often it recurs even after appearing to be healed. This emotional state is generally called depression. [p. 3]

What allows us, if we are characterologically capable of it, to mourn a loss and go on living productively? What is it in the way we live our losses that distinguishes normal mourning from pathological depression? Gaines (1997) suggests that healthy mourning encompasses *two* tasks: the detachment that Freud's drive theory emphasized, and the equally important task of creating continuity by maintaining and building on the connection to the inner object. Creating continuity is, as Gaines describes, a very interpersonal endeavor.

The creation and maintenance of continuity is not easily carried out alone. For many people it is difficult to maintain the internal image without opportunity to express it aloud and share it with others. Partly, this has to do with the role of language in preserving memory. Both the expression of feelings and images in words and the repetition and sharing of those narratives with others are known to enhance memory. Also, the very act of communicating one's experience of a lost relationship has the effect of "bringing it alive" that is different from inner contemplation. Further, other people's appreciation of the lost object validates and enriches the solitary mourner's inner image. Other's observations about the mourner's relationship to the lost object can add to an understanding of what the relationship consisted of, what it meant for the individual, and how it is relevant to his life now and in the future. The availability of other people with whom to share the connection to the lost object helps mourners to bring the relationship into the present context, making it part of their shared ongoing lives. In a very important way, inner construction of objects draws on shared social construction of those objects. [p. 559]

THE ANALYST'S UNRESOLVABLE MOURNING

This description of the interpersonal process of mourning highlights what is often missing for the analyst when his patient dies. Even if the analyst is characterologically capable of a healthy mourning process, the interpersonal context is not conducive to it. He may never be able to communicate with anyone about the patient, which may make it difficult to maintain the patient's image internally. Without the opportunity to talk about the patient, especially to others who also knew the patient, the analyst has only his own resources in his effort to understand what knowing and losing this patient meant to him.

But I believe that some of the role expectations embedded in our analytic culture interfere even more profoundly in the essential mourning process. As analysts we are part of the wider culture, but are also members of an analytic subculture, with its particular mores, injunctions, and assumptions (Buechler, 1988, 1992). The analytic culture dictates, sometimes in subtle ways, the emotional reactions deemed "appropriate" and acceptable. Although we might not be able consciously to formulate all the "rules," we could probably listen to a colleague's case presentation and agree on whether his involvement with the patient seems "excessive."

I feel that there are times when these mores inhibit the normal mourning process. I will break this process into its components, to suggest the specific elements of the normal healing process that are unavailable to us as analysts.

Healing requires recognizing the fact of the loss. Denial of the reality and meaningfulness of the loss interferes in normal mourning (see, for example, Riviere's, 1936, discussion of the relationship between denial and depression). Thus, to whatever extent our analytic culture discourages our seeing ourselves as personally invested in our relationships with patients, we may have difficulty admitting to ourselves what the loss of a patient means to us personally. In other words, any characterological tendencies we might have to use denial are enhanced in this context.

Mourning is complicated in the presence of unresolved aggression toward the object before the loss. (This, of course, was spelled out by Freud in his 1917 essay). To the extent that, as analysts, we ask ourselves to contain negative emotional responses to the patient, at least until it seems therapeutically appropriate to share them (Winnicott, 1949), we accept the burden of carrying our unresolved negative feelings during much of the course of the treatment. If the patient dies or terminates abruptly, we are left with these feelings.

The process of mourning is furthered by hearing about what the loss meant to others, and by maintaining communication with other mourners over time. This allows the mourner to create needed continuity in his relationship to the inner object (Gaines, 1997). All of this would generally be prohibited by the constraints of our roles as analysts. The absence of ongoing communication with anyone about what the patient meant to us may complicate our response when the patient terminates treatment as well. We do not see ourselves as needing any ongoing process, but seem to expect ourselves to behave as though patients are interchangeable, and the loss of one can be erased by the appearance of another.

A common component of mourning is identifying with the lost object, thus compensating for the loss (Freud, 1933; Jacobson, 1971). But this may be difficult for those analysts who maintain emotional distance as part of the frame.

The position of mourner requires temporary acceptance of passivity, which might be difficult to integrate with some analysts' conceptions of their role.

Thus, if we view mourning in Gaines's (1997) terms, as a process of both detachment from the object, to make room for new ties, and continuity, to preserve the meaningfulness of the ongoing inner connection, our roles as analysts interfere much more with the maintenance of continuity than with detachment. Our interpersonal context, which does not include anyone else who knew the patient, is not conducive to sustaining the inner tie. Our roles mandate some distance, encourage us to contain negative feelings about the patient, and heighten any tendency we may characterologically have to delimit appreciation of the personal significance of the departed patient to our own lives. Our workdays, lived in forty-five-minute segments, may encourage the illusion that we can emotionally "move on" every time the buzzer sounds. The analytic role may also exacerbate the discomfort we otherwise might be prone to have with the passivity of being a mourner. Our position, of having many other patients with pressing needs, seems to justify, even to ennoble, moving on. This encourages whatever defensive processes in us that might tend toward denying the impact of loss. It is as though our roles make it seem possible that we could "skip" some of the normal human mourning process. If we have any tendencies in this direction characterologically, the role reinforces them.

My experience analyzing, supervising, and informally talking to analysts over the years suggests that many of us have suffered the deaths of patients without making an active effort to process the loss in a meaningful way. We have no institutionalized rituals for dealing with these losses. It is as though the fact that the person was a "patient" makes a ritual unnecessary. We would be unlikely, if a colleague, or friend, or relative died or permanently left, to expect ourselves to "move on" without grieving. But because, in some fundamental sense, our role encourages the denial of the personal impact of our relationships with patients, we also deny the personal meaning of their death or departure.

There are added complications if a patient's death was the result of suicide. There is no question that a patient's suicide can haunt the analyst for life. Among other feelings, there can be a vague, guilty sense that the analyst might have prevented it. Most writers on the subject of mourning suggest that guilt, or any factor that could lower self-esteem, interferes in normal mourning (Arieti & Bemporad, 1978). Perhaps, like the patient's relatives and friends, the analyst is likely to mentally inspect every recent interaction with the deceased, looking for clues to the patient's desperate state that the analyst may have missed. But unlike friends and relatives, the analyst is, supposedly, an expert at reading human behavior. Unfortunately, of course, our expertise does not guarantee that we can always predict what a patient may do. But as analysts, perhaps especially if we look back and see ourselves as having been unwilling to extend ourselves for this patient, we may feel a special sense of responsibility and guilt.

TERMINATIONS, PLANNED AND ABRUPT

Even the well-planned termination involves several kinds of losses for the analyst: the loss of a partner in a significant relationship, an economic loss, and the loss of a reflection, that is, someone who could help the analyst assess his own professional progress. The literature on termination (e.g., Ferenczi, 1927; Freud, 1937;Reich, 1950) deals mainly with its timing and impact on the patient and focuses less often on the analyst's losses.

As all of us can do, I see, in my mind's eye, a parade of former patients. I would love to know what happened to them, if only out of natural curiosity. Of course, ours isn't the only field in which the practitioner works toward his own obsolescence. Consider foster care, and even parenthood. But for those of us who feel posttreatment contact should be very limited there is a unique kind of loss at the termination of an analytic treatment. Never to hear what became of someone you have known so intimately is an incredible loss. Yet it is a regular occurrence in our professional lives. Loss comes with the territory.

But we have only scratched the surface when it comes to the losses analysts bear. Aside from planned terminations, there are the abrupt departures. I would wager that no analyst completes his career without encountering at least one mystery patient who leaves in the middle of the work, giving circumstantial but insufficient reasons. Freud (1905) set an example for us in his open expression of pain and frustration in response to the abrupt departure of his patient Dora. As a graduate student, I remember watching a taped interview in which an "elder-statesman" analyst, commenting on mysterious terminations, said that "pieces" of these patients always "stuck with him." For the analyst, the story never ends; it remains unfinished. He can always wonder if he could have done something differently to make it possible for the work to continue. In addition to feeling responsible for any "mistakes" he committed, the analyst may not be able to absolve himself entirely of what he might have thought of.

Analysts who work with children often experience the exquisite pain of having the parent withdraw the child from treatment as soon as there is progress (from the analyst's point of view). The parent-child-analyst triangle is inherently complicated, and I will not belabor its difficulties here, but I can attest to the tremendous pain, most especially evident in young, idealistic therapists, who may deeply identify with their child patients, and must watch them return to abusive or neglectful family situations, with no recourse unless evidence can be presented that warrants intervention.

My comments on abrupt termination are meant to be evocative, not definitive. Each such event has its own particular impact. But unless our training and later experiences encourage us to self-examine how we are affected by these departures, I believe they can contribute to the destructive state of burnout I discuss in a subsequent section. Although each patient's treatment and departure has its own meaning, if an analyst reflects on her experience, it may be she will find that she does have a characteristic way of responding to abrupt terminations. For some of us, self-blame and a strong sense of guilt may predominate, while for others, shame and a painful feeling of inadequacy may prevail. Still others may experience mainly anger directed at the patient. Unless we find a way to face and truly deal with these experiences, I feel they can affect our commitment to the work and our faith in ourselves.

CULTURALLY BASED LOSSES AND "BURNOUT"

Without much effort, most of us can describe some of the array of losses experienced by analysts as a result of managed care. In many cases, we and our patients are put in untenable positions. We must either collaborate with a system that often shows no respect for the basic assumptions of our profession or risk losing, for our patients, reimbursement they need. Whether or not the treatment gets reimbursed can depend on the verbal skill of the "provider," who must couch the patient's "illness" in terms acceptable to the company. The losses for all concerned are too numerous to list, but too many times they include losses of dignity for both patient and analyst. Whatever choice the analyst makes, whether to "play the game" and try to guess the words that will bring reimbursement, or simply to report the facts or opt out of the system, patient and analyst have been forced into potentially troublesome roles with each other. The analyst's verbal skills, willingness to stretch the truth, political attitudes, resourcefulness in finding time for paperwork, and the like should not determine whether the patient gets reimbursed; but these and other equally absurd factors often make the difference.

So many analysts come to consultations or supervision having lost enthusiasm for the field, partially because of today's bottom-line-driven climate. Younger ones, just entering the field, wonder if they have chosen their profession wisely. Will there *be* analysis in ten, or twenty, or thirty years? How can they develop decent practices if that part of the public mind that wishes deep-seated problems could be eradicated with a magic pill, or in eight forty-five minute sessions, is given official sanction? Middle-aged analysts feel it is too late to change professions, and see their incomes and opportunities to use their skills dwindling, at the time of life when they expected to be reaching their professional peak. Older analysts look with increasing dismay at what has happened to the field to which they have dedicated their life's work.

So far, I have described the analyst's experience of loss from deaths, planned and abrupt terminations, and the demoralizing climate. Cumulatively, these experiences can, I believe, contribute to what is often called "burnout" (Cooper, 1986). For an analyst, burnout is symptomatic of the greatest loss of all—the loss of faith in the profession and in oneself. The burnt-out analyst no longer believes in the worth of what he does for a living. He feels, for whatever economic or other reasons, he must continue to go through the motions of doing treatment, but it has become an empty exercise. I believe that cumulative losses are one important source of burnout, although other factors, such as the unique stresses of the work and the individual analyst's particular character issues, play major roles.

In burnout, it is as though making the work not matter could offer solace, relief from repetitive experiences of stress, pain, and loss. If what I'm doing has no meaning, then losing patients and the discouraging climate would not hurt so much. Unconsciously, cynicism offers an illusion of protection from pain. Better to deaden oneself than to be continually assaulted by loss. Of course, this is not a real solution, and the burnt-out analyst has suffered the greatest possible loss—the loss of faith in the worthwhileness of what he can accomplish.

I would argue that for most analysts, most of the losses I have described usually evoke temporary sadness. The burnout reaction is, I believe, closer to depression than sadness (see the descriptions given earlier of the differences between the two). A definite loss of self-esteem is involved in burnout, and it is likely to be pervasive and extended, rather than a temporary response. Why do some of us burn out while others lead long, rich professional lives? As with any depression, underlying character structure is key (Jacobson, 1971). But I also believe that those of us who are involved in training have an obligation to talk and write openly about our loss experiences, so that younger analysts will feel free to reflect on and, if necessary, get early help dealing with the losses they encounter in the work. If we keep to ourselves what it is personally like to lose patients in one way or another, year after year, we don't offer an invitation to our younger colleagues to pursue these issues openly.

THE WELL-BORNE LOSS

Although repeated loss experiences are unavoidable in our work, we can learn to bear the losses as well as possible. Aside from permitting ourselves awareness of the meaningfulness of the losses, so that denial doesn't complicate the mourning process, we can turn, more often, to colleagues, to make these losses into shared experiences. We can also become more aware of the potential these experiences have for furthering our personal and professional growth.

I hope that by writing of the potential positive uses of these experiences I will not be misunderstood as making light of them. But I do feel they can contribute to the analyst's emotional life. Of course, I don't mean by this that losses should be sought. But we must collectively study how they can be borne in such a way that the analyst avoids burnout.

With every year I feel deeper appreciation of Sullivan's statement that we are all more simply human than otherwise. Participating in the painful moments of others' lives I have come to know how the most seemingly inexplicable behavior may, at bottom, be a convoluted expression of a grieving that is quite basic and universal. The intense losses that are part of everyday life, losses of loved ones, of health, of faith, of ideals, of dreams, are always near to the analyst. He knows of loss vicariously, through patients' experiences as well as through his own.

This heightened awareness of the pervasiveness of loss is not only a burden. It can also be a tremendous inducement to savor every waking moment. It can teach the same lessons that any brush with tragedy potentially affords. It can enhance appreciation of the smaller and bigger miracles of life, the ordinary pleasures so easily taken for granted.

Sadness is an emotion that potentially binds us together. It bids me to stretch to understand that which is initially alien. When I first began working as a therapist I was assigned to see a patient who was a member of the American Nazi Party. His beliefs were especially repugnant to me, and, initially, I had doubts as to whether I could treat him. But something pulled me to listen further, and, in hearing the story of his unbearably sad childhood, I found a human being I could connect with.

I could feel sorrow for his losses, for the gentler, saner childhood that would never be his. I could understand how it warped and embittered him, though I would never embrace the "philosophy" he developed. Eventually he came to repudiate that philosophy and its defensive strivings for absolute domination and superiority. Eventually we understood some of the complex determinants of his politics. Of course his party affiliation was more than merely a response to a severely abusive childhood, and cannot be so simplistically explained away. But without engaging in reductionism, I do feel that genuine sorrow for some of his early losses enabled me to empathize with aspects of his humanity, and to bear being with him long enough to get to know and help him.

Sadness eventually cleanses, allowing us to return to the fray. It acquaints us more nearly with all it means to be a human being, binds us to each other, and sharpens our appreciation of joyous moments. It lends perspective to the ordinary and the extraordinary vicissitudes of life. As an analyst, it is necessary that I develop a strong tolerance for sadness and loss, for they will always be close at hand.

I turn a corner and "see" the patient I mentioned earlier, who died years ago. I realize how often this has happened over the many years since she died. At first I thought it would be a fleeting phenomenon, a wishful fantasy expressing how much I miss her humor and courage. I understand that these moments meaningfully reflect on personal aspects of my ongoing relationship to loss. But for these brief instants she is here again, and not just alive but well, walking, out of her wheelchair. The fantasy gives me a momentary break from bearing the sad reality. And then the person in the street comes closer, and I realize it is not my patient. The pain of her loss is no less now than it was when she died, and my feelings of regret that she didn't have more time are unchanged. What *is* different is that years of self-reflection have clarified some of the personal meanings of her life and death to me. Now I bring this greater clarity to each instance of actively mourning her loss. And cumulative experience has taught me something about how much she contributed to my personal and professional growth. Every current clinical and nonclinical moment that the experience of her illuminates increases my appreciation of her. Every time remembering her helps me in some way, the balance of what I gained from her versus what I suffered changes. I know much more now about what seeing her did, and still does, for me professionally and personally, and how I would like to use that growth. The sadness is doing its essential job, of binding me more firmly to life.

References

Arieti, S. (1978), The basic questions and the psychological approach. In: *Severe and Mild Depression*, S. Arieti & J. Bemporad. New York: Basic Books, pp. 3–10.

——— & Bemporad, J. (1878), *Severe and Mild Depression*. New York: Basic Books.

Bonime, W. (1982). Psychotherapy of the depressed patient. *Contemporary Psychoanalysis* 18:173–189.

Buechler, S. (1988). Joining the psychoanalytic culture. *Contemporary Psychoanalysis* 24:462–469. http://www.pep-web.org/document.php?id'cps.024.0462a

———. (1992), Stress in the personal and professional development of a psychoanalyst. *Journal of the American Academy of Psychoanalysis and Dynamic Psychiatry* 20:183–191. http://www.pep-web.org/document.php?id'jaa.020.0183a

——— (2004). *Clinical Values: Emotions That Guide Psychoanalytic Treatment*. Hillsdale, NJ: The Analytic Press

——— (2008). *Making a Difference in Patient's Lives: Emotional Experience in the Therapeutic Setting*. New York: Routledge.

——— (2012). *Still Practicing: The Heartaches and Joys of a Clinical Career*. New York, NY: Routledge.

———(2015). *Understanding and Treating Patients in Clinical Psychoanalysis: Lessons from Literature*. York: Routledge.

Coltart, N. (1996), *The Baby and the Bathwater*. Madison, NJ: International Universities Press.

Cooper, A. M. (1986). Some limitations on therapeutic effectiveness: The "burnout syndrome" in psychoanalysts. *Psychoanalytic Quarterly* 55:576–598. http://www.pep-web.org/document.php?id'paq.055.0576a

Ferenczi, S. (1927), The problem of the termination of the analysis. In: *Final Contributions to the Problems and Methods of Psychoanalysis*, ed. M. Balint. New York: Basic Books, pp. 77–86.

Freud, S. (1905), Fragment of an analysis of a case of hysteria. *Standard Edition* 7:3–122. http://www.pep-web.org/document.php?id'se.007.0001a

————. (1917), Mourning and melancholia. *Standard Edition* 14:237–258. http://www.pep-web.org/document.php?id'se.014.0237a

———— (1933), New introductory lectures on psychoanalysis. *Standard Edition* 22:3–184. http://www.pep-web.org/document.php?id'se.022.0001a

———— (1937), Analysis terminable and interminable. *Standard Edition* 23:211–253. http://www.pep-web.org/document.php?id'se.023.0209a

Gaines, R. (1997). Detachment and continuity. *Contemporary Psychoanalysis* 33:549–571. http://www.pep-web.org/document.php?id'cps.033.0549a

Izard, C. E. (1971), *The Face of Emotion*. New York: Meredith Corporation.

———— (1972), *Patterns of Emotions*. New York: Academic Press.

———— (1977), *Human Emotions*. New York: Plenum Press.

Jacobson, E. (1971), *Depression: Comparative Studies of Normal, Neurotic, and Psychotic Conditions*. New York: International Universities Press.

Reich, A. (1950). On the termination of analysis. *International Journal of Psycho-Analysis* 31:179–183. http://www.pep-web.org/document.php?id'ijp.031.0179a

Riviere, J. (1936). A contribution to the analysis of the negative therapeutic reaction. *International Journal of Psycho-Analysis* 17:304–320. http://www.pep-web.org/document.php?id'ijp.017.0304a

Spiegel, R. (1960), Communication in the psychoanalysis of depressions. In: *Psychoanalysis and Human Values*, ed. J. H. Masserman. New York: Grune & Stratton, pp. 209–222.

———— (1965). Communication with depressive patients. *Contemporary Psychoanalysis* 2:30–34. http://www.pep-web.org/document.php?id'cps.002.0030a

———— (1967), Anger and acting out: Masks of depression. *Journal of the American Academy of Psychoanalysis and Dynamic Psychiatry* 21:597–606.

————. (1968). Supervisory collaboration in the treatment strategy for masked depression. *Contemporary Psychoanalysis* 5:57–61. http://www.pep-web.org/document.php?id'cps.005.0057a

———— (1980), Cognitive aspects of affects and other feeling states with clinical applications. *Journal of the American Academy of Psychoanalysis and Dynamic Psychiatry* 8:591–614. http://www.pep-web.org/document.php?id'jaa.008.0591a

Winnicott, D. W. (1949). Hate in the Counter-Transference. *International Journal of Psycho-Analysis* 30:69–74. http://www.pep-web.org/document.php?id'ijp.030.0069a

CHAPTER SIX

Joy in the Analytic Encounter:
A Response to Biancoli[*]

INTRODUCTION

You can still hear the voice of the emotion theorist in this paper. It focuses on just one emotion, joy, honoring the idea that each emotion has a history in an individual's life experience. Part of how I know myself is that I know what has frequently made me angry, or afraid, or joyful. We know ourselves and make ourselves known to others through our expressions of emotions, starting with the first cry. The paper also implicitly argues that the balance of positive and negative affects is crucial to wellbeing.

Joy has not received much attention in the psychoanalytic literature, although it is surely a highly significant human feeling. This paper distinguishes two potential sources of joy in psychoanalysis: focusing on our common humanity, and defining and affirming our unique individuality. These two joys can hearten both analyst and patient. Despite difficulties, a treatment can survive, and its participants can thrive, if there is sufficient joy.

The paper continues my conversation with Erich Fromm, comparing his view of joy with those of Schachtel and others. It also expresses my abiding love for poetry; the source, for me, of much joy.

---

[*] Contemporary Psychoanalysis, 2002, 38:4, 613-622.

JOY IN THE ANALYTIC ENCOUNTER: A RESPONSE TO BIANCOLI

> The analyst feels not only the patient, but also himself in seeking to discover his own humanity in the other, in experiencing the universal human in himself and in the other (Biancoli, 2002).

Experiencing the universally human is a potential source of joy in analysis. It is available to both participants. My response to Biancoli's essay is to explore the nature of this, and other sources of joy that I believe are at the heart of the analytic encounter.

Focusing on our common humanity can promote the sense that we can transcend our particular idiosyncrasies and circumstances and that can bring us joy. But there is a second fundamental source of joy in analysis, in the process of defining and affirming our unique individuality. Biancoli writes of analysis as "a dialogue between analyst and analysand aimed at clarifying who the latter is and why he is the way he is, that is to say, at unsticking his process of individuation." (p. 609). Biancoli goes on to describe how "the analyst's own process of individuation is also activated."

Thus I am differentiating two fundamental opportunities for joy in the treatment process. These two joys, the joy of affirming uniqueness and the joy of transcending it, can hearten both analyst and patient. Both, I believe, fortify the relationship, allowing it to weather its inevitable challenges. Despite difficulties, a treatment can survive and its participants thrive if there is sufficient joy.

I begin by exploring the nature of joy. First, I compare Fromm's and Schachtel's conceptions of joy with concepts drawn from emotion theory and the poetry of Wordsworth. Then, moving to the analytic encounter, I explore some of its potential joys. In a final section I reframe these sources of joy, in a further effort to clarify just what each celebrates.

SOMETHING THAT DOTH LIVE

Joy is often accompanied by a sense of harmony and unity with the object of joy and, to some extent, with the world. Some people have reported that in ecstatic joy they tend to lose individual identity, as in the case of some mystical experiences associated with meditation. [Izard, 1977, p. 271]

As this quote suggests, joy is often described by emotion theorists as an affect that connects us with something beyond ourselves. Izard notes that part of this joy can be the feeling of *shedding* individual identity. It is as though our sense of individuality usually blocks joyous connection, but in moments of intense joy we can transcend this limitation.

Similarly, Schachtel (1959) defines the highest form of "real" (as opposed to magical, omnipotent) joy as "a feeling of being related to all things living" (p. 42). He goes on to describe joy as a continuous turning toward the world. It is, in his words "the felt experience of the ongoing acts of relatedness" (p. 43).

Joyous moments, for the poet Wordsworth, prod us to remember our earliest years, when we had a more palpable connection to nature:

O joy! that in our embers
Is something that doth live,
That nature yet remembers
What was so fugitive!

Wordsworth seems to me to agree with Izard that our worldly sense of self can block the deepest joyous connection to ongoing life. He exhorts us to see "our noisy years" as but "moments in the being of the eternal silence" and bids us focus on the "truths that wake, / to perish never; / which neither listlessness, nor mad endeavor, / nor man, nor boy, / nor all that is at enmity with joy, / Can utterly abolish or destroy!" For Wordsworth, sensing that we are part of the vast fabric of life can bring profound joy.

Schachtel (1959, p. 43) says he is in essential agreement with Fromm's perspective on joy. Fromm (1947, p. 192) defined joy as "an achievement: it presupposes an inner effort, that of productive activity." Fromm writes of joy as though it rewards an active, healthy stance toward life. Both Schachtel and Fromm seem to me to imply a kind of hierarchy, with the active elevated over the passive. Even when Schachtel celebrates open receptivity to the world it is an *active* receptivity, a deliberate move. We might read in these authors more of a slant toward mastering life than we find in the poet, Wordsworth, or the emotion theorist, Izard. For Wordsworth it is enough simply to appreciate life, in all its forms. He doesn't need to act on anything or even turn himself toward anything. It is enough for him that when life presents itself his heart bears witness: "to me the meanest flower that blows can give / thoughts that do often lie too deep for tears."

CLEARING THE SILL OF THE WORLD

Among the sources of joy in analysis and other relationships is the thrill of witnessing a leap forward, or a significant step toward greater freedom. A patient begins to actively battle her depression. She suddenly seems to grasp the urgent necessity to fight for her life. She remembers personal strengths she has called on before, and also imagines developing new resources. It is an occasion for both patient and analyst to feel joy.

In *A Safe Place*, Leston Havens (1989) describes how he tries to avoid distracting or intruding when the patient is struggling to achieve new insight. To illustrate that "the neutrality of silence can also conceal a prayer" (p. 23) Havens quotes from a poem by Richard Wilbur. In this poem, "The Writer," a father is silently transfixed, listening outside the door as his daughter tries to write. He waits, hopeful that he will hear the clang of the typewriter, which will tell him she is able to find words. As he listens he recalls:

> I remember the dazed starling
> Which was trapped in that very room, two years ago;
> How we stole in, lifted a sash
> And retreated, not to affright it;
> And how for a helpless hour, through the crack of the door,
> We watched the sleek, wild, dark
> And iridescent creature

Batter against the brilliance, drop like a glove
To the hard floor, or the desk-top,
And wait then, humped and bloody,
For the wits to try it again; and how our spirits
Rose when, suddenly sure,
It lifted off from a chair-back,
Beating a smooth course for the right window
And clearing the sill of the world.
It is always a matter, my darling,
Of life or death, as I had forgotten. I wish
What I wished you before, but harder.

The quiet thrill of witnessing someone "clearing the sill of the world" is, for me, one of the clearest sources of joy as an analyst.

Why do we get excited when a child says her first words, or takes her first steps? Why does my heart leap when a patient, blocked for years, finishes her dissertation? I would call this "transcendent joy," in that I am identifying with the patient overcoming a limitation.

Interestingly, this transcendence seems to me the opposite of *anger*, rather than sadness. Anger, according to emotion research (Izard, 1977) is, at its essence, a response to being blocked. In infancy it first emerges in answer to frustrating obstacles. We swipe at the object in our way, facial muscles set in an angry grimace. In contrast, transcendent joy is a miraculous freedom from obstacles.

RIDING THE WAVES

There are times when the analytic process takes off. Many have described this experience (e.g., Levenson, 1991). I feel it is a source of an exhilarating joy in analysis (for both participants). We are carried along, still wondering (after all these years) at its power. Like something catching fire the reflective process builds, taking on a vibrant life of its own.

Somewhat similar to this, for me, is the joy when the strength of the life force becomes palpable. Sullivan (1953, 1954) referred to the drive toward health. Fromm(1973) wrote of biophilia. Ferenczi (1929), unlike Freud, thought we have to be initiated into caring about our lives, by being cared for. Regardless of how we believe it comes about there are moments when the patient's desire for life takes hold. The joy of this is more than just happiness or relief. It is, at least for me, a grateful surge of feeling.

I am reminded of Michelangelo's moving image of Adam, a central figure on the Sistine Chapel's ceiling. The artist captures the miraculous, magical moment of animation. What was inert is infused with spirit. We feel the joy of life asserting itself.

Like all other human beings, analysts celebrate when life wins. We may feel we ought to keep our celebrations to ourselves, or we may not abide by such constraints. But life renewed moves us as it does others. The patient who no longer considers suicide is a source of joy.

This joy has, for me, an element of greed. As children we probably all, at times, wanted a bigger portion of something. We urgently wanted to be "big," to stay up later, to surpass tomorrow what we could do today. Not content to crawl, we risked falling, because we needed to walk. Not content to walk, we ran.

I know I bring this greedy child to my work. She cheers the moments of ascendancy of the life force, and, still, she wants more.

LOSING MYSELF

In Winnicott's (1971) transitional space we are not bound by the usual rules. We don't ask the child to prove why his blanket comforts. We don't try to impress him with the fact that it is just a square of wool. We accept that it is, for him, what he makes of it.

Similarly, for me, as an analyst, my office, the patient, and my own mind often exist in a kind of transitional space. Like the child's experience of the blanket, my experience is unbound by the usual limitations. I am any age, we are any where, it is any time.

Of course, this is not the only truth. Just as the blanket has a size, in the treatment hour I still have an identity. But my awareness of it is intermittent. There are moments when I lose myself in the feel of the work. The patient and I are not bound by our histories and self-definitions. We are two instances of life.

For Winnicott, the child's transitional play becomes a template for the adult's engagement with culture. As the curtain goes up in the theatre I suspend disbelief. I don't ask whether what happens could be real. When I read Kafka's *Metamorphosis* I don't ask whether a person can become an insect. I enter the feel of the person becoming an insect. Engaging in that process I temporarily let go of my discrete, bordered self.

There is a kind of joy, for me, in this unmoored state. Perhaps it is simply the joy of letting go of the work of keeping track of things. Most of the time it is important to be clear about what is coming from inside myself and what is coming from outside. It is usually necessary to distinguish the real from the unreal, the likely from the unlikely. It is usually important to remember who I am and to behave accordingly. Keeping account takes effort.

A patient tells me about her weekend. Temporarily I imagine it, losing track of myself, just visualizing what I am hearing. Of course, I could snap back to a different kind of attention. I could focus on who I am, if I had to. But for the moment I let myself float in and out of the experience I am listening to. For moments I have entered her world, and I am looking around, like Alice in a wonderland that is governed by rules I have to discover. I am trying to get the feel of the place. I don't ask whether things are as they should be, whether it all makes sense. I just live it, and, in that moment, I am free of the constraints of time, place, identity. In that freedom there is, for me, a kind of joy.

FINDING MYSELF

"Joy, then, is what we experience in the process of growing nearer to the goal of becoming ourselves." (Fromm, 1976, p. 106).

Biancoli distills Fromm's challenge to human beings: individuate or you will regress! We are born into the human dilemma of having to face the loneliness of individuation or pay a heavy price for trying to avoid it. This vision of the human situation shapes the goals of analysis:

analysis must largely deal with exploration of the factors, in the analysand, that have inhibited or deformed this capacity—that is, deformed the expression of the analysand's own authenticity. "Authentic means original, and master of oneself" (Dolci, 1985, p. 139, translation mine); therefore authenticity is encountered along the road to individuation, and repeated experience thereof should occur in analysis on the part of both the analysand and the analyst. [p. 597]

I believe that individuation is, at its essence, an interpersonal process because we define ourselves, so often, through contrast. Frequently we clarify who we don't want to be before we know who we are. Raising or treating adolescents usually provides ample examples of this. As another example, let us briefly consider the process of becoming an analyst, with an individual style and voice. This is, obviously, an individuation process with which we are all familiar. In a paper on joining the psychoanalytic culture (1988) I described how in analytic training we recapitulate our own earlier adolescent individuation process, defining ourselves as analysts largely by contrast. Depending, partly, on the vicissitudes of the candidate's earlier passage through chronological adolescence the initial phases of professional identity development can take on tumultuous, idolatrous, or other qualities.

Of course, the development of a personal voice as an analyst does not end at the graduation ceremony. Colleagues can play a decisive role in nurturing each others' professional growth (Buechler, 2001). But we forge our own analytic style mainly in clinical interchanges. Doing supervision, teaching, and writing also contribute. In each of these professional activities we discover ourselves by contrasting our thoughts and feelings with the responses of others. Treatment affords both participants opportunities for self-discovery through contrast. I would say that contrast is an essential ingredient of the individuation process described by Biancoli (2002).

JOY IN THE DETAILS

For those of us who sometimes treat couples it is not uncommon to hear the irritated claim "You *always* ..." or "You *never* ..." The accused often objects to being so neatly summed up.

But when we are truly fond of someone (including ourselves) isn't it precisely his characteristic behaviors that we find charming, amusing, endearing? And when we lose someone we deeply loved, isn't it remembering his little personal quirks that often evokes tears? Wouldn't we give anything to hear him fumble with the lock, just once more?

Mourning is as much about remembering details and continuing the relationship as it is about relinquishing it (Gaines, 1997; Buechler, 2000). Henry James said that God is in the details, and Sullivan inquired vigorously about just when, and how, the patient's interpersonal interactions occurred. I believe that the triggers of individuation, interpersonal awareness, and bearable mourning, are also mainly in the details.

A patient who has had decades of professional experience tells me about attending an important meeting. I notice that although the topic for the meeting was quite familiar to the patient, and I know she has a strong point of view in this area, she didn't speak at all during the meeting. I focus on why. In retrospect I can see how overdetermined my response was. Transferential and countertransferential factors, in the broadest sense of both terms, led me to assume the patient's silence at the meeting was born of reticence, inadequate self-worth, truncated ambition, difficulty with assertion. Intuiting my assumptions from my focus, the patient confronts me. Why couldn't her silence at the meeting be, simply, her brand of participation, just as her forceful confrontation of me in the session reflects *her* values about when it is important to speak up?

As the patient and I examine our interchange we learn about ourselves and each other. Who is she, about speaking up? Who am I? We discover our potentially endearing (or maddening) peculiarities. Unlike the joy of finding human commonalities (as discussed above), this is the joy of knowing someone by appreciating small (and large) differences. We see ourselves and each other better through contrast. And such contrasts allow us to see that we could choose to respond differently to the world. Someone else already has.

Articulating differences in the details of an interpersonal response furthers the process of individuation. These exercises in contrast may sometimes involve some departure from traditional neutrality (for a discussion of the importance of neutrality versus the importance of these experiences of contrasting personal styles see, for example, Greenberg, 1991; Buechler, 1999).

I think the parent of an adolescent has to memorably express his beliefs and the details of his personal style of living, so as to provide *a* way (not *the* way) to live life. Similarly, I feel the analytic supervisor should clearly provide *a* model (not *the* model) for conducting an analysis. And the analyst should show enough of himself to give the patient a point of comparison. For example, a patient of mine noted that I didn't seem to be attempting to retaliate when he had deliberately tried to hurt me. The contrast helped him realize that he would have needed to even the score. I responded with some curiosity about why we had to keep score at all.

We come to know ourselves and others partly by noticing details. They endear and they frustrate us. They constitute an important aspect of what we often fear losing with aging or disease (will I still be me?). They form a part of what we can retain when someone is gone.

JOY IN THE STRANGE AND FAMILIAR

There can be joy in recognizing our common human nature, and there can be joy in appreciating our differences. Opportunities for these joys abound in the analytic process. For myself, I have often thought of analysis as a process that challenges both participants to know these joys fully enough to bear our inevitable frustrations, sorrows, and other erosions of the spirit.

Many years ago I took a course in metaphor, hoping to enhance my ability to write poetry. I don't think the course accomplished this goal, but it did give me some conceptual tools I have adopted in my analytic work. The course taught us to be able to "make the strange familiar, and the familiar strange." We were given exercises and asked, for example, to invent a new shape for an ice tray. How can we retain its essential "ice-trayness" but also change it?

Some of the analyst's tasks are similar. In the initially alien, strange, disturbing life stories we hear we must find the familiar earmarks to common humanity. But, just as often, we must notice the unusual where

212

the patient sees only what he assumes is universal. Heightened awareness of the profoundly human and the richly idiosyncratic provides some of the potential joys of an analytic life.

REFERENCES

Biancoli, R. (2002). Individuation in analytic relatedness. *Contemporary Psychoanalysis* 38:589–614,

Buechler, S. (1988). Joining the psychoanalytic culture. *Contemporary Psychoanalysis* 24:462–470.

——— (1999). Searching for a passionate neutrality. *Contemporary Psychoanalysis* 35:213–229. www.pep-web.org/document.php?id'cps.035.0213a

——— (2000). Necessary and unnecessary losses: The analyst's mourning. *Contemporary Psychoanalysis* 36:77–91 www.pep-web.org/document.php?id'cps.036.0077a

——— (2001). Coming of age in middle age. Presented at the spring meeting of the William Alanson White Society, May 19.

Dolci, D. (1985). *Palpitare di nessi.* Roma: Armando.

Ferenczi, S. (1929). The unwelcome child and his death instinct. *International Journal of Psycho-Analysis* 10:125–129. http://www.pep-web.org/document.php?id'ijp.010.0125a

Fromm, E. (1947). *Man for Himself.* Greenwich, CT: Fawcett Premier.

——— (1973). *The Anatomy of Human Destructiveness.* New York: Holt, Rinehart & Winston.

Fromm, E. (1976). *To Have or to Be?* New York: Harper and Row.

Gaines, R. (1997). Detachment and continuity: The two tasks of mourning. *Contemporary Psychoanalysis* 33:549–571. http://www.pep-web.org/document.php?id'cps.033.0549a

Greenberg, J. (1991). *Oedipus and Beyond: A Clinical Theory.* Cambridge: Harvard University Press.

Havens, L. (1989). *A Safe Place.* New York: Random House.

Izard, C.E. (1977). *Human Emotions.* New York: Plenum Press.

Levenson, E. (1991). *The Purloined Self: Interpersonal Perspectives in Psychoanalysis.* New York: Contemporary Psychoanalysis Books. http://www.pep-web.org/document.php?id'cps.028.0450a

Schachtel E. (1959). *Metamorphosis.* New York: Basic Books.

Sullivan, H. S. (1953). *The Interpersonal Theory of Psychiatry.* New York: W.W. Norton.

——— (1954). *The Psychiatric Interview.* New York: W.W. Norton.

Winnicott, D.W. (1971). *Playing and Reality.* London: Tavistock Publications. http://www.pep-web.org/document.php?id'zbk.017.0001a

Wordsworth, W. (1942). Ode: Intimations of immortality from recollections of early childhood. In: *A Treasury of Great Poems*, ed. L. Untermeyer. New York: Simon and Schuster.

CHAPTER SEVEN

More Simply Human Than Otherwise[*]

INTRODUCTION

Treatment can be seen as the interplay of two people, each with his or her own defensive structure. What impact might it have if the analyst's defenses closely approximate those of the patient? What if they greatly differ? This paper discusses what happened in a treatment where there was considerable overlap between my own defensive coping style and the patient's.

One question (p.489) in this paper, that is still a focus in my teaching and writing, is, "...who the analyst has to be, to facilitate growth in this treatment." I emphasize who we have to be, rather than what we need to say or do.

We encounter a version of this question each time we make a referral. Would you send a markedly obsessive compulsive patient to a colleague whose functioning veers in the same direction? Or would that be the last person you would suggest?

While there are challenges no matter how similar or different we are, this quote from Erich Fromm resonates with memories of my best moments as an analyst: "When you come to me, I will be completely open to you, and I shall respond with all the chords in myself which are

---

[*] *Contemporary Psychoanalysis,* 2002, 38:3, 485-497.

touched by the chords in yourself. That is all we can promise, and that is a promise we can keep" (Fromm, 2009, pp.26-27). If patient and analyst differ too much, in their culturally shaped implicit assumptions, defensive coping styles, fundamental values, it may be too difficult for the patient's "chords" to be "touched" by the analyst's. Each analyst may have a different capacity for stretching, for finding the other in him or herself. Questions about this process still fascinate me.

MORE SIMPLY HUMAN THAN OTHERWISE

A patient describes a recent conversation with his father. Once again, the patient is invited to join his father in financially providing extra resources for his younger siblings. Although the patient can afford to do this presently, the future looks extremely uncertain in his field. Of late, he has spoken often of his anxiety about his own financial security.

The patient recounts how he quickly agreed to help his siblings, so they would have the "peace of mind" of "extra reserves." Then he becomes noticeably uninterested in going over the details of the plan with his father, and equally uninterested in exploring it in treatment. His summary, in a nonchalant voice, is a repetition of the word "whatever." It wasn't that important.

The feeling I had was that this was a "fait accompli." I wasn't to question his acceding to the request. I wasn't to react as though this had much significance. I was merely to notice how his father assumed the patient hadn't needs of his own. Just as the patient was expected to unresistantly pay, I was expected to unresistantly accept he had no choice other than to go along with his father's plan.

What does this patient need most from me? Who must I be to help him? Can I be any competent analyst (harkening back to classical thinking, e.g., Freud, 1912)? Can I be any trained analyst able to "handle" her countertransference so it doesn't "disrupt" the process? Or are there human qualities, aside from technical competence, that are crucial to effective work with this patient?

In this clinical situation, I believe an important variable is my stance toward certain specific challenges in life. In what follows I elaborate some aspects of my own development as a person that I think are relevant to my treatment of this patient. I see as central to this work the encounter between the schizoid aspects of the patient and the schizoid aspects of the analyst.

Of course, it is not always the schizoid aspects of the analyst that are most relevant. Sometimes it is the narcissistic, or obsessional, or paranoid, or depressive aspect, as I elaborate. But treatment is not just the meeting of two people, each of whom has an unconscious. Treatment is an encounter between two people, each of whom has an interpersonal style, character issues, defensive proclivities. The process unfolds in this interchange between two people who have developed characteristic ways of dealing with the human condition.

I begin with a discussion of how I use terms such as "schizoid," what I see as the essential schizoid challenges, and how I believe they are lived out in treatment. This will take me back to the case vignette. What matters most about my character style at this moment in this treatment? What must the patient find in me to further our work?

For years we have acknowledged that all human beings, including analysts, are more simply human than otherwise. We have honored the intersubjective, seen treatment as cocreated, and noticed the importance of the match between the clinician and the patient (Lambert, 1983; Wolstein, 1983; Mitchell, 1997). But we are reluctant, I feel, to address some of the questions that would give these generalities more substantive meaning. Should we refer a strikingly obsessional patient to a prevailingly obsessional colleague, because she will intuitively understand the issues, or is this the *worst referral* we could make? Should we refer the patient to the overall best analyst we can find, trusting them to work out the important issues? In short, what aspects of the analyst's way of being human are relevant to the outcome of the work?

Clinically I have found terms like *schizoid, paranoid, narcissistic* most useful as adjectives describing coping patterns. They are like photographic portraits, capturing someone's style at a particular moment in time. Thus, for example, I may find that a patient who initially seemed narcissistic quickly settles into a schizoid pattern of relating. He may go through a schizoid "phase," only to emerge and then work on depressive issues. Diagnostic terms do not, for me, describe the static essence of someone. Rather, they capture fleeting patterns of coping with being human.

As an example, one part of being human is feeling an array of emotions (Izard, 1977; Buechler & Izard, 1983; Buechler, 1993). Schizoid coping patterns bear emotions by attempting to minimize their meaning and intensity (Guntrip, 1969; Bromberg, 1979). The patient in the initial vignette didn't merely try to *show* limited feeling in response to his father's idea. He actually tried not to *feel* much. At some level of consciousness he knew that if he carefully examined the plan with his father, or discussed it thoroughly with me, he might feel anxiety about his own financial situation, hurt that his father didn't seem concerned about the patient's "peace of mind," and perhaps angry at the longstanding expectations his family has had for him. Part of what I am calling "schizoid" is this patient's tendency to gloss over details that could evoke his strong feelings. His repeated "whatever" invited me to attach little meaning to his father's request and his own speedy acquiescence. His nonchalant tone also invited me not to "make a big deal."

Although many issues could be raised about this vignette, I feel the most important is how it could bring out my own schizoid proclivities. If I were to simply say little, for example, the moment would probably pass and the patient would go on to another topic. We would be spared intense emotional interchange. It is likely I could get through the session uneventfully. But at what cost?

The aspects of my own development as a person that I feel are most relevant here are my relationship to emotional intensity, my willingness to expend effort, my wish to make things go smoothly (at least on the surface), my need to comply with expectations, my courage, and my conviction about the worth of my immediate reactions. In other words, how much I rely on schizoid coping patterns affected the treatment interchange, just as the patient's reliance on schizoid patterns influenced his behavior with his father.

I further elaborate what I see as the essence of schizoid coping in order to consider what this patient needs to encounter in me. Is he best off if I am a veteran of my own personal battles with schizoid tendencies?

Or will the treatment thrive best if my character generally precludes schizoid behavior? Or, perhaps, is my patient lucky if he happens to encounter me at a time in my life when I am engaged in a profound schizoid struggle to survive? Or does all of this make no difference, assuming I am a competent analyst?

Schizoid tendencies have been variously described. Some (e.g., Impert, 1999) have focused on schizoid pleasure in self-reliance, while others have emphasized the patient's frightened retreat into an internal world of fantasy. Crowley (1980, personal communication) characterized schizoid existence as "living in the head." He described the patient as occasionally braving forays into the external world to collect impressions that will be used as "furniture" to fill the internal world. Guntrip (1969) contributed too many concepts to summarize, but emphasized the schizoid's belief that his love is dangerous, and the patient's struggle with inner deadness, empty depression, and the profound need to be taken care of.

My point of view is that schizoid strategies are available to us all, are employed at times by all of us, and are best thought of as "states" rather than traits. Some very early life experiences may predispose an individual to retreat more often to schizoid coping, but we all sometimes succumb to the Faustian bargain that if we would just want less, need less, feel less, depend less, connect less, invest less in the interpersonal world, we will be rewarded with relative peace and security. At times we all find ourselves hunkering down, trying not to care, in an effort to avoid hurt and disappointment. We mute our affective responses, as though resorting to emotional camouflage. We try to blend in or, as I would put it, "bland in." We hope only to get through (the session, the day, the week, our lives). We limit striving as though we will survive if we narrow the playing field enough. We limit direct engagement with others, but can feel deeply when the human drama is one step removed (e.g., in a movie theater).

I don't think anyone grows up immune to resorting to schizoid strategies. They seem to offer invincible, impregnable power to the powerless. And we have all been powerless. But for most of us, they are not our main line of defense. We have our schizoid moments, but much of the time we are too fully alive and engaged to fit the schizoid description very well. To me, the term is best used to describe a fleeting moment in a life, a phase in a treatment, or an emergency measure, resorted to in stressful times. No human being can be fully described as schizoid, but everyone has schizoid potential. Just as we all experience all of the fundamental emotions, such as anger, sadness, joy, and shame, so we each have moments of succumbing to schizoid retreat.

The analyst of a patient engaged in schizoid maneuvers is often profoundly lonely. In a paper on loneliness (Buechler, 1998) I commented on the challenge this can pose.

> The schizoid patient, perhaps rather like the unresponsive infant or caregiver, doesn't give his partner something to react to, and provides little feedback about how the therapist's interventions were received. The therapist may have images of trying to work in a vacuum, of sending messages in bottles into an expanse of sea, or of trying to play tennis when the ball doesn't come back. The loneliness with the schizoid may be particularly disorienting, since we use human responsiveness to know, literally and figuratively, where we are with each other. The absence of emotional response may make us wonder if there is any hope we can penetrate the patient's façade. Our own loneliness, under these conditions, would be tinged with whatever extreme separateness and isolation may mean to us. We each may have a different degree of need for human responsiveness. The analyst of the schizoid patient is bound to find out, more vividly than usual, just how much of that need he has. [pp. 99–100]

When a patient is engaging in schizoid defensiveness the analyst is often uncomfortable with his own needs. We may feel as if we are running after the patient. We may hunger to matter. We may find ourselves unusually willing to give advice and unusually uncomfortable with silences, as though they forebode the end of the relationship.

Because in schizoid moments the patient seems to have one foot out the door, how much should the analyst try to block the exits? Supervisees often ask whether to call patients after missed sessions, and, more generally, how much to focus on treatment-resistant behavior. We are equally afraid of putting too much or too little pressure on the patient to stay the course.

We could ask who the analyst has to be to facilitate growth in this treatment. Or we could reframe the issue of the therapeutic action, to ask how the analyst could help create a favorable balance of emotions in both participants. Freud (1926) wrote of signal levels of anxiety and Sullivan (1953, 1954) taught us to monitor shifts in the patient's anxiety, changing course when it becomes too intense. I think we can further extend these prescriptions. Analyst and patient *both* need adequate curiosity, hope, and joy in order to bear their burdens. They must not suffer too much shame, guilt, fear, anxiety, or depression. They must be able to bear some sadness, and allow themselves to be surprised (Stern, 1990). For each of these emotions there is probably an optimal range in treatment. Depending on the emotion, the range may or may not differ for the patient versus the analyst. Thus there is probably a range of anxiety that is tolerable for both participants. Too much would be disruptive to the process for either patient or analyst, but with too little anxiety, the sharp sense that something vital is at stake might be lost. With some emotions, such as curiosity and hope, it is easy to see how adequate levels are necessary for both participants to persevere. Whether there are optimal levels of love for patient and analyst, and whether these levels differ, would be an interesting, no doubt controversial question to pursue. When it comes to anger, shame, guilt, fear, and sadness we confront very difficult territory. Emotion theory(Izard, 1977) suggests that *all* the fundamental emotions play a crucial role in human experience. Must they not also have important functions, at bearable levels, in analysis? Don't *both* analyst and patient need access to their sadness about time, life wasted? Don't both need the motivating power all the fundamental emotions lend life?

At times when a patient is defending against affective intensity, how does the analyst promote the emotional climate that is essential to the work? Who must the analyst be to maximize the chance that the patient will become an emotionally alive participant in treatment and in other walks of life?

LIFE IN THE SCHIZOID LANE

Guntrip (1969) contributed many fundamental ideas to our understanding of schizoid functioning. And yet I believe this did not prevent his own schizoid potential from emerging in clinical work with schizoid patients. Even his advice to analysts invites us to go halfway:

> The patient does not do without personal relations, yet cannot do wholly with them, or cannot stand their being too close and involving. He takes up a halfway position in which he hopes to get by and remain relatively undisturbed. If the patient *can* survive in that way, it is not good to probe deeper, for it may mean asking him to face more than he can stand to go to the depths of his insecurity. [pp. 280–281]

Of course, there are times to halt probing, but here Guntrip is telling us to accept that the patient's relationships will be permanently limited, if we think the patient can survive that way! Isn't *Guntrip's* position in this similar to the *schizoid* emphasis on "getting through" life? Here are the words of one of Guntrip's patients:

> The height of my ambition now is to get through life without trouble. It's not that bad an aim, a bit negative; it has a certain vegetable feel about it, a kind of blankness. Under such circumstances you don't feel anything much at all. That's a preferable state to feeling awful. Big changes have gone on in me really. It's a tremendous relief not to feel so frightened, nor so excited in a bad way. Yet it feels also like losing something. [p. 281]

Every day, every hour we make difficult judgment calls. Maybe it was better, in the long run, to go along with this patient's compromise with life. I'm not suggesting this is always wrong. But I do believe that the patient's schizoidness can call out the analyst's schizoid potential, thus skewing the analyst's judgments.

In making these complicated judgment calls, several aspects of the analyst's personal progress in the schizoid arena seem especially relevant:

(1) The analyst's attitude about intense emotionality,
(2) The analyst's feelings about strong dependency needs,
(3) The analyst's willingness to expend effort,
(4) The courage to "upset the apple cart," that is, to say what the patient may not expect or want to hear,
(5) The analyst's firm belief that treatment is worthwhile.

FIERCE ANALYSIS

I am suggesting that the participants in an analysis both need access to a full array of emotions to do their work. While emotions *can* reach unbearable, unproductive levels, at lower intensities, and leavened by modulating emotions, they are essential ingredients in interpersonal life. For example, while there is an inevitable and, I would say, necessary loneliness for the patient in analysis, curiosity, hope, love, and joy should modulate the pain of it.

It should not be hard to see how my beliefs about the vital function of emotions in treatment complicate my approach to the patient in the initial vignette. This patient has spent a lifetime honing his ability to "not care." His cognitive and emotional equipment stand at the ready, prepared to ensure he doesn't focus much on what could hurt.

Perhaps it is time to call a moratorium on holding Freud responsible for our conflicts about expressing our emotions as analysts. It has been too easy to point to his prescriptions of neutrality and abstinence, and fail to confront the schizoid issues within ourselves that might make limited emotionality such an attractive professional requirement.

I would like to express more fully the invitation I felt from this patient:

(1) Don't get angry at my father on my behalf. Then I would feel *I* should be angry with him too.
(2) Don't notice, comment on, or have feelings about the inequalities in how I'm treated versus how my siblings are cared for.

(3) Don't raise questions that might worry me about how I'll provide the money.

(4) Let's talk about something else. Help me change the subject. Let's just get through this session without upset.

(5) Keep your tone matter-of-fact, with no sudden changes. No jolts. Nothing out of the ordinary should happen.

(6) Don't sound urgent, as though what I say to my father or what we say in the session really matters.

(7) Don't need anything from me, (e.g., to have an impact), just as I have learned not to need anything from my father.

How do I respond to this invitation? We could ask how I should have responded, how I should *not* have responded, or how I did respond. I'll start with how I did respond.

The strongest feeling I had was loneliness. I knew my patient wouldn't want to hear my full response and that I would be totally alone with it. The loneliness I felt was not merely the product of being alone with my thoughts (Fromm-Reichmann, 1959). I could have many thoughts in a session that, though impossible to share, would not make me lonely. I am reminded, again, of my earlier effort (Buechler, 1998) to understand the analyst's loneliness. Differentiating aloneness from loneliness I wrote, "loneliness with a patient, I suggest, stems from a sense of permanent, rather than temporary isolation. If the analyst feels cut off from the patient in some unalterable way, a deepening loneliness can develop" (p. 110). This is what I most keenly felt in the vignette. The patient won't *ever* want to hear my full response.

I think it is clear how the clinical material did recruit some schizoid potential in me, but not only that response. That is, it is *my* schizoid tendencies that turned aloneness into loneliness. By being unwilling to share experience with me the patient rendered me alone, but only I could render myself lonely.

Fortunately, I was also angry. How dare this patient's father be so unconcerned for his son! How dare this patient expect me to quietly go along, like a good little girl!

My point is that I probably had to be somewhat susceptible to schizoid responses, so that the treatment situation would adequately resemble the patient's position with his father. But I couldn't be too prone to schizoid defensiveness. Then I wouldn't have recognized that what happens with this father, and in this treatment, very much matters. I wouldn't have felt keenly hungry for the contact I wasn't getting. I wouldn't have been able to ask "why are you willing to do this?" in a tone that was probably closer to "why on earth are you willing to do this?"

In brief, I believe I had to be sufficiently but not prevailingly schizoid to help this patient. Like all the fundamental emotions (joy, curiosity, anger, sadness, shame, guilt, fear, surprise), the essential defensive strategies for coping with being human are in us all. I feel the patient needs to meet, in his analyst, someone who can be temporarily, partially induced to cope similarly. I am more risk-aversive when patients are paranoid, more prone to get into power struggles with obsessional patients. Hearing of a patient's sad dilemma should profoundly touch me, but not catapult me into an endless, despairing depression. I bring all my human experience to work with me. I have known every emotion and used every coping device at some point. My patient needs me to be willing and able to call on this backlog of experience without losing touch with *other* aspects of the current situation that are *also* true. He was inviting me to share his nonchalant attitude, in a cut-off, schizoid style. But, then, didn't he also make a different statement, just by telling me about the incident with his father? Isn't it just as important that I notice his more subtle expressions of dependency (on me and on his father) *as well as* his counterdependency?

If I were more schizoid, I believe I could have been too willing to say and do nothing, convincing myself I was neutrally letting the material unfold. I might have wanted to get through the session uneventfully. I might have refused to take the position that *my* response *does* matter, even when it's not wanted. I might have protected myself from feeling hurt by the patient's indifference to me (as he protected himself from his father's indifference) by "not caring" about any of this. I might have muted my anger, swallowed my loneliness, and allowed the patient to change the subject. I might have exerted as little effort as possible, explaining my schizoid detachment with theoretical rationalizations.

But if I were less schizoid, I don't think I would have felt the profound, cut-off loneliness that was such an informative signal. I couldn't have followed this patient as far as I did into his bleak isolation.

I would especially like to emphasize the issue of the analyst's effortfulness. Schizoid functioning, at its essence, is heavy-limbed. It expends just enough effort to lumber through. It conserves, like the energy-saving setting on an appliance. Just enough spark is created to get the job done.

I believe it is largely through our effortfulness that the analyst comments on the schizoid dilemma. By obviously working hard we clearly say that expending effort is worthwhile. By bothering to try hard to understand and respond we make a statement about the meaningfulness of human communication. By searching for just the right word to describe an experience we vote that the right word matters and, more broadly, that clarity matters, truth matters, treatment matters, the quality of a life matters. Our effortfulness is a personal statement about our values. It is conveyed in a variety of subtle and less subtle forms. How many times do we go over an incident to make sure we understand it? How often do we coast through a session, making only the obvious connections? How hard do we look for all the possible meanings of what we are hearing? How actively do we search our countertransferential responses for useful information? How avid is the interest expressed in our tone of voice? How much do we seem to try to remember the last session, the patient's history, current life situation, significant relationships, dreams?

Some analysts may not believe it is optimal to attempt all this. I am not trying to comprehensively outline the analytic task, but only to suggest that how we approach that task, however we define it, reveals our own attitudes about effort. Some analysts may believe they should listen more than they talk and follow more than they interpret. But they can still listen *hard* and try their *utmost* to follow. However one defines the analytic task, it can be approached with varying degrees of verve.

So much depends on the analyst's beliefs about the agent of change. In "Dead Mother, Dead Child," Bollas (1999) describes his treatment of Antonio, a man whose recollection of his traumatic early losses took the form of reliving them, over and over again, in his work life, in his love life, and in the analysis.

In one early session, the patient echoed the analyst's every word. Bollas remained silent for most of that hour, and said little for the next week. His only interpretation at the time was that the patient was trying to dislodge him from his analytic position, to mock it and to mock the analyst.

Much later, Bollas sees himself as clarifying the meaning of the patient's enactments because he can occupy a position

> outside the scene, outside the transference, outside the analysis and it was from there that I could speak to him and see his recognition of a need to speak to the other on that border. In the oddest of possible ways, by speaking from the outside, I gradually put Antonio back into life itself, a necessity forced upon me from communiqués transmitted from the strange country we call transference and countertransference. [p. 126]

Several of the analyst's assumptions seem to me to be crucial:

(1) The repetitive enactments are necessary to the work.
(2) Bollas's countertransference provides information about the *patient's* emotional truths.
(3) The analyst's "outsider" position allows him the perspective needed in order to clarify the genetic roots of the repetitions.

What would have happened if Bollas came to this treatment with a different set of assumptions about the process of change? Perhaps the eight-year interchange could have been briefer if Bollas believed that

(1) This patient was clearly inviting his analyst to repeat a dance of death, but how the analyst responds to the invitation depends, partially, on the characterological potentials *in the analyst*.

227

(2) The patient was not just repeating his trauma. He was also responding to Bollas's initial silence, initial sense of being mocked, and vision of himself as "speaking from the outside."

(3) Not all the repetitions were necessary, or helpful. Some may have been iatrogenic.

(4) Bollas's initial silence and "outsider" stance mirrored the patient's schizoid detachment. Instead of mirroring the detachment he could have contrasted with it. Active contrast would still have pointed out the patient's detachment, but not fed into it.

A patient invites us to join him in lifelessness. If we believe the treatment process requires us to be like litmus paper, absorbing and reflecting the patient's trauma, this belief profoundly affects the interchange. I don't know what would have happened, in this case, if the analyst had actively fought to stay visibly alive, every step of the way. Would crucial repetitions, necessary to the work, not have occurred? Or would change have been accelerated?

I will mention and briefly comment on a few possible objections to this way of thinking.

(1) It raises the spectre of the corrective emotional experience.

(2) It prescribes what can't be prescribed. The analyst can't tailor himself to suit the patient's character issues, even if that would be helpful.

(3) It deemphasizes the role of technique. The adequately trained analyst should be able to address the patient's schizoid (or other) proclivities through the competent application of the analytic method.

(4) It elevates some countertransferential responses over others, as though they were superior, when they are really just different.

To me, these objections hinge on the nature of the therapeutic action. What do we really "provide"? How much should we be "old" versus "new" objects? That is, how easy should it be for the patient to experience us transferentially (Greenberg, 1991)?

As people, more simply human than otherwise (Sullivan, 1953), analysts can not, and should not, try to enact any particular type of role, even if such an experience would be "corrective" for the patient. I don't believe I should play the role of the warm mother, even if my patient needed and still needs one. In that sense, the "corrective emotional experience" has a built-in inauthenticity. In my opinion it is this inauthenticity that is the main problem with many very popular analytic techniques. I can't, for example, decide to be "empathic," just because I believe certain patients need empathy. In the vignette presented here, it would be no more authentic for me to play the role of the nonschizoid than it would be to play the warm mother or the empathic listener. Analysis, to have meaning and impact, has to be an alive response to a real, unpredictable interchange.

But I feel that when I am in the presence of a detached, deadened schizoid patient I can actively search for the fighter in me. I can ask myself where she is today. I can remember her previous battles and their outcomes. I can think about those who have fought for life in my presence and, sometimes, on my behalf. I can recall moments, including some with my own supervisors and analysts, that have communicated their spirited intensity and determination to live every moment, in treatment as elsewhere, to its fullest.

REFERENCES

Bollas, C. (1999). Dead mother, dead child. In: *The Mystery of Things*. London: Routledge, pp. 106–127.

Bromberg, P. M. (1979). The schizoid personality: The psychopathology of stability. In: *Integrating Ego Psychology and Object Relations Theory*, ed. L. Saretsky, G.D. Goldman & D. S. Milman. Dubuque, I A: Kendall Hunt, pp. 226–243.

Buechler, S. (1993). Clinical applications of an interpersonal view of the emotions. *Contemporary Psychoanalysis* 29:219–236.

——— (1998). The analyst's experience of loneliness. *Contemporary Psychoanalysis* 34:91–111. www.pep-web.org/document.php?id'cps.034.0091a

———& Izard, C.E. (1983). On the emergence, functions, and regulation of some emotion expressions in infancy. In: *Emotions: Theory, Research, and Experience*, Vol. 2, ed. R. Plutchik & H. Kellerman. New York: Academic Press, pp. 293–313.

Freud, S. (1912). Recommendations to physicians practicing psycho-analysis. *Standard Edition*, 12:109–120. www.pep-web.org/document.php ?id'se.012.0109a

——— (1926). Inhibitions symptoms and anxiety. *Standard Edition*, 20:75–175. http://www.pep-web.org/document.php?id'se.020.0075a

Fromm, E. (2009). Being centrally related to the patient. In: *The Clinical Erich Fromm*, ed. Rainer Funk. Amsterdam: Rodopi, pp. 7–39.

Fromm-Reichmann, F. (1959). Loneliness. *Psychiatry*, 22:1–15. *Contemporary Psychoanalysis* 26:305–330, 1990. http://www.pep-web.org/document.php ?id'ijp.040.0001a

Greenberg, J. (1991). *Oedipus and Beyond: A Clinical Theory.* Cambridge, MA: Harvard University Press.

Guntrip, H. (1969). *Schizoid Phenomena, Object Relations and the Self.* New York: International Universities Press.

Impert, L. (1999). The body held hostage: The paradox of self-sufficiency. *Contemporary Psychoanalysis* 35:647–673. http://www.pep-web.org /document.php?id'cps.035.0647a

Izard, C.E. (1977). *Human Emotions.* New York: Plenum Press.

Lambert, M. J., ed. (1983). *Psychotherapy and Patient Relationships.* Homewood, IL: Dorsey Press.

Mitchell, S.A. (1997). *Influence and Autonomy in Psychoanalysis.* Hillsdale, NY: The Analytic Press.

Stern, D.B. (1990). Courting surprise. *Contemporary Psychoanalysis* 26:426–478. http://www.pep-web.org/document.php?id'cps.026.0452a

Sullivan, H.S. (1953). *The Interpersonal Theory of Psychiatry.* New York: W.W. Norton.

——— (1954). *The Psychiatric Interview.* New York: W.W. Norton.

Wolstein, B. (1983). The pluralism of perspectives on countertransference. *Contemporary Psychoanalysis* 19:506–521. http://www.pep-web.org/document.php?id'cps.019.0506a

* I am especially indebted to Dr. Mark Blechner for his helpful suggestions and encouragement.

CHAPTER EIGHT

The Analyst's Search for Atonement[*]

INTRODUCTION

The analyst's work furnishes ample opportunities to regret acts of commission and omission. In this paper I suggest that those that seem like consequences of our personal character are likely to evoke more intense painful feelings. For the analyst, atonement can be understood as a movement toward finding adequate expression for what we have learned.

This topic inspired some personal reminiscences of times I felt I did, and times I felt I did not, need to atone. I also take a position against overly harsh assessments of our analytic misdeeds. While it is important to hold ourselves accountable, it is also true that excessive guilt may make it harder to have the strength to atone.

I have often reviewed the events that occurred, many years ago, when a patient on my ward committed suicide. Could I have predicted/prevented it? In this paper I reflect that "...as I draw on what happened with the patient who committed suicide I modulate its meaning. Interpersonally, it becomes a vehicle for making future connections, though it also remains a deeply regretted experience. Intrapersonally it

---

* *Psychoanalytic Inquiry*, 2009, 29:5, 426–437. *Dr. Melvin R. Lansky thoughtfully contributed to this paper's development.

will be a resource as well as a guilt-inducing memory." The idea that we can atone through constructive uses of an experience has led me to think about the many ways we can change the impact of the past, to some degree.

THE ANALYST'S SEARCH FOR ATONEMENT

ABSTRACT:

Since an analytic hour presents infinite choices, it also provides infinite possibilities for retrospective regret. The analyst's work furnishes opportunities to regret acts of commission and omission. Missteps that seem like consequences of our personal character issues are likely to evoke shame and/or guilt, which can further complicate our feelings of regret. But genuine compassion and curiosity about ourselves can facilitate finding ways to atone. Atonement can be understood as a movement toward integration of all parts of oneself, or, more globally, a movement toward the inclusion of all human beings into the human community. For the analyst, atonement can mean becoming "at one" by finding a positive expression for what we have learned from our regrets. The challenge atonement poses is to face our shortcomings, yet retain self-respect and self love.

INTRODUCTION

I must have been about seven when, on a Yom Kippur, I emerged from reading a prayer with one of my persistent questions. The prayer asked for forgiveness for "coveting thy neighbor's wife." I felt outraged that I had to ask for forgiveness for this sin. Having dutifully looked up the word "covet" in our unwieldy dictionary, although I had not fully understood what I read, I was certain that I could not be guilty of this charge. Why did I have to atone for this, when I knew, for sure, that I did not even like my neighbor's wife?

I am amused, but also touched, by my child-self's search to understand. Although much about me has changed, I still have a strong wish to limit my atonement to forgiveness for misbehavior I have actually committed. A generalized *mea culpa* for any possible wrongdoing still strikes me as meaningless.

Accordingly, I often have a negative reaction to what I hear as a tendency toward excessive self-castigation in psychoanalysts today. I will provide examples of this shortly. In addition, I find a curious difference between how we are sometimes directed to deal with our own "sins" as analysts versus how we are told to deal with patients' wrongdoings. Sometimes I see an implicit grandiosity when an analyst holds himself or herself to extremely high standards. I will illustrate this, too, in the following sections. But here I would like to explore how we can have a compassion and curiosity toward ourselves that (hopefully) resembles our attitude toward our patients.

For example, how should I have responded when I forgot a makeup session with a patient? Would it have been sufficient to apologize and offer to make up the time? I don't think so. It would have said that I am responsible, proper, and willing to pay for my behavior. But as an analyst, I believe I should focus on the meaning of my behavior, and not just its occurrence. Wondering why I forgot is as essential as apologizing. Being genuinely curious is as important as showing sufficient contrition. In using the moment as an opportunity, I transform it (to some degree). Elsewhere (Buechler, 2004) I have discussed the values analytic work ideally manifests. Here I explore how our atonement can express some of these values. Briefly, I am suggesting that our response to our own "misdeeds" can be consonant with the spirit of analytic inquiry by opening up dialogue, privileging personal and interpersonal reflection, and re-contextualizing and thereby transforming the meaning of human experience.

I am reminded of a story, quoted in Estelle Frankel's book, *Sacred Therapy* (2003, p. 153):

A young man once came to Rabbi Yisrael of Rizhin seeking counsel as to how he might break or overcome his 'evil inclination' (sexual impulse or desire). The rabbi's eyes laughed as he looked compassionately at the young man and replied, "You want to break your impulses? You can break your back or hip, but you will never break an impulse no matter how hard you try. However if you pray and study and serve God with love and sincerity, the evil *in* your impulses will vanish of itself. In its place will remain a passion that is pure and holy. With this passion you will be able to serve God in truth.

As analysts, our task is to find ways to use our whole selves in the service of the work we do. An overly self-punitive stance could damage precious vitality. I can fantasize going back in time to tell the child that I was that, while she was correct in that she had never literally "coveted" the woman next door, she did have a great deal to learn about her own motivations, and how she could use them to develop herself as a clinical instrument. But I truly hope that as I delivered that message my eyes would laugh like the rabbi's.

ANALYSTS' CONFESSIONS

There is a rapidly proliferating analytic literature about our failures, enactments, crimes, misdemeanors, and delinquencies (see, for example, McLaughlin, 1995;Gabbard and Lester, 1996; Maroda, 1998). It is interesting to speculate as to why these accounts seem so prevalent now. Presumably analysts have always committed blameworthy acts. Are we confessing them more often, or are these accounts making it into print more readily? Does this reflect a more widespread societal shift? Certainly public confessions and personal revelations have become a mainstay in this information age. The boundary between private and public has eroded considerably, as autobiographical details are shared in public on cell phones, blogs, reality television, and more thoughtful, but no less personal, revelations at psychoanalytic conferences. Are analysts responding to a widespread change in the zeitgeist? Or are increases in our propensity for confession related to changes particular to the psychoanalytic climate? Are we, for example, trying to change an outdated impression of analysts as Olympian, anonymous, faceless authorities?

In any case, one example of the current trend is a paper by Joyce

Slochower, "The Analyst's Secret Delinquencies." This paper was distributed for an online IARPP discussion in November 2005. Since I was a participant, I carefully followed the unfolding commentary, from interested professionals literally all over the globe. Two other papers were offered for discussion, as well. Slochower's paper was presented as part of a larger work in progress.

One of the important contributions this paper makes is its effort to distinguish between delinquencies or misdemeanors versus enactments. It goes further, attempting to delineate the boundary between these less serious breaches and more serious "crimes." I quote from some of the passages that provide definitions of these behaviors on the part of the analyst.

> I use the term misdemeanors to refer to relatively minor breaches wherein we momentarily, but with apparently conscious intent, deliberately disengage from the treatment process to satisfy a personal need [p. 153].

> In minor and more egregious ways, we exploit an opportunity to secretively withdraw affectively or cognitively from our patients. In doing so, we violate implicit professional norms but keep that violation to ourselves [p. 154].

> It is not always easy to delineate the boundary between enactments, misdemeanors, and more serious analytic crimes. These categories are more often overlapping than entirely distinct; what constitutes a misdemeanor to us may feel like a crime to our patient or colleague, or vice versa [p. 158].

> Enactments that emerge in the emotional or erotic heat of an analytic encounter involve breaches of the therapeutic frame that are briefly, rather than permanently, destabilizing [p. 159].

> An analyst who commits a serious 'crime' exploits the patient's emotional vulnerability thereby transforming the patient from subject to object [p. 161].

Finally, in an effort to describe the entire range of analytic misbehaviors, Slochower (p. 161) suggested that they exist on a continuum.

I locate misdemeanors along a continuum marked by major boundary violations at one pole and enactments on the other. In contrast to the spontaneous affective 'eruption' that typically characterizes analytic enactments, it is my impression that most misdemeanors are deliberately committed and contain less affective charge; the analyst is not engaged in reverie (Ogden, 1994, 1997) but in purposeful inattention…misdemeanors involve the analyst's attentional and affective *withdrawal* from the arena of the patient's need.

Although it is unquestionably important to examine these issues, and the effort to differentiate various kinds of analytic behaviors is useful and evocative, I worry about the impact of the legalistic language. Must we call some shifts in the analyst's attention a *misdemeanor*? What do we gain from this?

I think it is important to decipher the moral code embedded in this continuum. I am reminded of Dante's rings of hell, in that an effort is made to distinguish more from less blameworthy intentions and fit the severity of the punishment to the crime. This continuum presumes a list of commandments for the analyst. These *dos* and *don'ts* seem to me to define the analytic role in terms not unlike the old-fashioned ideal of the self-sacrificing mother.

1. We are expected to want to keep our attention and affective focus fixed on the patient, and to succeed in so doing.
2. We are also, of course, expected to keep track of our own feelings, but keep them in check.
3. The more the analyst intends to interrupt focusing on the patient and the more long-standing the interruption, the more serious the breach.
4. An action that does not result from intense passion is more egregious.

I feel myself returning to the rabbi's words that "you will never break an impulse no matter how hard you try." I wonder whether setting such stringent standards for our processes of attention might create an obsessive battle for the analyst. By an obsessive battle, I mean an ongoing conflict between urges versus internalized standards. I think these standards might put us in an inevitably guilt-inducing bind. Failing to live up to being who we think we should be might contribute to our rate of burnout. Or, possibly, we might be too easily convinced that our patients are untreatable, thus taking out our feelings of frustration and failure on them. Having set standards we can't meet, we might be prey to pessimism about our "impossible profession." We might be tempted to embrace the wider culture's tendencies toward quick, pharmaceutical, cognitive, or behavioral fixes.

Personally, I am not comforted by the end of the story Slochower tells (p. 168) about Dr. M, a supervisee who confessed that she had looked at a magazine during a patient's phone session.

> Facing these facts for the first time, Dr. M expressed intense guilt, shame, and anxiety about what she identified as a failure of professionalism and an abandonment of her patients. As we attempted to leave judgment aside and explore the dynamics underlying her delinquencies, Dr. M became conscious of a heretofore disowned, chronic sense of depletion and strain that pervaded her working life. The need to support her family had led her to take on a maximum number of patient hours and then attempt to counterbalance that strain in little ways. ... Ultimately, she decided to guard against the danger of taking advantage of her patients by increased vigilance to her own tendency to sneak what she needed [p. 168].

I don't think it allows us to "leave judgment aside" when we continue to call the behavior *delinquencies*. Given that she already feels intense guilt, shame, and anxiety, what might help Dr. M? I go back to Frankel (2003, p. 182).

> At first God thought to create the world through the quality of judgment (*din*), but realizing that the world could not endure at

this level, God added on the quality of compassion (*rachamim*).
Midrash Bereishit Raba 12:15.

I don't know exactly what form compassion for Dr. M might take, but
I would like to propose a few components I think it should include.

1. The best resolution of this situation doesn't rely on Dr. M's
    "increased vigilance." Again, this strikes me as likely to lead
    to an obsessive effort toward a self control that inevitably
    will be marked by ambivalence and conflict.
2. What is best for Dr. M ultimately coincides with what is best
    for her patients. They are all much better off if she can be
    genuinely curious about them, and involved in her work.
    Thus, in my view, there is no real conflict of interest here.
    Dr. M is not serving herself at her patient's expense. She is
    serving no one, because she is burned out.
3. We all, sometimes, mistakenly reach for the television re-
    mote when we are tired, looking for respite in something
    mindless. I don't think it generally works. What would really
    refresh us is involvement in something interesting.
4. I imagine I might want to tell Dr. M about times I have
    done, or felt pulled to do, similar things with my own pa-
    tients.
5. Given the painful feelings Dr. M has expressed to her super-
    visor, perhaps she could be helped to find ways of atoning,
    or better integrating what happened (these concepts are
    elaborated below).

ATONEMENT

In response to this emphasis on our analytic *crimes*, a clear conception
of atonement might come in especially handy for analysts today. The
concept of atonement has been understood (Bokser, 1978) as, literally,
being "at one," that is, integrating oneself internally, as well as joining
others to form a community of selves.

Yom Kippur, or the Day of Atonement, prescribes rites that symbolize the oneness of the Jewish people. For example, as Frankel (2003) described, on that holiest of days the high priests perform an incense offering, which is called the *ketoret*. The ketoret is made of eleven different spices, one of which is, by itself, foul smelling. Its inclusion symbolizes unity and the interconnectedness of all of us. We must welcome the vulnerable, as well as our own, personal weaknesses, so that we don't fragment ourselves as a people, or our own, inner selves. What we reject or deny becomes an adversarial force, which will take away from our strength. Frankel conclude that, "Despite whatever has been broken or shattered through our own mistakes or fate itself, Yom Kippur, the day of at-one-ment, gives us a chance to heal and be whole once more" (p. 163). Thus, according to this way of thinking, personal atonement is integration of the "foul" in ourselves, and interpersonal atonement is inclusion of the weakest members into the human community.

A PATIENT'S SUICIDE

An experience of my own, early in my career as a clinician, acquainted me with how intensely I could feel the need to atone. I was young to be a non-medical team leader in the increasingly politically correct state hospital system. Until that day, I had been proud of moving up the ladder so quickly, to become the first state psychologist in charge of a team of psychiatrists, nurses, social workers, and psychiatric aides. My job included running ward meetings, working with the team to create treatment plans for new patients, deciding together which patients could go on leave, or be discharged.

My first task one morning was to interview James, a newly admitted patient, and then run a team meeting, where we would discuss how to work with him. I remember little of the interview, except that James seemed unresponsive, head down as though fascinated with the floor. Nothing I asked, nothing I could think of, seemed to interest him enough to engage him in the interview. Did I give up too easily?

The team meeting was held in my office, a huge, dingy square room whose only advantage was that it had a door that closed. This gave us all temporary relief from the day room, where televisions blasted and patients kept up a steady stream of invective, punctuated by sudden, threatening, unpredictable outbursts. To do my job at all took a well-practiced blindness to the revolting smells and heart-rending sobs.

The meeting was going smoothly until a wild-eyed aide called me out, telling me they had found James in the men's bathroom, having succeeded in hanging himself from the overhead light fixture. He was dead.

I remember being numb and grateful that there was so much to do. How will I know what I must not leave out? I called the police first, thinking they would tell me. Then I followed the aides who were going into the bathroom to cut James down. They tried to get me to leave, but I would not, although what they had to do was physically beyond my strength.

Before I called the family I thought about how to tell them. Best to blurt it out right away? James is dead. Sorry. Maybe it would be better to tell them more slowly, easing them into understanding. Something bad has happened to James.

What I remember is doing one thing after another, focusing on the details; the reports to be made out, the paperwork of death. At the end of my shift I drove off the hospital grounds. I parked without any conscious plan of what to do next. I walked all night, passing through towns, apparently intent on keeping moving. In the many hours before morning, before going back to the parking lot and my work, I asked myself what I had missed in the interview with James. There must have been clues to his desperate state of mind. A more experienced clinician would have picked them up, and could have prevented the tragedy, somehow. Perhaps I could have persuaded James to hope, or, at least, put him on surveillance. I shouldn't have this job. I wasn't ready. What did I know? Why hadn't I taken more time, instead of giving up on reaching him? Was it because it was time for me to run the team meeting? It was time to discuss his care, so there was no more time for me to talk to him? Reviewing these snapshots of myself, on a day many years ago, I recognize regret mingled with sadness and guilt. My regret was for danger I had not recognized. My sadness was for life spilt. My guilt was for the selfishness of taking a job because I needed it, not because I really felt qualified. I think guilt and regret mingled in my sense of myself hurrying to tick off the day's tasks, so that missing signs of James's desperation reflected, for me, a truth about my character. I was always too much in a hurry. I accepted James's unresponsiveness too easily, because it shortened an interview that was keeping me from conducting the next meeting on time. My impatience showed itself in the hour with James and, more generally, in how I have conducted my career. Moving up, moving on, that's me. But, I might still ask, at what price and who, besides myself, has paid for it?

REFLECTING ON EARLY FAILURES

Others have reflected on what they failed to notice and, more generally, on how their character issues affected their work early in their careers as clinicians. Irwin Hirsch has provided a particularly candid example. Speaking on September 20, 2005 at the W. A. White Institute, New York, Hirsch recounted his analytic work with B, a patient he had treated 25 years earlier. Briefly, the patient and analyst created a comfortable stasis, a kind of holding pattern that had benefits for each of them, but failed to take full advantage of treatment's potential for promoting change. B left analysis after eight years, having gained in some areas, but remaining limited in his interpersonal, intimate life.

As I heard and later read this essay, I thought about whether analysts regret their acts of omission any differently from their acts of commission. I believe analysts pay more public attention to our regrettable acts of commission, in which we do something irresponsible or inappropriate to our role. Here, I would like to consider our regret for opportunities we missed, such as those discussed by Hirsch, and my own self-questioning in the case of the patient who committed suicide. In Hirsch's (2005) presentation (p. 8), the "road not taken" included a more direct confrontation with the mutually comfortable "deal" that allowed patient and analyst to avoid truly engaging each other. Hirsch eloquently described the terms of this unspoken arrangement.

The two of us created equilibrium—I was well paid and adored, and he came at the times most convenient to me. He let me take respite from my demanding life and to sink into a self-absorption that was familiar to me. I never considered myself a particularly exploitative person, but I knew that I was engaging B at about 50% of my capacity. I rationalized that this was all he could integrate, but I knew otherwise—I was not pushing myself to be sufficiently present for him [Hirsch, 2005, p. 8].

Later, Hirsch summed up how two people can opt for convenience over challenge, "Our manifest tepid connection seemed just the right temperature for the two of us" (p. 8). Listening to Hirsch's self-reflections, I felt moved by the struggle of an analyst with integrity. Such acts of omission seem so inevitable to me, and yet, for analysts, they can be so deeply regretted. There are always many roads not taken in analysis. Every moment of every session, we focus selectively, choosing to respond to a part of the material, remaining silent, or even unaware of other aspects. Being human beings with human limitations, we lack the energy for some encounters, are too confused, or lack the courage for others. It can't be otherwise. And yet, the quality of human lives is at stake. If we feel we missed significant opportunities to nurture a richer life in someone we care about, the need to atone seems to me inevitable.

But how we think about this makes a difference, because it affects the array of emotions we will feel. Do we attend to the information about the patient that our failure feelings may reflect, as well as the information about ourselves? Do we approach the clinical situation with shame about the inadequacies it reveals? Do we see our acts of omission as defining us? Do we feel that mourning and atonement are possible? What resources can modulate our regret, making it bearable enough to preserve its presence in our awareness as a useful reminder?

I would like to express how strongly I feel that we must temper our zeal for uncovering analytic sins with compassion for ourselves and our colleagues. Although it is crucial that we face all the negative aspects of our impact, and all the ways we fail our patients, I think it is equally important that we use insight to promote our own health, as we (hopefully) would do with our patients. Insight can be used destructively, demolishing self-esteem without extending help toward rebuilding it. We can, I believe, get lost in a frenzy of reproach and/or self-reproach. Like Savonarola setting fire to Renaissance masterpieces because they were not sufficiently "pious," we can get carried away with an intense need for purification. We live in self-righteous times, which, I feel, can make it especially easy to succumb to extremism. Whether or not the condemned is ourselves, we owe her compassion.

I must stress that I do not mean these comments to be taken prescriptively. I am not suggesting that we can order ourselves to feel less shame with our regret, or more curiosity, or any other felicitous emotion. Nor can we manufacture meaningful chances to atone for what we feel are our failures. But I do believe we can be mindful of the human need to atone, and ready for every opportunity.

PATTERNS OF FEELINGS IN THE ANALYST

For all human beings, the emotions that accompany a feeling can drastically alter its impact (Izard, 1977). I would suggest that compassion toward ourselves requires us to pay particular attention to these patterns when we feel we have failed, since some of these combinations can be especially paralyzing. I believe that one such configuration is shame, or a sense of insufficiency/inadequacy, and regret, understood as sorrow and guilt about a clinical outcome that could have been better. I believe that when we are ashamed, as well as regretful, the strength we need to face our regrets may be sapped. Instead of being able to rise to the occasion of courageous self-confrontation, we feel shame's need to hide ourselves. It is impossible to simultaneously satisfy the essential tasks set by shame and regret. We may not be able to fully confront what we also deeply need to cover up.

From this point of view, interpersonal/relational psychoanalysis has done our field a great favor. At least for many of us, I think it has changed the balance of the analyst's feelings about having intense countertransferential feelings. Shame about countertransference, the need to cover it up, and the sense of inadequacy for intense emotionality have been altered by placing a premium on the analyst's ability to disclose affect to colleagues and, at least at times, to the patient. Today, because I am less ashamed of having profound regrets about some of my work with patients, I am not as paralyzed by them. I am sure this is partially a product of my greater experience in the field, but, I think theoretical shifts have also had an impact on me.

Returning to Hirsch's self-reflections, I ask what fosters his ability to publicly express his regrets about how his character issues limited his earlier treatment effectiveness. My belief is that one factor is an analytic climate that fosters unashamed disclosure of countertransference affect. Without shame about feeling and revealing regret, we can, at least, more fully have our regrets. Hopefully, this allows us more opportunity for atonement, in Frankel's (2003) sense (as discussed above). That is, if we are less ashamed of our feelings, whether they are regret, anger, enjoyment, anxiety, or other emotions, we may be able to integrate them within ourselves, and use awareness of them interpersonally. I return to Frankel's description of the Yom Kippur rite, which, for me, takes on new meaning in this context. Just as the spices of the ketoret are foul in isolation but not in combination, the analyst's emotions can be more problematic when intrapersonally and interpersonally unintegrated. I find Frankel's description of this rite remarkably apt, as I work on integrating my regret about my patient's suicide.

> In order for us to come into our wholeness, all parts of the self must be held together as one. And when we join together as a collective, something greater constellates than the simple sum of individuals. Joined together, we atone for one another, for what one of us may lack another makes up for, and one person's weakness may evoke another's strength. In community, then, we find our wholeness and healing [Frankel, 2003, p. 162].

Thus, if I am not too ashamed about my guilty, regretful and other feelings about James's suicide I can, for example, integrate them with my love for teaching. I can find new uses for them in our analytic community, as well as in my personal development. Intrapersonally and interpersonally, my regret changes as it is transformed by its new uses. If my regret teaches me, and teaches others, I may find greater at-one-ment. A shorthand way of expressing this might be that love (of teaching) potentially transforms my regret, making it more bearable. But, on the other hand, too much shame could preclude my experiencing this intrapersonal and interpersonal healing. I believe that only by thinking about regret as part of a system of emotions, affected by the other feelings it joins, and affected by the interpersonal context, can we approach its complexity, and its potential transformation.

In sum, I am suggesting that, as analysts, we are no different from other human beings in our need to be able to atone. I am highlighting two components of atonement in the clinical situation.

1. We must attend to patterns of emotions we feel, not just single emotions, as we often do in papers on transference and countertransference. For example, because I feel that how I conducted the session just before my patient's suicide meaningfully reflects important aspects of my character, I am more than just regretful about the outcome. I am ashamed and guilty and regretful. I think it is very important to recognize this.

2. Compassion for myself means, to me, that I strive to atone by integrating what I regret with other, more positive aspects of my self. For example, if I use what I have (painfully) learned to enhance the teaching I love, I am integrating the *foul* in me, both intrapsychically and interpersonally.

NEEDS FOR ATONEMENT IN ANALYTIC SUPERVISORS

There has been relatively little written about any of the supervisor's emotional reactions in supervision. Whether we wish to call this *supervisory countertransference*, or a supervisor's transference to the supervisee, there can be no doubt that supervisors have emotional reactions to supervisees, as well as responses to the patients being presented. Of course, they reflect aspects of the supervisor's character style, as well as reflecting on the supervisee and the treatment they are discussing.

I am sure that I am not alone in sometimes feeling regret, among my other emotional experiences as a supervisor. I can look back on work I have done and wish I could atone for its limitations. Although there are supervisory acts of commission for me to regret, I believe, at least for myself, that in supervision, regrettable acts of omission have been more frequent. Supervision can present even more temptations to "coast" than treatment does. I think it is all too easy to slide into shortchanging supervisees, in one way or another. What may start out as a positive, collegial atmosphere can easily become a subtle collusion to avoid anything potentially uncomfortable. This slippery slope is especially tempting for me when a supervisory hour comes in the middle of a long day of back-to-back sessions with patients. Seeing a supervisee in the waiting room, it is sometimes hard to stay as focused as I would with a demanding or worrisome and highly disturbed patient. There are so many convenient rationalizations available to the supervisor. Useful discussion of theory can slide into something like gossip about its originators. An hour that begins with genuinely helpful career advice can morph into an unfocused social chat.

What makes this regrettable is not so much the content, but the feeling (for both people) of getting through the hour and avoiding something more challenging. It is rather like the experience we have probably all had, of escaping into the television or computer, wishing time away, rather than fully living it. Ultimately it feels empty. We emerge as though from a time warp, perhaps a bit disoriented, certainly unfulfilled.

Many have written of the strains of an analytic life (for example, Cooper, 1986). Some may blame the current managed care culture, and its consequences for the analyst; others look within the process to understand why it can be so draining (Buechler, 1992; Coltart, 1996). Elsewhere (Buechler, 2000, 2004), I have suggested that the unmourned losses of patients that accumulate over a career can be a factor. I have also explored (Buechler, 1998) the particular kind of loneliness we may suffer, doing this work. Although never alone in sessions, we may nevertheless be peculiarly lonely, although often (consciously) unaware of it.

The strain of focusing intently, the bearing of feelings intuited, the paradoxes built into the role, vicarious traumatizations (Pearlman & Saakvitne, 1995) and, I am sure, many other factors contribute to our depletion. Of course, that is only one side of the experience of being an analyst. There are also significant pleasures and fulfillments (Maroda, 2005) and potential stimulants of curiosity (Buechler, 2004).

Perhaps all of this can help us have compassion, as well as ashamed regret, for the supervisory hours we attempt to slide through. Seeing a supervisee can seem like just the thing to assuage the loneliness. Here is someone who may understand, who won't demand the impossible, who is "one of us." But giving less than 100% of my attention cheats a super-visee just as much as it would a patient. It should elicit my regret. But that regret should, I believe, point me toward atonement. Regret can be among our most potent teachers, focusing us on what can be lost when we merely glide, and what can be salvaged when we turn away from opportunities to coast, and face each other.

THE INTERNAL CHORUS

Elsewhere (Buechler, 1997, 1998, 1999, 2004), I have developed the concept of the clinician's *internal chorus*. This is my phrase for the internalizations of aspects of teachers, supervisors, colleagues, and, often, most especially, our own analysts. I think of analytic training as, fundamentally, a process of identity formation/acculturation. We each enter this process with personal legacies from previous experiences of trying to forge a sense of self.

With our personal history as a backdrop (and template), we form an identity as a member of the analytic community. As is true in any such process, certain individuals make more of an impression than others. I think of these influential figures as, collectively, an internal chorus that is constantly auditioning potential new members.

For me, over the years their voices have blended more smoothly, alt-hough some still ring with distinct, quirky tones. My chorus now includes supervision that I have internalized from patients, as well as gleanings from my other walks of life.

Perhaps this chorus is a professional version of the "ideal self" of Sandler et. al (1963). In any case, I know it is my ballast. Like home, it is the place that has to take me in. When I feel lost, I hear Ralph Crowley (my first analytic supervisor) saying, with his faint smile, "Let's look at what you do know about the patient." When I am worn down, I listen to the lilt of Rose Spiegel (my training analyst), with her unique blend of kindness and absolute resoluteness. When (for whatever reasons) I feel flawed and alone, they comfort me. Their presence heartens me. Their unswerving dedication inspires me. They give me strength by reminding me to look toward the far horizon. Right now, my own and my patient's or my supervisee's emotional balance may be off kilter. There may seem to be no way to balance what is *foul* in us. Perhaps I have simply let us both down, out of insufficient courage to truly meet some challenge. But Rose, Ralph, and others assure me that, eventually, I will become more integrated. That is, my shame, guilt, and regret will be modulated by positive feelings as I watch myself use painful experiences to teach others. Serving this purpose, the *foul* in me becomes *fair*, as well as *foul*. That is, as I draw on what happened with the patient who committed suicide, I modulate its meaning. Interpersonally, it becomes a vehicle for making future connections, though it also remains a deeply regretted experience. Intrapersonally, it will be a resource, as well as a guilt-inducing memory. By using what still hurts, I will more fully integrate myself into my community, as I also integrate my own limitations with more positive aspects of who I am. By accepting and using what is *foul*, I soften my shame, guilt, and regret. More *at one*, I will atone.

References

Bokser, B.B. (1978). *Abraham Isaac Kook*. Mahwah, NJ: Paulist Press

Buechler, S. (1992). Stress in the personal and professional development of a psychoanalyst. *Journal American Academy of Psychoanalysis* 20:183–191

——— (1997). The right stuff. *Contemporary Psychoanalysis* 33:295–306 http://www.pep-web.org/document.php?id'cps.033.0295a

——— (1998). The analyst's experience of loneliness. *Contemporary Psychoanalysis* 34:91–115 www.pep-web.org/document.php?id'cps.034.0091a

———— (1999). Searching for a passionate neutrality. *Contemporary Psychoanalysis* 35:213–227 www.pep-web.org/document.php?id'cps.035.0213a

———— (2000). Necessary and unnecessary losses: The analyst's mourning. *Contemporary Psychoanalysis* 36:77–90 http://www.pep-web.org /document.php?id'cps.036.0077a

———— (2004). *Clinical Values: Emotions That Guide Psychoanalytic Treatment.* Hillsdale, NJ: The Analytic Press

Coltart, N. (1996). *The Baby and the Bathwater.* Madison, NJ: International Universities Press.

Cooper, A. (1986). Some limitations of therapeutic effectiveness: The "burn-out syndrome" in psychoanalysis. *Psychoanalytic Quarterly* 55:576–598 http://www.pep-web.org/document.php?id'paq.055.0576a

Frankel, E. (2003). *Sacred Therapy.* Boston: Shambhala

Gabbard, E.P. Lester, E.P. (1996). *Boundaries and Boundary Violations in Psychoanalysis.* New York: Basic Books

Hirsch, I. (2005). More human than otherwise. *Clinical Services.* New York: September : W. A. White Institute.

Izard, C.E. (1977). *Human Emotions.* New York: Plenum Press.

McLaughlin, J. (1995). Touching limits in the analytic dyad. *Psychoanalysis. Quarterly* 64:433–465. www.pep-web.org/document.php?id'paq .064.0433a

Maroda, K. (1998). Enactment: When the patient's and the analyst's pasts converge. *Psychoanalytic Psychology* 15:517–535. http://www.pep-web.org/document.php?id'ppsy.015.0517a

———— (2005). Legitimate gratification of the analyst's needs. *Contemporary Psychoanalysis* 41:371–389. www.pep-web.org/document.php?id'cps .041.0371a

Pearlman, K.W. Saakvitne, K.W. (1995). *Trauma and the Therapist.* New York: W.W. Norton.

Sandler, D. Holder, D. Meers, D. (1963). The ego ideal and the ideal self. *Psychoanalysis Study of the Child* 18:139–158. http://www.pep-web.org/document.php?id'psc.018.0139a

Slochower, J. (2005) *The analyst's secret delinquencies. IARPP Online Colloquium* November. http://www.pep-web.org/document.php?id'pd.013.0451a

CHAPTER NINE

No Pain No Gain? Suffering
and the Analysis of Defense*

INTRODUCTION

If the clinician functions in accordance with an attitude that pain is a symptom that should be reduced as quickly as possible, this has a significant impact on the analyst's focus in treatment, most especially on the timing of interpretations of defense. In contrast, the analyst may be (wittingly or unwittingly) operating under the assumption that pain is an inevitable part of human experience, best accepted rather than avoided. A third stance embraces suffering as not only unavoidable, but a significant source of wisdom and personal identity. This paper explores how each of these inclinations affect the analyst's treatment approach.

I see this paper as an outgrowth of my ongoing efforts to grapple with sorrow, both personally and professionally. Contemplating my personal attitudes toward grief, and other forms of psychic pain, has led me to wonder how these attitudes affect my functioning as a psychoanalyst. How would my work be different, if I could wholeheartedly ascribe to the popular goal of eradicating pain through pharmaceutical solutions? Might I be

* *Contemporary Psychoanalysis* 2010, 46, 334-355. I am indebted to Dr. Kenneth Eisold for his helpful comments on an earlier draft of this paper.

more inclined to support, rather than analyze, defensive maneuvers? And what if I fully embraced the (spiritual/philosophical) attitude that suffering is the royal road to wisdom?

Of course, some would say that the analyst should maintain a careful neutrality that avoids taking any of these positions. But I have long felt that, whether or not that would be optimal in theory, in practice (in more than one sense of the word) it is impossible. What we hear, remember, respond to, take as too commonplace to notice, and assume is worthy of further attention, is inevitably shaped by our (fully and less fully recognized) cultural, personal, and clinical values.

ABSTRACT

This article describes three attitudes toward psychic pain and suffering, and their clinical implications are explored and illustrated. When analyst and patient differ fundamentally in their understanding of the place of suffering in psychic life, treatment destructive clashes may result. The attitude that pain should be reduced as quickly as possible has a significant impact on the analyst's focus in treatment, most especially on the timing of interpretations of defense. A different orientation is that pain is an inevitable part of human experience and is best accepted rather than avoided. A third possibility embraces suffering as not only unavoidable, but as a primary source of wisdom and personal identity.

NO PAIN NO GAIN? SUFFERING AND THE ANALYSIS OF DEFENSE

When I was in graduate school, I had a teacher who was much admired, theoretically knowledgeable, and intellectually sharp. He could debate anyone, in any analytic lingo. He had high standards and expected his students and patients to devote much of our resources (financial and otherwise) to a steadfast search for enlightenment. I remember thinking, "This man doesn't understand how hard real life is." I look back, much more aware today that it is possible to love theory *and* appreciate life's hardships. But, in our working methods and public statements, do we fully manifest this appreciation? Do our actions, in sessions—that is, what we highlight and what we ignore—reflect compassionate understanding of just how outnumbered, overwhelmed, and unprepared people often feel when faced with serious illnesses, deteriorating parents, financial struggles, clamoring children, maxed-out schedules, competing priorities, the difficulties of aging well, along with many other everyday challenges? Are we somehow failing to transmit our grasp of these issues? Or, like my graduate school teacher, are some of us lost in theories that are intellectually compelling but not sufficiently grounded in life as it is lived?

True, we all experience suffering, but we may not have fully formulated our attitude about its place in psychic life. When is suffering to be borne, rather than medicated, muted, or eradicated? When should it be taken as a sign of a full appreciation of the human condition, rather than as a sign of pathology? Our attitudes about suffering have a significant effect on much of our behavior in a session, most especially, on our approach to the analysis of defense. It can be valuable for us to reflect on our attitudes about suffering, their personal, theoretical, religious, and philosophical origins, and their impact on our clinical approach.

First, let me note that I am using the words pain, suffering, emotional pain, and psychic pain interchangeably. Here is a brief description of the three attitudes I am discussing:

1) Primarily, emotional pain is a symptom. Its reduction or elimination is a pivotal aim in treatment. Therefore any method that might delimit suffering, such as medication, should be employed.

2) For the most part, suffering is a human inevitability. An important goal of psychological treatment is to facilitate both participants' efforts to become better able to accept suffering as a part of the human condition, to endure it courageously and with dignity.

3) For centuries suffering has been seen by many as the royal road to some form of enlightenment, wisdom, or personal identity. Suffering is viewed as *the* path toward redemption and self-knowledge. Treatment should further both participants' capacities to learn from their suffering.

Of course, all these attitudes have currency. I suggest, however, that clinicians differ as to whether we focus mainly on suffering as a symptom, as an inevitable burden, or as a window of opportunity. What inclines each of us toward our attitude about psychic pain? Perhaps our age, possibly our gender, help shape our often unformulated outlook. Our own life experience seems certain to have an influence. But I think the wider culture and the psychoanalytic culture also play roles in our slant toward suffering.

Should We Aim to Alleviate Suffering Quickly?

I think the attitude that suffering should be alleviated as quickly as possible is much more acceptable in analytic circles than it used to be. In previous eras, partially because of a concern that medication would reduce their patients' motivation for the psychological treatment that could profoundly and permanently cure, analysts were reluctant to have patients take medications to alleviate suffering, Today, I think it is fair to say that many analysts and nonanalytic therapists, as well as patients, believe that suffering should be alleviated wherever possible, that it is neither noble nor inevitable. Here I want to differentiate attitudes about suffering's cause from attitudes about its cure. A clinician or patient may believe that how we experience our lives causes much of our suffering, or they may see it as more often a product of external forces. Either way the clinician and patient can aim for its rapid alleviation.

Whether or not pain should be ameliorated as soon as possible has probably most often been raised in relation to medications, but it does come up in countless other ways. In an article about how clinicians might integrate decisions about medication in a psychoanalytic treatment, Glick and Roose (2006) explore the differences between psychopharmacologists and analysts in how we are often taught to view the alleviation of suffering:

> There is nothing in the training of psychopharmacologists that cautions them to be wary of the wish to cure the patient or of feeling pleasure when it happens. In contrast, the analyst must struggle with a paradox. While the therapeutic aim of analysis is to relieve suffering, in day-to-day practice the analyst is supposed to monitor, examine, and not act on desires to cure [p. 754].

So, although it seems self-evident that simple kindness and compassion require us to try to limit human suffering (as well, of course, as animal suffering), the analyst may be taught to *monitor first* rather than act on this aim. We can certainly understand how such monitoring could lead to clashes between analyst and patient. It seems obvious that much of the time (although not always) the patient would want his or her suffering quickly alleviated rather than simply monitored. Feeling *any* kind of pain might, on some level, return human beings to our early days of helplessness. Adam Phillips (1995) puts the infant's plight succinctly: "Pain makes us believe that other people have something we need. When we suffer first, as children, we seek people out; and our wish to communicate, and our will to believe in comfort, is urgent" (p. 33).

Thus the analyst, taught to be wary of impulses to alleviate pain, and the patient, wishing to be relieved of pain quickly, are often in an unavoidably conflict-laden situation that inevitably evokes parent—child analogies. We have all been infants, overwhelmed by hunger, thirst, and other insistent needs. The power of those who can grant or refuse to grant gratification is absolute.

We know that patients often see clinicians as withholding needed comfort or relief from suffering, whether or not the clinician feels that he or she really has that power. It is interesting to speculate on the part this issue plays in forcing the participants into the traditional transferential roles. In any case, I think repeated experiences of clashing with patients who want instant relief may eventually persuade many analysts to adopt a "pain minimizing" stance. Of course, some need no prodding to take this position, for they have entered the field with personal and professional proclivities toward alleviating suffering as quickly as possible. (I will shortly elaborate on how that might play out clinically.) I would like to emphasize the complexity of the forces that can pull even those trained to "monitor" pain, eventually to move closer to a pain-minimizing stance. Analytic politics, and even the likelihood of getting referrals, can favor those with a reputation for more quickly relieving suffering. Some analysts feel torn between their training as pain "monitors/explorers" and the benefits of a reputation as a "pain reliever." Also, I think it is easy for conferences to become battlegrounds between these two positions. Attendees frequently resort to splitting and devaluation of each other, and idealization of their own position. Those who favor quickly minimizing pain are often told they are not "real" analysts, while those who take a slower approach may be branded as holdovers from a more authoritarian age. When it comes to the analyst's attitude toward suffering, infighting can get ugly fast. The political can get insultingly personal, and the personal can unwittingly shape the political.

I suggest that, for each of us, our attitude toward suffering probably correlates with our posture toward intense emotionality in general. Because I have addressed the issue of emotional intensity extensively elsewhere (2004, 2008), I will just mention here that I believe each of us has a rough idea of fitting expressions of sadness, rage, anxiety, and other feelings. However unformulated these notions may be, I think they have tremendous effect on our behavior in sessions. We may not have reflected much on how we arrived at our particular profile of appropriate emotionality. My own belief is that it is generally influenced by our individual character style, as well as our training analyst(s), supervisors, teachers, patients, and personal relationships. For example, life experience, professional training, and personal characteristics have rendered some of us more comfortable than others when we are in the presence of intense rage in ourselves or in another person. These differences influence our focus on the material in a rage filled session.

The Effect of Attitudes toward Suffering on the Interpretation of Defense

With respect to the more specific question of how the analyst's attitude toward suffering affects defense interpretation, first I want to emphasize that I believe this discussion pertains to adherents of *all* theoretical schools. For example, I think an analyst who inclines toward minimizing suffering could hold to a classical Freudian, Sullivanian, Jungian, or any other orientation, although I speculate that personal attitudes about suffering may be one factor in the analyst's original choice of a school of thought. Elsewhere I (2004, ch. 9) have spelled out how I think various currently popular schools of thought fulfill some of an analyst's particular emotional needs. But I am sure that many factors determine which orientation appeals most to each of us. In what follows I describe several possibilities for how attitudes toward suffering might influence defense interpretation, regardless of the analyst's theoretical allegiances.

How does the assumption that suffering should be minimized as quickly as possible affect defense interpretation? I think it could incline the analyst to hold off interpreting defense, regardless of his or her theoretical persuasion. Briefly, I am suggesting that, to the degree that an analyst prioritizes minimizing pain, defenses could seem (at least temporarily) like allies. An adherent of this point of view might argue that, since most of us have accepted the notion of dissociation as an aspect of normal functioning we could say the same for denial, repression, splitting, projection, and the other defenses. And, if we believe these defenses are part of healthy functioning, shouldn't we avoid (at least, early in treatment) disrupting them? I believe that analysts who are unwilling to consider this issue drive many prospective patients into the arms of practitioners of Cognitive Behavioral Therapy (CBT), where their defenses are given a more cordial welcome. In fact, some nonanalytic treatment modes promote, and even teach patients defensive strategies, such as compartmentalization. I am not advocating that we join this throng for the sake of the survival of our profession. But I think we should carefully consider how our (perhaps unexamined) attitudes about pain color our responses to patients' defenses and our own.

Every moment of every session provides myriad choices about what to focus on. I hear a patient recount an instance of her husband's "emotional generosity." The memory comforts her. I could be silent. I might, by that action (or inaction), be expressing an inclination to leave well enough alone. But perhaps I believe that her vision of his generosity is a defensive distortion. Perhaps I see it as a therapeutic opportunity to acquaint her further with her idealization, splitting, denial, or other aspects of her psychic functioning. Do I value the comfort she is getting from this memory so much that I postpone (for the moment or indefinitely) closer examination? It is not enough to say that we just follow the patient's lead in these matters. Some would like to think that we do not have to decide for our patients whether or not to pursue their increasing awareness of defensive processes, since in their associations, in the train of their thought, *they* tell *us*. While this is true, it is not the whole story. I think I may have a very different effect if I simply ask how she felt, when her husband was showing his "generosity." Such a seemingly innocuous question might begin a line of inquiry that results in an altered picture of their interaction. I believe that when the patient tells of her husband's generous action, my silence, my seemingly routine question, or any other choices inevitably reflect what I am prioritizing. If I see myself as primarily working to minimize pain, I will be less likely to focus on a defense that may help to preserve the patient's equanimity. I might tell myself (if I am consciously aware of this choice) that it is "too early." But this judgment, too, reflects my priorities.

When I first entered graduate school, we learned a basic dictum: with neurotic or healthier patients, analyze defenses so as to make them superfluous. With borderline or more disturbed patients, shore up the defenses. In extreme states of pathology, repression is too weak and the patient may be flooded with terrifying possibilities. Of course, this rule oversimplified professional life in many senses. We are not omniscient; we cannot decide who needs what defense and choose to supply it when necessary. Real people do not fall neatly into categories. Yet, I believe that with every word we utter, or do not utter, in treatment, we are taking a position about consciousness, defenses, and, more generally, emotional well-being. But do we know what that is?

I can not overstate the complexity of defining concepts like emotionally "healthy" functioning and "normal" responses to pain. I am not suggesting that I have adequate definitions of them. But I am saying that those of us practicing treatment should consider our points of view about the role of defenses in healthy functioning and what that should suggest about the goals and techniques of therapy.

If we do not know how to define healthy functioning, how can we know which set of defenses to interpret, to try to undo their limitation on what can be conscious? If we cannot be clear about health, how do we know that where id is, ego should be? Maybe where id is, id should remain!

A textbook geared to medical students (Carol Donley and Sheryl Buckley, 2000) asks in its title, *What's Normal?* The editors, in their introduction, suggest, "When the ideal is taken as the norm, variation becomes defined as disease. Too often we convert normal and healthy variabilities into diseases or disorders because they differ from the ideal norm. This reluctance to accept normal variations makes people who are only slightly different from the norm feel unacceptable" (p. 3).

What are some possible clinical applications of these thoughts about normalcy? Are there normal variations in defensive patterns; and, if we believe there are, how would those translate into a treatment technique? For a patient who relies on repression, is ignorance bliss or merely a part of her psychological equipment for living? Should her therapist point out the footprints of repressions in her dreams? Or is it wiser to let those sleeping dogs lie?

I have often thought that the more experienced the clinician, the less eager she is to interpret immediately everything she thinks she sees. Timing and tact are part of the art of the work. They are difficult to teach but not so difficult to recognize. Are we supporting a defense when we do not interpret what may then remain unconscious? When is that omission a product of our cowardice, and when is it a product of our wisdom? It is impossible to consider these issues without reference to the personal attitude toward suffering that each of us develops, whether or not we ever spell it out.

SHOULD SUFFERING BE ACCEPTED?

The second attitude sees suffering as inevitable without, necessarily, seeing it as potentially ennobling. Unlike the first attitude, which unequivocally aims to reduce or eradicate suffering, according to this point of view, the recognition and acceptance of suffering is what is crucial. This recognition can alleviate wasted efforts to deny suffering's existence. According to this attitude, the central problem is not suffering itself, but the human effort to deny its presence. Freud can be counted among the proponents of this idea. I still get a chill when I read his famously modest claim for the effect of a successful treatment. Speaking to the recipient of such a treatment he predicted that "you will be able to convince yourself that much will be gained if we succeed in transforming your hysterical misery into common unhappiness. With a mental life that has been restored to health you will be better armed against that unhappiness" (Breuer and Freud, 1895, p. 305).

I can't help thinking of combat. Years of work yield better armor for the endless battles ahead. We help to mend the chinks in the armor. Freud's statement suggests an attitude toward suffering that focuses on its inevitability. The analyst should address *the way people try to avoid pain, rather than the pain itself*. Defensive avoidance of pain can greatly complicate life. I suggest that analysts aiming for the acceptance of pain would be likely to interpret defenses earlier than would analysts aiming for pain's eradication or reduction.

Of course, Freud was not alone in this emphasis. Analysts generally probably value facing pain squarely. But at times this attitude can morph into an idealization of stoicism. An extreme example of this, from my point of view, can be found in Richard Taylor's (2002) book, *Virtue Ethics*. Describing pride as a virtue that differs from conceit, he illustrates the behavior of the healthily proud person in adversity.

One of the great tests, for example, is the individual's response to acute danger, or his or her reaction to a life-threatening disease or to humiliation at the hands of enemies. One type of person bears these things with a natural, unpracticed fortitude and nobility while, at the other extreme, some collapse into whimpering and self-pity. With respect to death a proud person knows that even his or her own life is not worth clinging to at the cost of pride or honor; would never want it prolonged beyond the point where the virtues upon which pride rests have become debilitated; and would, for this reason, prefer to die ten years too soon than ten days too late. And there are other great tests, such as one's reaction to the death of a son or daughter who was intelligent, and strong, and filled with promise of great achievement (p. 103).

When I try to apply that advice to myself, I feel sure that I would fail most of Taylor's tests. Even if a son or daughter of mine were not exceptionally intelligent, strong, or filled with promise, on his or her death I would certainly whimper, and do plenty more. Taylor's language contrasts nobility, at one end of a spectrum, with whimpering self-pity at the other. What he elevates as healthy pride and fortitude I see as a kind of schizoid narcissism.

But it is not necessary to idealize suffering in order to believe in making it more conscious. For example, a patient came into treatment years after her mother died. This mother and daughter had been extremely close, and yet the patient, an intelligent, middle-aged professional, had never shed a tear about losing her mother. When I asked about this, her answer astonished me. In a muted voice, she told me that she couldn't mourn her mother's death because she hadn't yet taken in that it really happened. This was not a psychotic patient. Yet it seems as though her psyche took the position that mourning this loss would be too much to bear, so she kept the full experience at bay. Should I see her reaction as problematic? If I belonged to the first group, the "pain reducers," I might think it best that her defensive equilibrium stay intact. But, if I believe that how we try to avoid pain is a central psychological problem and a major source of pathology, I might focus on making the defensive maneuvers conscious. I would be assuming that the patient would be better off when she can experience, rather than avoid, the pain of mourning.

For historical precedents, we can begin with Breuer and Freud (1895). Both authors suggested that the failure to remember an event and its associated affect can create conversion symptoms. First, in Breuer's words: "The 'wearing away' influences, however, are all of them effects of association, of thinking, of corrections by reference to other ideas. This process of correction becomes impossible if the affective idea is withdrawn from 'associative contact.' When this happens the idea retains its whole quota of affect" (p. 214).

Later, Freud discusses how conversion symptoms result from ideas torn out of their contexts and away from their accompanying affects.

> A reversal of this process, however, can restore health: each individual hysterical symptom immediately and permanently disappeared when we had succeeded in bringing clearly to light the memory of the event by which it was provoked and in arousing its accompanying affect, and when the patient had described that event in the greatest possible detail and had put the affect into words [p. 255].

Thus, a disturbing thought or memory must be remembered if it is to be modulated by other cognitive processes, and its associated affect must be abreacted. A fundamental potential conflict between analyst and patient could result from this process. The analyst wants the patient to remember and feel fully, whereas the patient may want to forget and avoid feelings. Put another way, this premise has the potential to create a clash of wills. The patient's will to defend against memory and emotion will be seen by the analyst as resistance.

This battle of wills follows the analytic couple through the next century and beyond. Sullivan's (1956) "happy idea" and Farber's (1966) "disorders of the will" are labels analysts have used for their patients' willful avoidances. We can see vestiges of this thinking in Abby Stein's (2003) poetic descriptions of violated men who become violent criminals. She tells us that she believes that their "perceptions, trace memories, inchoate thoughts and images surrounding abuse instead grow into awesome poltergeists" (p. 180) when they have not been subjected to a healing associative process. In a further description of the course of these unmoored poltergeists, Stein suggests, "These primitive ideas and affects swirl madly in search of an elaboration that will anchor them somehow to the host's ongoing narrative reality" (p. 180). In other words, torn out of context, torn out of an ongoing, autobiographical narrative, our memories can haunt us. This danger gives some clinicians a clear directive: help the patient overcome resistances to remembering and connect the memory with its affects and context, and this truth will then set the patient free.

In short, we must overcome the patient's willful avoidance of suffering so as to free him from his unprocessed and disconnected memories. We know that a fundamental difference between Breuer's conception of hysteria and Freud's was that Breuer emphasized the notion that the patient cannot remember what occurred in a hypnoid state, whereas for Freud remembering would engender conflict and is therefore resisted. Freud put will at the center of a struggle between clinicians and patients; a struggle that has taken various forms, including seductions on the part of either or both participants. Färber (1966) has a particularly witty description of the battle:

> When this particular absorption with the willful possibilities of sex occurs at the feverish beginnings of psychotherapy, it is apt to be called "positive transference," and to be mistakenly considered a good omen for cure. During this phase, before the two wills begin to oppose each other, the hysteric makes sexuality out of the therapist's science, while the therapist makes science out of sexuality. In this affair, the hysteric has the advantage, there being more sex to science than vice versa [p. 109].

Although analysts these days have broadened the subject matter of what should be remembered so that it is no longer exclusively sexual in nature, we still generally try to persuade patients that remembering *something* will set them free. For example, Bromberg (1998) emphasizes that Freud's patient Emmy von M needed to get all her selves into the relationship with Freud. According to Bromberg, Emmy had to be helped to overcome the dissociation of some of her self-states from the rest. This pattern of dissociation was, originally, defensive. As Bromberg puts it, "[W]e do not treat patients such as Emmy to cure them of something that was done to them in the past; rather we are trying to cure them of what they still do to themselves and to others in order to *cope* with what was done to them in the past" (p. 237).

As I see it, the concept of the therapeutic action, or the reason we get patients to remember, has shifted, but the battle remains the same. Now it is not simply remembering and putting the memory back into its affective context that cures. It is overcoming a willfully defensive dissociation. In effect, we make patients a promise. We tell them that bringing all their self-states together will not harm them, but, rather, will set them free. Whereas full self-awareness may have been dangerous in the past, it will be curative now. It will spare the energy that has kept self-states apart, now saving it for more constructive purposes. It will foster the joy of integrity or appreciation of one's wholeness. It will facilitate awareness of lifelong interpersonal patterns. In our presence, we tell patients, it is safe and desirable to remember, once more, with feeling.

It seems worth mentioning again that how we regard emotional intensity in general can affect our views about painful memories. Do we think that ideally all negative emotions (including pain) should be minimized or eliminated? Would we human beings be better off if our intense anger were excised, along with our intense guilt and other feelings? Who would we then be, and what would be the "side effects" of such a procedure? Without our guilt, how might we behave? This stance negates emotion theory's assumption (Izard, 1977) that all the emotions have useful functions, at least potentially. I am underscoring the complexity and the many implications of our often unexamined beliefs about human feelings in general, and human suffering in particular. For example, I think that our attitudes about suffering affect what patients and clinicians are willing to bear for the sake of the work, as well as the extent of time the treatment can be sustained. Someone who expects all aspects of life and growth to involve pain might be less urgently insistent on a "quick fix."

I remember being told, in my training, that patients often want the outcome of their way of life to improve without their having to change the way they live. I think of a patient, a young lawyer, who came into treatment complaining of tiredness. When I asked her how long her work-day was, she answered, "Around 15 hours"! When I suggested that the hours of her workday would have to change if she wanted to feel better, she said they couldn't be changed. This is an extreme example, but I do not think it is uncommon at lesser degrees. Patients often do want better outcomes without paying the price of changing how they live. And they want those changes now, not next year. I think this expectation sometimes elicits a negative reaction in me. It is as though the patient were demanding a result but not allowing us the means to accomplish it. And, I think, many of us become judgmental in response to these pressures. We take the attitude that patients are short sighted, greedily wanting dessert without first eating their spinach. We blame the culture for encouraging impulsivity. For example, Fiscalini (2009) described the clash between the wider culture's values and analytic values:

> A new problem, however, looms on the horizon. I refer here to the repudiation of psychoanalytic values by a culture that is impatient, nonreflective, and passively insistent. The complex, much longer, and far more subtle psychoanalysis is abandoned for the seemingly briefer, quicker, less painful, and less expensive, though ultimately less effective, behavior therapies and pop psychologies [p. 327].

I think I understand the frustration those sentiments express. Yet I want to make a plea for striking a balance between our investment in the long-term reflective process of increasing awareness and the human need to limit suffering now. Wanting less pain, now, is simply more human than otherwise. If we do not find ways to embrace it, I feel we may consign ourselves to an isolated ivory tower.

DEPRESSION AND ATTITUDES TOWARD SUFFERING

The patient is a woman in her early 40s. We will call her Emily. She entered treatment well aware that her childhood had been unhappy, but she wished to avoid dwelling on the past. The rhetorical question, What good would it do? often seems to hang in the air. For Emily, an only child and still single, her greatest fear is that she will miss out on the joys of partnership and parenthood. With each week her fear increases, as she sees the window of opportunity rapidly closing. But it is too painful to think about. The signals she gives me seem contradictory. Talking about the situation is too painful, yet addressing it is absolutely necessary. Changing it is crucial, but thinking about it is impossible. Not today. It would be too hard. It would make her feel worse. It is not the right time. The week was too difficult, and she must be calm for tonight's event. She can't function if she gets upset. Emily is especially shaky and can't take any more, right now. It is too close to one of the holidays that serve as markers of her lonely status. On the other hand, maybe she should have been harsher with her last therapist, who unconscionably let so much time go by. How could she do that? Didn't she care? Maybe the patient should take medication, so she wouldn't be so anxious about time going by. But would that only allow her to let it go by less uncomfortably?

Emily comes to a session complaining about a colleague at work. I feel it would be easy to pursue this topic; since the patient has brought it up, it is genuinely meaningful and causes her real frustration. But, as the minutes go by, I start to feel uncomfortable. The biological as well as the chronological clock is ticking. Is the topic of the work problem a defensive diversion from more salient material? If I join in a discussion of work, am I colluding in avoiding more painful, but more essential issues? Is that wrong? Isn't it all related, anyhow? The patient clearly wants to avoid talking about extremely painful subjects. My formulated and unformulated attitudes about suffering are likely to affect my focus in general in the session and, more specifically, the degree to which I focus on the patient's defenses.

Examples of attitudes about whether suffering should be avoided, reduced, or made more conscious abound in clinical work. They affect many of the moves we make or do not make in a session. They frequently permeate clashes between clinicians and their patients. While it is probable that there are consistent differences between the analytic culture and the wider culture on this score, I can also recognize differences within each culture on attitudes about suffering. Nowhere are these differences more confusing than in relation to depression. Is depression to be fully experienced, mined for its potential to make us more whole, more ourselves, and more connected with each other? Is it to be fully felt, so that defensively running away from it does not permeate the rest of our lives? Or should it be limited as much as possible, pharmacologically and psychologically? Depression is probably the type of suffering that most often elicits (in clinicians as well as patients) strong opinions about whether pain should be limited as quickly as possible, tolerated as well as possible, or mined for what it can teach us. Of course, each participant in a treatment might have any attitude, but here I am focusing on the potential clash of an analyst who leans toward accepting or embracing suffering and a patient who wants to avoid it as much as possible. Stephen Mitchell (1993) succinctly summarized this frequent culture clash:

> The patient and analyst both surely want something to be different and better; both want the patient to have an experience of living that is richer and fuller. But it is not clear that there is much congruence between the patient's original ideas of what that would entail and the analyst's; rather, as the work proceeds, it generally becomes apparent how different those visions really are [p. 209].

EMBRACING SUFFERING

We are all familiar with versions of the point of view that suffering is the route to salvation. Religious thought, of course, provides many clear illustrations of this idea. Here I can mention only some of the more contemporary versions, draw a few comparisons between the religious belief in salvation through suffering and some tenets in emotion theory, and suggest some clinical implications of this attitude. Is suffering the royal road to understanding ourselves and others?

We might begin with the religious vision of attaining salvation by participating in Christ's suffering. In a sense, Christ can be seen as having brought us salvation through our compassion. An analogy can be drawn with Estelle Frankel's (2003) "baptism in despair" (p.66). Her understanding of some Hebrew texts is that pain, and most especially the pain of losing a loved one, can connect us with the infinite, and potentially helps us heal our essential wound of separateness. She sees this healing potential as a reason that loss was frequently the gateway to spiritual awakening for ancient mystics. She writes of the 13th-century Sufi poet, Rumi, whose teacher, Shams, disappeared, and may have been murdered. In Frankel's words, "In his grief, however, his heart didn't just break. It broke open, and thereafter his love knew no boundaries" (p. 64). This way of thinking suggests that profound suffering, and especially the pain of loss, is the condition that most facilitates our development of love, compassion, and self-transcendence. Frankel (p. 66) quotes the mystic philosopher, Andrew Harvey, who said, "From the deepest wound of my life grew its miraculous possibility" (p. 66).

Not unrelated is the emotion theory (Izard, 1977) conception of sadness as having as its function drawing human beings closer together, with a heightened appreciation of our common human condition. Suffering, in other words, is not just something to be courageously and forthrightly endured, but, rather, it is an essential part of us. Potentially it is the great humanizer. Not only are our ties to each other highlighted by suffering, but life itself may be affirmed through it. A few more quotations remind us of the many incarnations of this age old idea. Jeremy Safran (2003) suggests, "Buddhism places the confrontation with death, loss, and suffering at the heart of things. And ultimately it offers refuge, not in the promise of a better afterlife or protection by a divine figure, but in the form of a pathway toward greater acceptance of life as it is, with all its pain and suffering" p. 29). He goes on to say that this is what can enhance our ability to truly cherish life.

Another version of what is precious in suffering is that suffering transformed becomes beauty, joy, and art, as well as compassion and self-transcendence. Psychological expressions of this idea abound. For example, Jungian analyst James Hollis (1996) asks, "Could we even imagine the possibility of joy if we could not contrast it with its opposite? Yet in modern culture we have distorted reality in an addictive search for unalloyed happiness. Such a search can become demonic" (p. 67).

Michelle Stacey (2002) says:

Is our Prozac-inspired happiness just window-dressing, an easy, mindless glide through life? This is where the question of psychoactive drugs begins to intersect with the divine, with our larger ideas of why we're here on this earth. Religious belief is rooted in struggle: against evil, against meaninglessness, against the uncaring, unethical part of ourselves [pp. 295–296].

Stacey goes on to describe the Walker Percy novel, *The Thanatos Syndrome*, in which a drug called Heavy Sodium is put into the water supply and removes everyone's angst. The drug is seen as robbing people of their souls.

My favorite poet, Rilke, says succinctly (in Baer, 2005), "What, finally, would be more useless to me than a consoled life?" He advises us, "to elevate suffering to the level of one's own perspective and to transform it into an aid for one's way of seeing" (pp. 112–113).

I will end this glance at the vast literature on the uses of suffering with words from Joseph Campbell's (1988) conversations with Bill Moyers. Campbell said, "The secret cause of all suffering...is mortality itself, which is the prime condition of life. It cannot be denied if life is to be affirmed" (p. xi). Suffering, in other words, has been seen across many cultures, eras, philosophies, and religions as potentially moving us to connect with other human beings, with our own humanity, with sources of personal creativity, with our souls, and with God.

My own version of a clinical application of the idea of suffering as humanizing is that patients can sometimes benefit from seeing me suffer. Of course, I don't deliberately set out to suffer. But sessions can sometimes present opportunities for suffering out loud. Elsewhere (2008) I have suggested that the openly suffering analyst has become a "fool for love." That is, especially with patients who bear self-esteem wounds, seeing the analyst struggle, sometimes become overwhelmed, unable to cope, willing to feel pain openly, perhaps to cry, can be very significant therapeutically. Not only might it serve to forge connection and compassion, but it might also negate the patient's sense of being inferior because of his or her suffering. The shame of being unable to think, speak, understand, or remember can provide occasions for forms of suffering. Simply understanding the patient's suffering can sometimes signal to the patient that I must have known similar pain at some point in my life. In addition, at times of illness or other difficult circumstances, my suffering may become a shared experience.

Stuart Pizer (2009) has written of his work with a patient during a time that Pizer had to have emergency surgery and then a complicated period of convalescence. I (2009) discussed his paper and wrote of a time when my own illness felt different hour by hour, depending, in part, on the patient I happened to be with. Without planning, or sometimes without awareness, I believe that I reveal my attitude toward suffering if I try to suppress signs of pain, ill health, or sorrow, as well as when I "wear suffering on my sleeve," so to speak. My experience is that the patient's compassion often plays an unnoticed but significant role in the work, even when I think I am not showing any suffering. Compassion for my intense effort can also be a factor in treatment. Aside from compassion, sometimes my intensity inspires a greater willingness to meet me halfway. In short, I wonder how many treatments really take off when the patient begins to identify and feel compassion for a suffering, and undeterred, unashamed, emotionally responsive clinician.

THE ATTITUDE THAT SUFFERING HUMANIZES, ENNOBLES, AND DEFINES

A.C. Bradley (1966) gives us a particularly poetic description of pain as the royal road to wisdom, in more than one sense of the word royal. His portrayal of emotional growth through suffering is so evocative that I quote it at length. He says that King Lear

> comes in his affliction to think of others first, and to seek, in tender solicitude for the poor boy, the shelter he scorns for his own head; who learns to feel and pray for the miserable and houseless poor, to discern the falseness of flattery and the brutality of authority, and to pierce below the differences of rank and raiment to the common humanity beneath; whose sight is so purged by scalding tears that it sees at last

how power and place and all things in the world are vanity except love; who tastes in his last hours the extremes both of love's rapture and its agony, but could never, if he lived on or lived again care a jot for aught besides- there is no figure, surely, in the world of poetry at once so grand, so pathetic, and so beautiful as he [p. 235].

I have already sketched some of the roles that suffering has been thought to play in emotional growth. Here I expand on suffering's educative potential and suggest some ways this attitude might affect an analyst's approach to working with his own and the patient's defenses.

Until this point I have described how some have seen suffering as the teacher that can best humanize, redeem, even exalt. I think we can add to the list of its enhancing possibilities its capacity to define us and provide our lives with a sense of purpose. Thus, some of us think of ourselves as "survivors" (of cancer, rape, war, concentration camps, torture, incest, and other painful experiences). Today, many insist on language that emphasizes the personhood of the sufferer (e.g., persons with disorders, not "the disordered"), but this formulation still includes the suffering in the person's self-definition.

There is a curious rift in the wider culture that perhaps filters into our own psychoanalytic culture. On one hand, many have a bias toward chemically eliminating suffering wherever possible. Of course, the pharmaceutical companies have a stake in persuading us that suffering is unnecessary, avoidable, and totally unproductive. Commercials picture the satisfying life that is possible if only sufferers have the good sense to pop the right pill. But, on the other hand, our "Oprah" entertainment industry can make suffering into a cultish badge of honor. If I have suffered, I am interesting, noteworthy, newsworthy, and, in a sense, special. My suffering may not exalt me spiritually, but it helps to define me psychologically, singles me out, and gives me social status. Whereas, at least much of the time, pain used to be a private affair, today we have reality TV, the cell phone, and the paparazzi. Some still prefer a private cry, but many seem intent on exploiting pain to get publicity. Others simply do not seem to care whether or not casual eavesdroppers can hear their cell phone conversations about their cheating partners or miserably lonely lives. *Jerry Springer- The Opera* made delicious fun of our propensity for putting our pain on display.

Exhibiting pain is not new, but I think it is more evident in our information age, with its blogs, Facebook, and other means of instant, wide ranging communication. But there are many precedents. I remember being struck, as a child, with a television program called "Queen for a Day." At least as I recall it, contestants would vie for who had the most miserable sob story. The "winner" got a prize. Tabloids are another example of how human misery can serve as a ticket to glamour. Pain is the great equalizer, in a sense. The Hollywood star, the politician, and the ordinary citizen who suffers mightily, or who sins dramatically can achieve fame (or infamy).

How does all this affect the analysis of defense? I have already suggested that those who (because of their character and personal and professional experiences) believe that ignorance can be bliss are the analysts likely to be friendliest toward defense, reluctant to interpret it early, regardless of their theoretical orientation (although this attitude about suffering may incline them toward adopting some orientations more than others). I have also discussed the likelihood that, in contrast, analysts who believe that only the truth can set us free will interpret defense early. They will see the defense as, itself, a central problem, taking up energy that could be better spent and adding dissociative disconnections and hysterical symptoms to the patient's miseries.

But for those who see suffering as the royal road to enlightenment, humanistic wisdom, or personal identity, defenses are neither friend nor foe. They are simply not the point. Unlike their colleagues in the first two groups, these analysts are neither loath to interpret defense nor eager. Their focus is elsewhere. They are looking for hurt, not for what blocks awareness of pain, but for the humanizing function of the pain itself.

Analysts are not alone in viewing suffering as a potentially great educator and reformer. I would like to quote from two firsthand accounts, from people who have each survived periods of intense psychic suffering, and have chosen to write about the subsequent effects on their lives. The first is Lee Springer (cited in Casey, 2001), who stresses pain's function as a wake-up call.

One grows older and more knowing over time; life's more facile charms grow dim; the soul yearns, seeking more than could ever be had on this earth, more than could ever be wrought out of three dimensions and five senses. We, all of us, suffer some from the limits of living within the flesh. Our walk through this world is never entirely without pain. It lurks in the still, quiet hours which we in our constant busyness, steadfastly avoid. And it has occurred to me since that perhaps what we call depression isn't really a disorder at all but, like physical pain, an alarm of sorts, alerting us that something is undoubtedly wrong, that perhaps it is time to stop, take a time-out, take as long as it takes, and attend to the unaddressed business of filling our souls [pp. 112–113].

The second is Susanna Keysen, herself a sufferer from bouts of painful depressive episodes, who wrote an aptly titled essay, "One Cheer for Melancholy" (cited in Casey, 2001). Keysen highlights how creativity can arise from a will to make sense of one's suffering:

I think melancholy is useful. In its aspect of pensive reflection or contemplation, it's the source of many books (even those complaining about it) and paintings, much scientific insight, the resolution of many fights between couples and friends, and the process known as becoming mature [pp. 38–39].

CONCLUSION

I have considered how three attitudes about suffering may affect the timing of an analyst's interpretations of defense. I suggest that those who would vote for accepting, rather than either avoiding or embracing, suffering have the greatest tendency to interpret defensive maneuvers early in treatment. I want to be clear that I am referring to an attitude that I think affects the timing of defense interpretation. I assume that, on the whole, we all hope eventually to help our patients integrate much that has been dissociated, for example. But I think we might differ about the timing of when to focus on what we see as the "footprints" of dissociation.

Candidates in training frequently want help developing confidence in their timing. For example, one asks me if I think that it is too soon to pursue signs of a patient's disturbing early memory. There is no "guide to technique" that is isolated from personal, cultural, and professional attitudes about suffering. A general feeling that suffering should be minimized, or accepted, or embraced will affect how an analyst hears the material in a session. It may even color which psychoanalytic theories she favors, as well as how she understands therapeutic action, psychological health, and the goals of treatment. All this is, of course, related to the familiar concept of the effect of the observer on what can be observed.

Analysts are human beings, influenced by countless personal and social pressures. But elsewhere I (2004) have suggested that analysts are also trained in a profession with its own culture. Certain mores, values, hopes, and dreams characterize most analysts to some degree. We value truth, sometimes for itself. Most of us are still fans of insight, even though our field has lost its absolute allegiance to it as the vehicle of cure. We are brought up to be troopers. We would not get through our training if we could not put something ahead of immediate gratification. And we could not get through one day of clinical work if we did not value something other than ease. On any random day we may participate with people we have come to care about in life's most painful trials, in the unanswerable, the unbearable, in tragic losses and unimaginable suffering. That experience makes us unusually familiar with pain's contours. But we are also in danger of taking it for granted and perhaps forgetting that there are people who may just want help to get through the night. A kind of nonchalance about human suffering could contribute to consigning us to a lonely ivory tower.

In summary, although all analysts have had to learn to tolerate being in the presence of pain, I think we differ in our fundamental attitudes about the place of suffering in human psychic life. Those of us who prioritize pain alleviation are not going to focus on clinical material, or on our own countertransference, in the same way as those of us who prize other changes more than the reduction of suffering. I think it is imperative for each of us to examine our own tendencies to treat human suffering, first and foremost, as an obstacle to living fully, or as an inevitable part of human existence, or as a vehicle to gaining the fullest understanding of the human condition and our own particular, psychic life.

REFERENCES

Baer, U. (2005), *The Poet's Guide to Life: The Wisdom of Rilke*. New York: Modern Library.

Bradley, A.C. (1966). *Shakespearean Tragedy*. New York: St. Martin's Press.

Breuer, J. & Freud, S. (1895). Studies on Hysteria. *Standard Edition 2*.

Bromberg, P. (1998). *Standing in the Spaces: Essays on Clinical Practice, Trauma, and Dissociation*. Hillsdale, NJ: Analytic Press, 2001. http://www.pep-web.org/document.php?id'cps.032.0509a

Buechler, S. (2004). *Clinical Values: Emotions That Guide Psychoanalytic Treatment*. Hillsdale, NJ: Analytic Press.

——— (2008). *Making a Difference in Patients' Lives*. New York: Routledge.

——— (2009). Love will do the thing that's right. *Psychoanalytic Dialogues* 19:63–68. http://www.pep-web.org/document.php?id'pd.019.0063a

Campbell, J. & Moyers, B. (1988). *The Power of Myth*. New York: Anchor Books, 1991.

Casey, N., ed. (2001). *Unholy Ghost: Writers on Depression*. New York: HarperCollins.

Donley, C. & Buckley, S., eds. (2000). *What's Normal?* Kent, OH: Kent State University Press.

Färber, L. (1966). *The Ways of the Will*. New York: Basic Books.

Fiscalini, J. (2009). A community of clinicians. *Contemporary Psychoanalysis* 45:322–330. http://www.pep-web.org/document.php?id'cps.045.0322a

Frankel, E. (2003). *Sacred Therapy*. Boston, MA: Shambhala.

Glick, R.A. & Roose, S. (2006). Talking about medication. *Journal of the American Psychoanalysis Association* 54:745–762. http://www.pep-web.org/document.php?id'apa.054.0745a

Hollis, J. (1996). *Swamplands of the Soul: New Life in Dismal Places*. Toronto: Inner City Books.

Izard, C. (1977). *Human Emotions*. New York: Plenum Press.

Mitchell, S.A. (1993). *Hope and Dread in Psychoanalysis.* New York: Basic Books.

Phillips, A. (1995). *Terrors and Experts.* Cambridge, MA: Harvard University Press.

Pizer, S.A. (2009). Inside out: The state of the analyst and the state of the patient. *Psychoanalysis Dialogues* 19:49–63. http://www.pep-web.org/document.php?id'pd.019.0049a

Safran, J.D., ed. (2003). *Psychoanalysis and Buddhism: An Unfolding Dialogue.* Boston, MA: Wisdom.

Stacey, M. (2002). *The Fasting Girl.* New York: Penguin Books.

Stein, A. (2003). Dreaming while awake: The use of trance to bypass threat. *Contemporary Psychoanalysis* 39:179–197. http://www.pep-web.org/document.php?id'cps.039.0179a

Sullivan, H.S. (1956). *Clinical Studies in Psychiatry.* New York: W.W. Norton.

Taylor, R. (2002). *Virtue Ethics.* New York: Prometheus Books.

CHAPTER TEN

My Personal Interpersonalism: An Essay on Sullivan's One-Genus Postulate[*]

INTRODUCTION

This paper took me more than thirty five years to write. It expresses how much I value the work of H.S. Sullivan. I explore some of the clinical implications of Sullivan's one genus postulate that "everyone is much more simply human than otherwise" (1953, p.32). I then compare Sullivan's notion with seemingly similar ideas from philosophers, poets, and emotion theorists, to clarify the meaning of Sullivan's statement. Finally, I offer clinical illustrations of some applications of the postulate.

Even before my analytic training, Sullivan was one of my heroes. During graduate school, while many of my teachers introduced me to fascinating theories, only Sullivan illuminated my bewildering experience as a neophyte psychologist on inpatient wards. He helped me enter into the frightening inner worlds of my psychotic patients. I was (and remain) grateful.

Like Fromm, Sullivan had a humanistic intention. The regressed, psychotic person is, first of all, a human being. By insisting on this, Sullivan encouraged me to look for commonalities, as well as noting

---

* *Contemporary Psychoanalysis*, 2014, 50:4, 531-548.

differences. The differences are easier to recognize, perhaps because they (seem to) offer a way to maintain a relatively undisturbed distance. But, as another of my heroes, the poet Rainer Maria Rilke (1934, pp. 67-68) wrote, the easier way is not always the better way. "Most people have (with the help of conventions) turned their solutions toward what is easy and toward the easiest side of easy; but it is clear that we must trust in what is difficult; everything alive trusts in it, everything in Nature grows and defends itself any way it can and is spontaneously itself, tries to be itself at all costs and against all opposition. We know little, but that we must trust in what is difficult is a certainty that will never abandon us..."

These words, together with Sullivan's outlook, have come to mean so much to me. I can sometimes see how a psychic equilibrium ("in" myself, my patient, and/or our interaction) "defends itself in any way it can, and is spontaneously itself, tries to be itself at all costs and against all opposition." I can sometimes see that fierce determination to remain oneself, regardless of the cost, as more simply human than otherwise.

ABSTRACT

This article explores some implications of Sullivan's (1953, p. 32) postulate that "everyone is much more simply human than otherwise. . . ." Comparisons with seemingly similar statements by philosophers, poets, and emotion theorists may clarify what Sullivan meant. The author discusses her own theoretical and clinical applications of Sullivan's concept and focuses on the emotions of joy and sorrow, as quintessentially "simply human" experiences.

Hath not a Jew eyes? Hath not a Jew hands, organs, dimensions, senses, affections, passions? — fed with the same food, hurt with the same weapons, subject to the same diseases, healed by the same means, warmed and cooled by the same winter and summer as a Christian is? If you prick us, do we not bleed? If you tickle us, do we not laugh? If you poison us, do we not die? And if you wrong us, shall we not revenge? (William Shakespeare, *The Merchant of Venice*, Act III, Scene 1, lines 54-62).

In Shakespeare's *The Merchant of Venice*, Shylock declares a Jew emotionally more simply human than otherwise. "If you prick us, do we not bleed?" When we are injured, isn't our pain the same as anyone else's? Isn't our laughter, our anger, the same?

Photography declares our common humanity graphically, silently. We see a picture of a crying infant whose hungry belly is distended. No words are required. We have all known abject, powerless, desperate need. We have hungered for something or someone. Our recognition of this infant's passion confers compassion. In an instant, we feel hunger's yawning, churning limitless rumble.

One way we can understand Sullivan's one-genus postulate is that, as human beings, we share a potential for joy, sorrow, shame, and other feelings. In this article, I expand on this reading of the postulate, and add some other possibilities.

SULLIVAN'S ONE-GENUS POSTULATE

Sullivan (1953) provided several versions of the one-genus hypothesis or postulate. In *The Interpersonal Theory of Psychiatry* he said, "I have become occupied with the science, not of individual differences, but of human identities, or parallels, one might say. In other words, I try to study the degrees and patterns of things which I assume to be ubiquitously human" (p. 33).

The more memorable version (Sullivan, 1953, p. 32) states that, ". . . everyone is much more simply human than otherwise. . . ." Scores of papers have been written on the implications of this sentence. I will merely mention a few of the issues it raises. What does it say about Sullivan's view of individuality? Personally, I don't think Sullivan is denying the significance of individual differences, but I think he is saying two important things in this postulate.

1. He has a humanistic intention. The regressed schizophrenic is a human being who can, potentially, be understood by other human beings, and deserves the respect we expect to be accorded to ourselves.

2.   The unique individuality of the patient is not the psychiatrist's primary focus (but that does not mean it doesn't exist).
We get further in treatment if we assume that human living
occurs in characteristic patterns that we can know, and use,
in understanding a particular person. It should be noted that
some interpersonalists, such as Wolstein, have disagreed
with this emphasis, privileging the discovery of the unique.
But for Sullivan, the analyst's awareness of common human
patterns plays a major role in directing inquiry. If a patient,
for example, never mentions having any playmates as a child
we make the assumption that this is something to inquire
into.

This may sound like it merely states the obvious, but I think that is
far from true. For example, think about the word "simply." What does it
mean to be simply human? Contrasting Sullivan's statement with two
others clarifies what it does and does not imply. Terence (1987) stated
that "I am a man: I hold that nothing human is alien to me" (p. 236).
Likewise, Goethe (1987) said "[t]here is no crime of which I do not
deem myself capable" (p. 325). I take both Goethe and Terence to mean
that I have the potential for the actions of any other human being. In
contrast, Sullivan is referring to the ubiquity of certain patterns of
behavior, which make us all more alike than different. He is not commenting on what we are capable of, but merely on what we have in
common. The analyst's expertise is, partially, in his or her familiarity
with these recurrent patterns. What are the patterns we all share? In my
own work, I have concentrated on three: emotional motivations, character styles, and defenses. I will briefly discuss each of these three aspects
of being human.

HUMAN EMOTIONAL MOTIVATIONS

It is meaningful to me that Shylock bases his plea for recognizing the
Jew's humanity on the universality of human emotions. One way that we
are all more human than otherwise is that each of us is capable of joy,

sadness, anger, shame, fear, and all the other basic emotions. From my research, with Cal Izard, on the first expressions of each of the fundamental emotions, I took the idea that the emotions are the primary motivational system in human beings. Although the potential to feel all the fundamental emotions is universal, our life experience patterns them differently in each of us. You and I are both capable of shame. But maybe very intense early taunting has tinged your shame with rage. My shame comes with a different history, perhaps bringing more anxiety than rage in its wake. Of course, these would be relative, not absolute, differences.

Seeing emotions as the primary motivational system in human beings is fundamentally different from a drive theory. Drive theories suggest a limited number of predetermined possibilities, but emotions can interact in extremely varying ways, and at different levels of intensity. Along with the idea that feelings are our principal motivators, I have taken from emotion theory the concept that the emotions form a system in human beings, with changes in any feeling affecting all the others. Thus, because our feelings exist in us in a kind of balance or system, it follows that a shift in the *intensity* of any one emotion affects all the others. The liberating thing about thinking of the emotions as forming a system is that it allows us to have an impact on the whole array by affecting the intensity of any emotion. We know how this works from our own personal experience, but I believe we don't apply it often enough to an understanding of clinical exchanges. When we are saddened by sobering news, the world takes on a somber cast, the fight is out of us, and other feelings are muted. But joy and love can also permeate experience, lending all of it a glow. Likewise, if we can deepen the patient's curiosity, we are also having an impact on the patient's anger and anxiety level. A human being's experience of life itself shifts when any emotion is heightened or diminished. This means when I am with a depressed patient, I don't have to feel stuck focusing endlessly on the depression, which can be painfully unproductive. Instead, I can wonder about the patient's shame or curiosity. The assumption that *emotions form a system* frees us to range over *all* the emotions when we encounter any one of them.

I want to take this further to suggest that in an interaction, the emotions of one person form a constantly oscillating system with the feelings of the other person. As Irwin Hirsch (2002, p. 582) suggests, the work of Harold Searles, among others, gave us examples of how sharing the patient's emotional impact on the analyst can be integrated into an analytic approach. My own way of expressing this is that, for example, the patient's anxiety may be affecting my curiosity, and my anger might be modulating their depression. To say that influence is bidirectional doesn't do full justice to the complexity of the system of mutual emotional modulation that is always going on between two people in an interaction. Thus, at any moment in time, my own fear and the patient's escalating rage might both be diminishing my curiosity, or, if my life experience is different, my fear and her rage might augment my curiosity. Because no one really feels only one emotion at a time, the permutations are virtually endless. So much for simplistic theories of human motivation!

Working with feelings in treatment includes, for me, an emphasis on my own and the patient's histories of experience of each emotion. Each of us brings to the present moment a lifetime of knowing how we feel when we are angry, fearful, joyful, and sad, among other feeling states. Shortly, I discuss some implications of this for notions of projective identification. In brief, I believe that no one can project his or her experience into me without it being shaped by my personal emotional history. I see this understanding of the limits of projective identification as one of the unique contributions of an interpersonal approach. We are simply human in that we have all known fear, shame, and anger, and can recognize their faces, but-for each of us-their meaning is shaped by our particular life experiences.

Thinking about this leads to an interpersonal understanding of the difference between empathy and sympathy, and, in particular, of empathic processes in treatment. In my 2008 book, I discuss this in more detail but, in brief, one way to look at the emotional interplay in treatment is that the analyst is continuously losing and regaining an emotional balance that privileges curiosity. One hopes, simultaneously, that the analyst is observing what is making maintaining this balance difficult, as well as what can make it possible. These observations can be used to learn about both participants. Of course, the patient may be making the same or different observations. Thus, my understanding of empathy is inherently interpersonal, in that it centers on the seesawing emotional impact of one person on another person's emotional balance. In an empathic process, I do more than merely passively mirror the patient's feelings. For example, if my patient, Mary, expresses hate I may momentarily register *her* hate, but then, it quickly morphs into *my* way of feeling this emotion. I can only know hate in my way of hating. Another way to say this is that the experience alters inside my milieu. It is embedded inside the context of my lifetime of experience of hating. I have a personal hating history, just as I have a personal history of living through moments of grief, anger, joy, surprise, and other feelings. Thus, I may initially register Mary's hate, but it quickly becomes my hate. That's the only kind of hate that is possible for me to sustain. This is quintessentially interpersonal in that it is shaped by both participants. That is, I don't believe that I just pick up Mary's hate and sympathetically feel it Mary's way. That would say that Mary could project her hate into me. My understanding is interpersonal in that once Mary's hate enters me it changes into a hate consonant with my lifelong hating history. For example, if hating generally makes me anxious, I will feel anxiety along with the hating. If it evokes my shame, then shame will be part of the experience.

As I go through this process, I automatically begin to struggle toward balance, in a way that is also shaped by my life history. However I overtly reacted, I hope that I become curious about what is going on, which modulates my feelings. This state of mind and heart would prime me to hear the subsequent material differently. That is, the process of feeling Mary's hate, which morphs into my hate, and recovering my capacity to be curious and work analytically brings some aspects of the material to the foreground. For example, it might make me especially ready to hear about internal battles between feeling hate and maintaining a familiar sense of oneself.

My way of understanding empathy is at the crux of my personal interpersonalism. It is an active process, and not merely a passive sympathetic joining or seamless mirroring. It differs in important ways from projective identification as it is often understood, although there are also commonalities. If I say I feel your pain, I am both accurate and inaccurate. I may feel something *like* your pain, and I probably feel something *triggered* by your pain, but no one can feel pain that is an exact copy of yours. Once the pain enters my system, it is colored by my life experience. My pain is a product of me and you, a mix that is neither purely your pain nor purely my own, but something new. And it is this newness that allows for change to occur. Your pain is transformed as it enters my milieu, and it is further transformed as I struggle to recover from it, using my resources. This transformed version of your pain allows me to know you to the extent that I can. It is an inexact version of what you feel, but it is the best I can do. Who I am colors my empathy: shapes, limits, but also empowers it.

Extending this one step further, I believe that each emotion is a separable self state when it is intense. That is, when I am very angry, I experience the moment differently from when I feel intense joy. Not only does intense anger remind me of my whole history of experience in that emotional state, but it also affects my cognitive and other functioning. This, of course, has implications for the one-genus hypothesis. One of the ways we are all more human than otherwise is that, for example, we have all known fear, in some form. To take another example, culture has a big impact on what shames us, but all human beings have known shame.

When I was in training, I was taught that an important function we serve is to monitor the patient's level of anxiety by carefully observing his or her nonverbal and verbal expressions of it. We should strive to help the patient stay within bearable levels of anxiety because when it escalates it blocks further progress. In other words, anxiety can operate like a blow on the head. I would broaden this, to suggest that the analyst keeps track of all intense emotionality felt by both participants. There are bearable and unbearable levels of shame and loneliness, for example. And some combinations of feelings are unbearable, although each emotion might be bearable by itself. Shame can be particularly troublesome in combination with other intense feelings, because it motivates human beings to hide, which can interfere in the interpersonal process. Whether to merely keep track of intense emotions, such as painful loneliness, or to strive to help the patient modulate them, is a difficult clinical judgment call that can not be prescribed in advance, but we should be aware that intense emotions of all kinds affect the treatment exchange. This is another way we are all "more human than otherwise." The analyst, too, can suffer from painful shame, loneliness, anxiety, and other intense feelings in a session, with significant consequences. For example, I would suggest that in states of loneliness we are more likely to take an active stance in a session. We might, then, explain our behavior with a rationalization, drawn from theory, about why this patient needed us to be active.

Although all of us feel all the fundamental emotions at one point or another, are any more significant than the others in shaping who we are? Are any more important than the others as a focus for the clinician? Sullivan emphasized the role of anxiety in human experience. The patient will learn more from his or her experience in treatment if anxiety is kept at a tolerable intensity.

Other theorists have privileged different emotions. Kohut and Morrison, among others, emphasized shame, and, of course, Freud and Klein contributed their slant on the power of sexual and aggressive motives. I quote William James (1902/2004) in *The Varieties of Religious Experience*, for a lively statement of a different point of view. "If we were to ask the question: 'What is human life's chief concern' one of the answers we should receive would be: 'It is happiness.' How to gain, how to keep, how to recover happiness, is in fact for most men at all times the secret motive of all they do, and of all they are willing to endure" (p. 78).

I would say that any emotion, if intense enough, can affect our quality of life. In treatment, *all the human emotions can play substantial roles.* Being a patient or a clinician requires enough curiosity, hope, joy, and love to sustain the work. It is sometimes necessary to be able to bear surprise. Anger can be a motivating force, driving the work forward. People fight for their lives, partly in angry response to obstacles. But shame, guilt, contempt, sadness, depression, and loneliness must not exceed bearable levels for treatment to continue. Too much loneliness in a treatment hour can sap the will to go on. Too much shame can make the self-exposure inherent in treatment too painful. If anxiety is too intense, experimentation feels too risky. *There is a range of each emotion that permits us to do treatment or to receive it.*

Because each emotion is qualitatively, and not just quantitatively, different, I believe that we can't talk about working with "countertransference" emotions without being more specific. For example, when the patient is extremely sensitive to shame, it seems to me especially important for the therapist to try to be aware of fluctuations in his or her sense of self. Of course, we would each approach this task differently. Some approaches include sharing the patient's shame, much as, I think, a Shakespearian "fool" would. Not unlike the clinician, this character sometimes softens shame by being willing to look "foolish" if that contributes to creating a new perspective. I will just mention a few emotions besides shame that play key roles in treatment and the rest of life.

JOY AND SORROW

Although each of the fundamental emotions is an aspect of our common experience, joy and sorrow seem to me to be especially suited to express what it means to be simply human. That is, joy and sorrow are not just emotions we all feel. They are emotions we all feel that (at least to some extent) are *about* being part of the human community. In joy we feel enriched by our membership in the human race, whereas in sorrow we join the impoverished. Sorrow reminds us not to ask for whom the bell tolls. When it tolls, it tolls for us all. Thus, as I see it, joy and sorrow are quintessentially "more simply human" emotions. Feeling like part of humankind is a vital way to understand what brings some moments of joy. I (Buechler, 2008) call joy the "universal antidote," because I believe it can play a vital role in modulating all of our most painful emotional experiences. Joy makes us feel we can soar over frustrating obstacles. It counters the paralysis in depression and the diminishment in grief. Its potential for moments of timelessness frees us from anxious constraint. Interludes of joy help us shed shame, guilt, sorrow, and fear, and invest more fully in life again. As clinicians, it seems to me to be important to wonder how we can help others, and ourselves access the power of joy.

Schachtel (1959/2001) defined joy as "a feeling of being related to all things living" (p. 42). He went on to describe joy as a continuous turning toward the world. It is, in his words, "the felt experience of the ongoing acts of relatedness." For me, the poet Wordsworth (1805/1988) best captured the joy of connecting to life in his "Ode: Intimations of Immortality from Recollections of Early Childhood." For Wordsworth, sensing that we are part of the vast fabric of life can bring profound joy. When life presents itself to him, in any form, his heart bears witness. As he expresses it, "to me the meanest flower that blows can give/thoughts that do often lie too deep for tears." Pablo Neruda wrote of the life changing moment when he suddenly felt a kind of love between himself and strangers, a feeling that "widens out the boundaries of our being and unites all living things." That exchange brought home to me for the first time a precious idea: that all of humanity is somehow together ..." (as quoted in E. Hirsch, 1999, p. 262).

In joy we celebrate life augmented, whereas in sorrow we mourn for life lost. At the heart of my writing, in many senses, is a meditation on human grief. To me, it is crucial for the analyst to be attentive to opportunities for grief work. How we each understand grief reflects, perhaps more clearly than anything else, our analytic allegiances. Nowhere does an interpersonal approach matter more to me than in our attitudes about grief. It shapes what we emphasize. Thus, although I agree with the idea of an ongoing interchange with the internalized object, my interpersonal emphasis points up the limitations of that approach. As I have written elsewhere:

> ... I believe that a true grasp of our interpersonal natures forces us to conclude that the Joss of actual, specific, intimately known others is irreplaceable. We need to feel their breath, to hold their hand, to watch them laugh, to experience them in the living moment, through every sense, and not just in memory. This need is given poignant voice by survivors like Didion and Bayley who will settle for nothing less than the continuing presence of their beloved. Anything else denies the importance of the body, of sur-

prise, of the unpredictable moment. No matter how mature and well developed our inner life, there is no object relational substitute for an alive partner when you want to go dancing. (Buechler, 2008, p. 150)

I think of loss as an ongoing process, in treatment and the rest of life. The ultimate losses crystallize our feelings about the more subtle but pervasive ones. How many times in a session does each participant lose a bit of hope of being really understood? When we open the newspaper in the morning, how much of our belief in a sane humane world is shattered? These "micro-losses" gather at the point of termination of treatment, or at other times of concrete loss. At those moments, grief is formulated partially, perhaps, because there will be no more chances to recoup what has been lost along the way. I would suggest that the analyst's transparent registering of sadness can be a potent force. When we are palpably affected by the patient's losses and our own, it is apparent that we are all simply human. Clinicians have many opportunities to appreciate one sorrow, in particular. I (Buechler, 2008) have called it the "death of the unharmed self." For example, when we treat someone who was abused as a child, what can emerge is a picture of the freer, livelier, more joyous, and trusting person the patient might have become had the abuse not occurred. For me, it has often felt as though I am participating in this person's burial. I am one of the mourners. I can be deeply affected in the presence of the loss of life that could and should have been. Many interpersonalists, including Searles (1965, 1979) and Ehrenberg (1992), have emphasized the potentially mutative power of the patient's awareness of having an emotional impact on the analyst. I would extend this to suggest that we think about how transparency about our sadness may impact differently from transparency about our shame, guilt, anger, loneliness, hope, anxiety, and other feelings.

When we meet another in sorrow, the connection that exists between us all can be palpable. Writing about *King Lear*, Edmundson (2000) notes that "[b]efore the play is over, Lear, tutored by the fool, will show us how humane a vision can arise from losing all outward trappings, and seeing the essential fragility and preciousness of everything that lives" (p. 35).

CHARACTER STYLES

So far, I have suggested that we are all more simply human than otherwise in our emotions and their motivating forces, and most especially in our joys and sorrows. A second broad area of human commonality is our potential for coping with life in all the basic ways available to us. That is, given circumstances conducive to it, I can become somewhat paranoid, or depressive, or obsessive, and so on. Elsewhere (Buechler, 2012) I have suggested that diagnostic terminology lags behind some of our other conceptualizations in that it is conceived of in one-person, rather than two-person terms. We think of people who are paranoid, rather than paranoid interpersonal interactions. To some extent that is inevitable, given the exigencies of insurance forms and other practicalities. But, in our own minds, we can preserve an ability to remember that different interpersonal situations call out different potentials in each of us. I am more obsessive in some interpersonal situations and more depressed in others. In 2002, I wrote about a schizoid patient, who brought out my own schizoid potential. For me, terms like schizoid, paranoid, and narcissistic are most useful not as nouns, but as adjectives describing coping patterns. They are like photographs, capturing a moment in time, in a particular context. Thus, for example, I may find that a patient who initially seemed narcissistic quickly settles into a schizoid pattern of relating as we work together. Perhaps this patient will go through a schizoid "phase," only to emerge to work on depressive issues. Had he or she been working with a different analyst or, even, with me at a different time, the picture might have varied somewhat. Diagnostic terms are not most useful as descriptions of the static essence of a person. Rather, they capture fleeting patterns of coping with human vulnerabilities. One of the ways we are all more human than otherwise is in our implicit knowing of how to obsess.

I think of all the "diagnostic entities" as elements in healthy functioning. We all have some potential for schizoid withdrawal, obsessive controlling, and paranoid suspicion. Coping with the human condition inevitably fashions these tendencies in us. But if they are in something like equilibrium, we won't suffer from a severe distortion of living.

Although it is sometimes necessary for the clinician to refer to someone as a schizoid person, it can be more useful to think about schizoid moments in a session created by both participants. A truly interpersonal understanding of human functioning necessitates thinking about how one person's way of coping affects the other, when the two are interacting. With a particular patient I may focus, feel, and interact in my most paranoid fashion, but another patient, that same day, may elicit a different coping style from me. I live different aspects of my potential with different people. Although my basic profile, my characteristic style, endures, a patient and I might bring out each other's capacity for paranoid feeling, thinking, and interacting. But if I am not prevailingly paranoid, I will soon be able to recover and tilt in another direction.

DEFENSES

Aside from our common human emotions and character styles, we have the potential to use all the basic defenses. That is, at times, we each use projection, selective inattention, sublimation, and so on. Once again, a significant part of what the clinician has to offer is familiarity with these patterns. My understanding of the defenses and coping styles has led me to a way of thinking about health. Just as Bromberg has written about normal dissociation, I see all the defenses as playing some role in psychic life. We couldn't focus without selective inattention, and we certainly couldn't function without compartmentalization. The notion of a balance of defenses makes sense to me. Overreliance on any one of them becomes problematic, but some denial, repression, dissociation, etc. makes psychic survival possible.

So far, I have seen us all as simply human in our motivating emotions, and potential for using basic defenses and character styles to cope with our vulnerabilities. I would say that, in one sense, interpersonalists take a position that differs from seeing all human beings as alike. From an interpersonal point of view, the path toward health may be different for any two people. Unlike the classical notion of a resolution of the Oedipal complex, or the Kleinian notion of achieving the depressive position, in an interpersonal understanding there is no specific issue that people in general need to resolve. An implication of this is that the analyst can not know the particular goals of a treatment or the therapeutic action that can achieve these goals until they are constructed by the participants. They are not known in advance. Thus, in each treatment we have to discover what needs to change and create a means to change it. This is, to me, radically different from any theory that includes a static conception of health, whether health is pictured as mentalizing, resolving a particular conflict, or developing a positive sense of self.

In this context, I will just mention that, although I agree that each treatment has to discover what relative health can mean for this patient and how it could be achieved, I also feel that some challenges are built into the human condition, and, therefore, are highly likely to play roles in an individual's strivings. For example, what I often find most clinically relevant about the Oedipal situation is that each generation comes into its peak as the last one is losing its grip. Thus, I frequently focus on the offspring's grief for the declining parent, although there are times when competitive wishes to replace the parent, envy, jealousy, and guilt play more prominent roles than grief. Sometimes Oedipus comes to mind as a human being who didn't understand a vitally significant crossroads until he had made a terrible mistake. Even a brilliant riddle solver is still simply a human being. We often realize our blindness too late. In short, just as Winnicott declared that there is no such thing as the baby, we can say that there is no such thing as the Oedipus complex. Each human being lives the interaction with an earlier generation in his or her own way, and the selective focus of the analyst brings to the fore specific aspects of the situation. Although I often privilege its grief, another analyst might bring a different slant. It follows that each analyst would understand the therapeutic action somewhat differently. I might focus on the centrality of mourning as part of healing, whereas another analyst might conceive of the treatment process with the same patient very differently.

To add just one more way we are simply human, the idea that "... man requires interpersonal relationships, or interchange with others" (Sullivan, 1953, p. 32) can be seen as another extension of the one-genus postulate. It posits a universal need for interaction. A similar thought, with a somewhat different emphasis, was stated by Fromm (1968, p. 72) in his famous declaration that, "[b]ecause I have eyes, I have the need to see, because I have ears, I have the need to hear, because I have a mind, I have a need to think; and because I have a heart, I have a need to feel. In short, because I am a man, I am in need of man and of the world." Fromm emphasizes that a reason we need interpersonal relating is that it is a capacity within us, and, like other human potentials, it can be problematic if it is not lived. This aspect of Fromm's thinking integrates easily with existentialism. It has been beautifully expressed by the poet and scholar Edward Hirsch (1999). Hirsch describes the part of Plato's *Symposium* in which each of us is seen as half of a knucklebone, forever seeking our other half. I love how Hirsch portrays the process between poet and reader. I ask you to listen, substituting analyst and patient.

> We make meaning together, we wrestle with what we read and talk back to it, we become more fully ourselves in the process. We activate the poem inside us by engaging it as deeply as possible, by bringing our lives to it, our associational memories, our past histories, our vocabularies, by letting its verbal music infiltrate our bodies, its ideas seep into our minds, by discovering its pattern emerging, by entering the echo chamber that is the history of poetry, and, most of all, by listening and paying attention. *Attentiveness is the natural prayer of the soul.* (E. Hirsch, 1999, p. 260, emphasis added).

In addition to the idea that we *need* interpersonal relating, I take Sullivan to further imply that the *meaning* of an interpersonal experience is created through interaction. Thus, development is seen as a process of having experiences with real others and internalizing emotionally salient aspects of these experiences. In a similar vein, the Spanish philosopher Jose Ortega y Gasset wrote, "[h]ow unimportant a thing would be if it were only what it is in isolation" (as quoted in Dowrick, 2011, p. 167). I believe this to be consonant with Sullivan's thinking, and it is certainly consonant with my own. I have already described how Edward Hirsch (1999) makes a similar point in reference to poetry, where meaning is interpersonally created through the interaction of writer and reader. He refers to Berkeley's idea that the taste of an apple lies in the contact of the fruit with the palate, not in the fruit itself (p. 29).

MORE SIMPLY CLINICAL THAN OTHERWISE

I appreciate that the theories we hold matter, but I am going to argue that we spend too much time trying to pin down our differences, and not enough time looking at our commonalities as clinicians. First, I do feel that our theories matter in that they affect our focus. This is true in all of life. By its nature, focus is selective. The world we each experience is, in part, the world we create through our focus. Likewise, for the analyst, the patient we experience is, to some extent, the patient we create. In other words, as we all know, the analyst experiences the patient subjectively. Our theories privilege certain aspects of who the patient is, and help determine what we ask about, remember, and evoke.

But I also believe that there are important values we all share, as clinicians and as human beings. These clinical values were the subject of my first book (Buechler, 2004) and remain especially meaningful to me. The therapeutic culture values courage, curiosity, hope, integrity, and other qualities. We cherish the patient's pursuit of whatever truths can be known. We love this for itself, and not as a means to an end. We want to help people know themselves better, and live their potential. We are all fans of the little engine that could. We believe that the past can be prologue, and that those who are ignorant of it are more often doomed to repeat it.

By saying that we are more simply clinical than otherwise, I am implying that I think we have to be very wary of generalizations about how analysts from a particular school work, especially when these characterizations include emotionally evocative qualities like whether or not they are sensitive, kind, or empathic. Categorizing schools with value-laden binaries inevitably provokes intense feelings. Although it is true that our theories play a role in our focus in sessions, I think my choices—for example, about whether to say something at any particular moment— result from an often unformulated and extremely complicated calculus about the potential value of the words as against their potential negative impact. Theory affects my decision about when to speak, but so do many other factors. It is probably true that, out of the thousands of choices I make in a session, more of my choices could be seen as following interpersonal theory than following self psychology. But I think it is equally true that my choices are shaped by my clinical values, such as my belief that curiosity is a valuable attribute to nurture in myself and others. I think my self psychological colleagues and I are more simply clinical than otherwise in that we all tend to value curiosity, integrity, courage, and hope.

So, my suggestion to those just entering the field is that, instead of trying to figure out which way of working is right, ask yourself which supervisors, teachers, personal analysts seem likely to help *you* maximize *your own* personal strengths. I'm too emotionally intense to make a good blank screen, and somehow, I knew it early on. I was lucky enough to encounter a few teachers who helped me hone my particular set of strengths, to some degree, and understand some of my personal limitations. I will always be grateful to these teachers, many of whom were at the William Alanson White Institute.

To close, I would like to return briefly to the question of our more simply human motivations. How similar are we, in this respect? The distinction between Sullivan's emphasis on patterns and Goethe's declarations that he is capable of any crime loses clarity for me in some contexts. In Primo Levi's (1988) last book, *The Drowned and the Saved*, published the year before he died, he considers the question of who his Nazi torturers were. At the end of his efforts to answer this question he writes:

> . . . we are asked by the young who our "torturers" were, of what cloth were they made. The term torturers alludes to our ex-guardians, the SS, and is in my opinion inappropriate: it brings to mind twisted individuals, ill-born, sadists, afflicted by an original flaw. Instead they were made of the same cloth as we, they were average human beings, averagely intelligent, averagely wicked: save the exceptions, they were not monsters, they had our faces,

but they had been reared badly. They were, for the greater part. diligent followers and functionaries, some fanatically convinced of Nazi doctrine, many indifferent, or fearful of punishment, or desirous of a good career, or too obedient. (p. 202).

I cannot comment on the voluminous literature that examines the banality of evil. But, in brief, if we are more human than otherwise in our defenses, character styles, and emotional motivations, what does this say about our potential for crime? For example, if we are all potentially fearful, hateful, paranoid, and capable of projection, dissociation, and denial, does that mean nothing human is alien to me, and there is no crime of which I should deem myself incapable? Far from a simple statement, I think the one-genus postulate can lead us to examine profound issues about what it means to be a human being.

REFERENCES

Buechler, S. (2002). More simply human than otherwise. *Contemporary Psychoanalysis* 38:485–497.

——— (2004). *Clinical Values: Emotions That Guide Psychoanalytic Treatment.* Hillsdale, NJ: The Analytic Press.

——— (2008). *Making a Difference in Patients' Lives: Emotional Experience in the Therapeutic Setting.* New York: Routledge.

——— (2012). *Still Practicing: The Heartaches and Joys of a Clinical Career.* New York, NY: Routledge.

Dowrick, S. (2011). *In the Company of Rilke.* New York, NY: Penguin.

Edmundson, M. (2000, April 2). Playing the fool. *New York Times Book Review,* p. 35.

Ehrenberg, D. B. (1992). *The Intimate Edge.* New York: W.W. Norton.

Fromm, E. (1968). *The Revolution of Hope.* New York: Harper & Row.

Goethe, J. W. von. (1987). In R. I. Fitzhenry (Ed.), *Book of Quotations.* New York, Barnes & Noble Books.

Hirsch, E. (1999). *How to Read a Poem and Fall in Love with Poetry.* New York: Harcourt.

Hirsch, I. (2002). Beyond interpretation: Analytic interaction in the interpersonal tradition. *Contemporary Psychoanalysis* 38:573B589.

James, W. (2004). The *Varieties of Religious Experience.*. New York: Barnes & Noble Classics, 1902.

Levi, P. (1988). *The Drowned and the Saved,* trans., R. Rosenthal. New York: Summit Books.

Schachtel, E. G. (2001). *Metamorphosis: On the Conflict of Human Development and the Psychology of Creativity.* Hillsdale, NJ: Analytic Press, 1959.

Searles, H. (1965). *Selected Papers on Schizophrenia and Related Subjects.* New York, NY: International Universities Press.

——— (1979). *Countertransference and Related Subjects. Selected Papers.* New York, NY: International Universities Press.

Shakespeare, W. (1959). *The Merchant of Venice.* In A. R. Braunmuller, ed, *The Pelican Shakespeare.* New York: Penguin, originally published in 1598, pp. 1–208.

Sullivan, H. S. (1953). *The Interpersonal theory of Psychiatry.* New York Norton.

Terence, P. T. A. (1987). In R. I. Fitzhenry, ed. *Book of Quotations.* New York: Barnes & Noble Books, p. 236.

Wordsworth, W. (1988). Ode: Intimations of immortality from recollections of early childhood. In: Heaney (Ed.), *Essential Wordsworth.* New York: HarperCollins, pp. 147–155.

CHAPTER ELEVEN

Henry James' Middle Years and My Own[*]

INTRODUCTION

In this paper I voice personal regrets for roads not taken, that have now vanished. Although well past the middle of my own life, I suggest that mid life is a perfect time for regrets. We have an increasing awareness of time's limitations, and our own. In this paper I reflect on some of my regrets, as well as reasons to celebrate. I draw some parallels with Henry James' (1992) short story, "The Middle Years," which sympathetically describes the torment of an aging writer, who realizes that "He should never again, as at one or two great moments of the past, be better than himself. The infinite of life was gone..." In the story the writer, Dencombe, feels great pain that he hadn't quite gotten where he most wanted to go, as an author.

As I think about this paper now, a different perspective occurs to me. I remember the end of C.P. Cavefy's (2009) great poem, "Ithaca."

Ithaca gave you the beautiful journey.
without her you wouldn't have set upon the road.
But now she has nothing left to give you.

---

[*] Paper presented at Division 39 of the American Psychological Association meeting, April, 2015.

And if you find her poor, Ithaca didn't deceive you.
As wise as you will have become, with so much experience,
you will understand, by then, these Ithacas; what they mean.

I want to tell Dencombe to value the journey, and not just grieve the loss of the destination. But, of course, this is also what I want to tell myself.

HENRY JAMES' MIDDLE YEARS AND MY OWN

Division 39, 2015

Midway on our life's journey, I found myself
In dark woods, the right road lost. To tell
About those woods is hard-so tangled and rough

And savage that thinking of it now, I feel
The old fear stirring: death is hardly more bitter.
And yet, to treat the good I found there as well

I'll tell what I saw.....

The Inferno of Dante, Translated by Robert Pinsky, Canto I, lines 1–7
(New York: Farrar, Straus, & Giroux, 1994)

So begins Robert Pinsky's translation of Dante's Inferno. While these lines hardly apply to my life, which is far from an inferno and way past its middle, I do want to speak of the dark woods, the tangled and rough, the savage and fearful, and treat the good I found as well.

In "The Middle Years," (1992) Henry James explores an aging author's regrets and longings. Dencombe is no longer a young, promising writer with all the time in the world to bring his talent to fruition. As the story opens, he has just received a copy of his new book and realizes that he doesn't remember what he wrote. What does this mean about the functioning of his mind, at present and in the future?

As I see it, Dencombe mourns a series of painful losses. The luxurious feeling of unlimited time is gone. Little remains of his reliable memory, sharp senses, and thrilling discoveries of newfound powers. As he loses young Dencombe he also says goodbye to a protesting chorus of unlived Dencombe's.

Dencombe vividly mourns waning opportunities. "He should never again, as at one or two great moments of the past, be better than himself. The infinite of life was gone, and what remained of the dose a small glass scored like a thermometer by the apothecary." Tears fill Dencombe's eyes, as he reflects that, for him, "...something precious had passed away. This was the pang that had been the sharpest during the last few years-the sense of ebbing time, of shrinking opportunity; and now he felt not so much that his last chance was going as that it was gone indeed. He had done all he should ever do, and yet hadn't done what he wanted." (p. 173).

What moves me is that Dencombe simultaneously understands what he most wants to say, and envisions that he won't have enough time to say it. Similarly, the middle years have been my season for precipitously escalating regrets. Roads not taken are rapidly vanishing. There are worlds I would like to have explored, books I wish I had written, and selves I wanted to be. Earlier in my life I wrote poetry, studied art history, researched facial expressions of emotions, and treated psychotic children. I promised myself I would return and rescue these unfinished selves from oblivion, but, I now believe, I will break all those promises.

Mourning selves that once were, and those that never will be, can become a full time job. I may look like a person on her way somewhere, but, like Dencombe, I am most keenly aware of the dreams that will remain unrealized. This paper stands at the convergence of professional and personal lives just foreclosing, selves that never had their chance, and some that have. It sketches my perspective from this "post middle" vantage point, and offers it to those still in early phases of their careers, as well as cohorts in the "middle years" and beyond.

At the outset let me say that, while Dencombe and I are similar in many respects, unlike him I don't want to lose my regrets. Any sharp hunger is a sign of life. My aim is to make my regrets keen, and live them as fully as possible, while I have the chance.

At the outset of Henry James' story, Dencombe is aging prematurely, staying at a health resort, and trying recoup the strength he has lost to a debilitating illness. He sits on a bench, looking at his newly published book as though he had never seen it before. He reads, and is dazzled by the author's brilliance, which only further perplexes him.

To his amazement, he spots a young man, Doctor Hugh, who is also reading the new book. In subsequent conversations Dr. Hugh tries to reconcile Dencombe to his situation, with approaches familiar to clinicians. Dr. Hugh exhorts Dencombe to have a more positive outlook. He praises this latest book, attempting to convince the author that his mission was, indeed, accomplished. But this only heightens Dencombe's sorrow over the promise that he has not fulfilled, from his perspective. Dr. Hugh argues that Dencombe needs more vanity, but Dencombe sadly asserts that what he needs is time. He pleads with life, for what he calls an "extension." It is as though Dencombe believes that life, like a fair minded authority, will give him more time if he deserves it. But life, impervious to Dencombe's pleadings, does not grant his wish. Dr. Hugh's logic and positive assertions do nothing to alleviate Dencombe's sorrow, though the reader can wonder whether Dr. Hugh's intense interest and offer of a relationship gave Dencombe some solace as his life ended.

I relate to the irony I read at the heart of this story. It takes Dencombe most of his life to understand who he might have become. It takes time to grow into the wisdom to separate what really matters from what really doesn't. And when, at last, he stands ready to live wisely and well, his turn is over.

Losses of shelved selves are a lot like losses of people we have loved. In perhaps the most extreme example of the loss of another person, if a child dies, her parents lose her smell and her radiant smile, but they also lose being her parents, and helping her grow up. They lose this aspect of themselves. While it is true that they can parent other children, it is not the same. The Saturdays are a little different. The strengths Mary's parents need to develop in themselves are not quite the same as the strengths Amy's parents must call upon. So three kinds of sorrows, losing a person, mislaying an old self, and failing to develop a potential self seem to me to have in common an impoverishment of who we could have been.

So far I have concentrated on the loss column. But the middle years can also be a time of consolidation of strengths. For example, my way of doing my work is more clearly formulated now than it has ever been. What it gives me, what it means to me, is with me. While it is still true that treatment has to be invented, in each session, with each patient, it is not invented from scratch. I know I believe that life experience is the most powerful agent of change. Life cures people. Treatment can make more life possible for someone, but it is mainly life experience that has the power to create profound changes. Along with Sullivan (1953) I believe in a primary, inborn drive toward health. Treatment often serves to facilitate removing obstacles, or defensive complications in functioning. When they become relatively less necessary, life forces have a better chance to hold sway. I know I am grossly oversimplifying, but I believe that our role as clinicians is to promote life, and each of us finds a theoretical stance that maximizes our therapeutic talents for doing so. For me, that has been an interpersonal slant, greatly influenced by Sullivan, Fromm, and Fromm-Reichmann, but also affected by Guntrip, Winnicott, and many patients, clinicians, teachers, supervisors, writers, poets, and artists I have loved.

After decades of living with these voices in my head, or, what I call my internal chorus, they have blended into a personal style. I suggest that having a relatively reliable personal style is an achievement that is most often accomplished in the middle years. This doesn't, and shouldn't eliminate uncertainties, anxieties, second guessing, and other difficulties endemic to our profession. But it makes me better able to bear the inevitable quandaries.

My own style relies on phrases I find helpful, like Guntrip's "schizoid compromise," "schizoid futility," "half in, half out relating," "schizoid bargain," and the "need/fear dilemma." These evocative phrases are beacons of light in my work with some people, at some junctures. With a phrase like "schizoid futility" I have a label for a moment in a session that helps me connect it with other moments in my work with that patient, in my own life, and in supervising, reading theory, reading fiction, poetry, and so on. Such collections of moments, with their headings, have helped shape my identity as a clinician. It was in my middle years that I learned who I tend to be, when I am in the presence of schizoid futility. Having this clearer sense gives me a reference point. It doesn't, and shouldn't tell me what to say or do. But it anchors me. Having a home base grounds me and helps me adventure more in any particular session. Recalling phrases from Guntrip has often come to my rescue. I once described that process as follows.

> But I feel that when I am in the presence of a detached, deadened schizoid patient I can actively search for the fighter in me. I can ask myself where she is today. I can remember her previous battles and their outcomes. I can think about those who have fought for life in my presence and, sometimes, on my behalf. I can recall moments, including some with my own supervisors and analysts, that have communicated their spirited intensity and determination to live every moment, in treatment as elsewhere, to its fullest. (2002, pp. 496–497).

For me, it was in my post analytic training middle years that I was able to integrate internalized mentors into something approaching a style of my own. Some mentors became especially meaningful, partially because they resonated enough with who I already was as a person. To resonate they had to have integrity, that is, how they treated me had to be consonant with what they advocated doing with patients. The medium had to match the message. Otherwise, at least for me, the experience was more perplexing and disturbing than enlightening. Perhaps another way to say this is that only voices that sounded authentic to me made it into the choir.

In our middle years we often evolve from being an offspring to being a parent, and from being a student to being a teacher. How do we accomplish these leaps? I don't know if this is true for others, but, in my experience, someone had to already see me as a teacher, for me to begin to inhabit the role. I remember, at the very onset of my career, a psychiatrist who trusted me with some referrals that I scarcely thought I could handle. Later on, I recall a young student who asked me to supervise her, when I was just finishing training myself. These people saw beyond where I was, to where I could go. They lent me their fantasies of me, and dreamt me into my future.

Stephen Mitchell was one person who furthered my middle years' transitions, simply by believing them possible. He encouraged me to write my first paper on hope (1995) which was inspired by his book, *Hope and Dread in Psychoanalysis*, (1993). I think developing a voice of one's own can be facilitated by someone believing in us enough to imagine us as innovators. Whether or not we choose to write, we need to author an authentic point of view.

Aside from developing a personally resonant perspective, there are three other accomplishments that I think most often take place in the middle years. The first is what I call my secret stash. It is the array of people I have tried to teach or treat. They live in my mind's eye. In my younger years I wondered how much I would get to do. My middle years have brought a partial answer. Some people reached, some books written are no longer in question.

My middle years have also brought me faith in my resilience. I am not immune to despair, but I believe I will always eventually bounce back. In *Still Practicing* (2012) I tried to express the toll of years of losing patients and hearing about every imaginable form human suffering can take. I wrote about how shame can accumulate and pool, on the days I fail people hour after hour. I tried to express the sharp pain of lost opportunities, of lost time, of seemingly endless misunderstandings. I can't think of a profession with more chances to feel like a coward or to feel dense, or impatient, or unkind. But my middle years have honed faith in my own resilience. There will be hours that I am discouraged and, perhaps, rendered inarticulate. But I'll be back.

Finally my middle years have given me a good feeling about the future. I don't mean my own future, but, rather, the future of our field. I know there are causes for real concern. But I have met many avid newcomers to clinical work. The shape of our profession may shift. But I feel a great confidence in the generation coming up. There will always be a need for people who can tend the life force. And I have faith that there will always be people who will make that their life's work.

REFERENCES

Buechler, S. (1995). Hope as inspiration in psychoanalysis. *Psychoanalytic Dialogues* 5:1, 63–74.

——— (2002). More simply human than otherwise. *Contemporary Psychoanalysis* 38:485B497.

——— (2012). *Still Practicing: The Heartaches and Joys of a Clinical Career.* New York: Routledge.

Cavafy, C. P. (2009). Ithaca. In: *Collected Poems by C. P. Cavafy*, trans. D. Mendelsohn. New York: Alfred A. Knopf.

James, H. (1992). The middle years. In: *The Oxford Book of American Short Stories*, ed. J. C. Oates. New York: Oxford University Press, p. 171–190.

Mitchell, S. A. (19903). *Hope and Dread in Psychoanalysis.* New York: Basic Books.

Pinsky, R. (1994). *The Inferno of Dante.* New York: Farrar, Straus, and Giroux.

Sullivan, H. S. (1953). *The Interpersonal Theory of Psychiatry.* New York: W. W. Norton.

EPILOGUE

While doing research for my last book (2015) I came across an enchanting short story, called "Little Selves," by Mary Lerner (1999). Old Aunt Margaret is clearly dying. She longs to recapture her former "selves" and portray them to her niece, before it is too late. She fears her fierce need won't be understood but her niece, Anna, has no trouble comprehending it. Anna, herself, has had similar thoughts. Margaret gets her heart's desire when she comes upon a special memory of herself, as a child of 9 or 10, wearing a red coat of her own making. Remembering this "little self" brings Margaret great joy (p.15). "With its fullness of detail, it achieved a delicious suggestion of permanence, in contrast to the illusiveness of other isolated moments. Margaret O'Brien saw all those other figures, but she really was the child with the red coat."

Re-reading the papers in this volume has brought me closer to my own former selves. Like Margaret, I am especially keen on communicating those that are still vivid enough to experience in the present tense. Many of those "selves" were inspired by generous mentors, who passed on their love for psychoanalysis.

In an Op Ed piece (New York Times, Tuesday, August 23, 2016, p.A23) David Brooks defines a vocation, as distinct from a career. "...a vocation involves falling in love with something, having a conviction about it and making it part of your personal identity." Psychoanalysis is my vocation, in this sense. I have always felt grateful that it allows me so many forms of self expression. Teaching, supervising, treating, and writing inform each other. Psychoanalysis has never made me choose which of these selves to inhabit. It has encouraged me to live them all.

In these pages I meet myself as a newly minted analyst. That "little self" yearned to find a professional home. While she relied on the theories impressed upon her in her training, she was determined to create a personally resonant voice of her own.

Another professional "self" coalesced around efforts to find better ways to prepare candidates. Issues raised by this effort still preoccupy me.

At a fork in the road, I chose analytic training over continuing my work as an emotion theorist. I didn't want to leave that more academic "self" behind, but I felt impelled to try to become a better clinical instrument.

Since then, I have spent much of my time trying to integrate ideas from emotion theory with concepts drawn from various psychoanalytic schools. Thinking about the emotions still nourishes me. It has brought stimulating challenges, such as how to forge a "passionate neutrality."

In the introduction to the last paper, on "Henry James' middle years and my own," I quoted from Cavefy's poem, "Ithaca." Its wondrous, infinitely gentle wisdom stuns me, every time I read it.

Ithaca gave you the beautiful journey.
without her you wouldn't have set upon the road...

I feel sure you understand what my Ithaca has been, and the beautiful journey it has given me.

REFERENCES

Buechler, S. (2015). *Understanding and Treating Patients in Clinical Psychoanalysis: Lessons from Literature.* New York: Routledge.

Cavafy, C. P. (2009). Ithaca. In: *Collected Poems by C. P. Cavafy,* trans. D. Mendelsohn. New York: Alfred A. Knopf.

Lerner, M. (1999). Little selves. In: The *Best American Stories of the Century,* eds. J. Updike & K. Kenison. New York: Houghton Mifflin Company, pp. 7–18.

CPSIA information can be obtained
at www.ICGtesting.com
Printed in the USA
FFOW04n2205171017
41245FF